Referendums around the World

Referendums around the <u>World</u>

The Growing Use of Direct Democracy

Edited by David Butler and
Austin Ranney

The AEI Press

Publisher for the American Enterprise Institute
WASHINGTON, D.C.

1994

To order call toll free 1-800-462-6420 or 1-717-794-3800. For all other inquiries please contact the AEI Press, 1150 Seventeenth Street, N.W., Washington, D.C. 20036 or call 1-800-862-5801.

Library of Congress Cataloging-in-Publication Data

Referendums around the world : the growing use of direct democracy / edited by David Butler and Austin Ranney.

    p. cm.
    Updated ed. of: Referendums. © 1978.
    "Except for the editors, all the authors are new, and our own sections are completely rewritten. The only repetitions are the appendixes, which list all known nationwide referendums and referendums in subordinate territories held up to the end of 1993"- -Pref.
    Includes bibliographical references and index.
    ISBN 0-8447-3852-2 (c). — ISBN 978 0-8447-3853-6 (p)
    1. Referendum. 2. Comparative government. I. Butler, David, 1924– . II. Ranney, Austin. III. Referendums.
JF491.R393 1994
328.2—dc20   94-13296
                                                    CIP

1 3 5 7 9 10 8 6 4 2

THE AEI PRESS
Publisher for the American Enterprise Institute
1150 17th Street, N.W., Washington, D.C. 20036

Contents

LIST OF TABLES

LIST OF FIGURES

Preface

Referendums, published in 1978 by the American Enterprise Institute, was the first attempt since 1926 to summarize the world's experience with various forms of the referendum device. We invited specialists to discuss in detail how the institution had affected the politics of the countries (and the American states) that had used it most.

Since 1978, referendums have assumed new prominence in many places: in the United States, where in many states referendums have been exploited by different political groups to pursue moral or constitutional goals; in Western Europe, where the evolution of the European Community has turned critically on referendum outcomes in some member nations; in Eastern Europe, where boundaries, sovereignties, and governing institutions have been extensively tested following the disintegration of the Soviet Union; in Chile and South Africa, as new regimes emerge from old tyrannies; and in New Zealand and Italy, where referendums have exposed the unpopularity of politicians and helped to transform the governing system.

We focus on these new situations in the pages that follow, but we continue our effort to consider referendums in a comprehensive historical perspective. The present book is far from being a revised version of *Referendums*. Except for the editors, all the authors are new, and our own sections are completely rewritten. The only repetitions are the appendixes, which list all known nationwide referendums and referendums in subordinate territories held up to the end of 1993; and even they have had to be greatly expanded to comprehend the hundreds of referendums held since 1977.

We are grateful to the authors of our chapters on the referendum device in the various regions of the world for their tolerance for the editors' peculiarities as well as for the high quality of their contributions. We also thank Pilar Domingo, Keith Ovenden, Adam Steinhouse, and Pier Vincenzo Uleri for their help.

Contributors

VERNON BOGDANOR has been a fellow of Brasenose College, Oxford, since 1966. He has published a number of studies of constitutions in Europe and the United Kingdom, including *Constitutions in Democratic Politics* and *Multi-Party Politics and the Constitution.*

HENRY E. BRADY is professor of political science at the University of California, Berkeley. He has written on research methodology and on Canadian politics in elections. He recently directed a survey study of political attitudes in some republics of the former Soviet Union.

DAVID BUTLER has been a fellow of Nuffield College, Oxford, since 1951 and is currently an adjunct scholar of the American Enterprise Institute. He has published books on electoral systems and politics in Australia, India, and the United Kingdom and was coeditor of *Referendums: A Study in Practice and Theory* (1978).

COLIN A. HUGHES is professor of political science at the University of Queensland and author of several books on politics in Queensland and Australia. From 1984 to 1991, he served as Australia's chief electoral commissioner.

CYNTHIA S. KAPLAN is associate professor of political science at the University of California, Santa Barbara. She has published studies of policy making in the former Soviet Union, including *The Party and Agricultural Crisis Management in the USSR.* She collaborated with Henry E. Brady in the survey of political attitudes in some republics of the former Soviet Union.

KRIS W. KOBACH received his D.Phil. from Nuffield College, Oxford. He has recently published *The Referendum: Direct Democracy in Switzerland* and is currently enrolled in Yale University's College of Law.

DAVID B. MAGLEBY is professor and chairman of the Department of Political Science at Brigham Young University. He has published several studies of referendums in the United States, including *Direct Legislation: Voting on Ballot Propositions in the United States.*

AUSTIN RANNEY is professor emeritus of political science at the University of California, Berkeley, and currently an adjunct scholar of the American Enterprise Institute. He has published several books on parties and elections in the United States and was coeditor of *Referendums: A Study of Practice and Theory* (1978).

1
Practice

David Butler and Austin Ranney

In a referendum, a mass electorate votes on some public issue.[1] A referendum can be initiated in many ways and take many forms, but most democracies have at some time held referendums. In a few countries, these have been institutionalized into a regular part of government. In most, they have been ad hoc affairs designed to solve a specific problem. Half the eight hundred or so referendums that have taken place at the national level in the history of the world have been in Switzerland, but the number of other countries in which they have played a continuous role in politics is very small. On the whole, they have been crisis instruments, invoked to solve a particular problem or to justify a particular solution.

A referendum may be advisory or mandatory. On the one hand, its outcome may be treated merely as a comprehensive opinion poll on a significant issue, with a verdict that can be translated into law or policy as the government or legislature may see fit. On the other hand, it may be part of the statutory process: a popular Yes may be required before a law or a constitutional change is put into effect. In some cases, the vote may be an "initiative," made necessary by a petition from a stipulated percentage of voters. Initiatives may be allowed only to nul-

---

1. Two points of definition should be made. We speak of *referendums;* in some countries the term used has been *plebiscites.* Plebiscites got a bad name when the device was abused by Adolf Hitler, but in any case no one has produced a clear distinction between the two terms. Therefore, we use the more popular word throughout this book.

We speak of referend*ums,* not referend*a,* on the advice of the editors of the *Oxford English Dictionary:* "Referendum is logically preferable as a plural form meaning ballots on one issue (as a Latin gerund referendum has no plural). The Latin plural gerundive referenda, meaning 'things to be referred,' necessarily connotes a plurality of issues."

lify a law; more frequently provision is made for voters to put forward new legislation.[2]

Forms and Functions

Referendums have had many different forms and functions. With varying sincerity, governments or political groups have invoked referendums to decide or to give legitimacy to a change in constitutions or in boundaries or in policies. Almost every polity has at some time or other considered involving the people directly in settling practical or moral questions. Appendix A, which lists all known nationwide referendums in the history of the world to the end of 1993, presents many surprises. The subject matter, the frequency, and the outcome of referendums have not been what most people coming to the subject—the present authors included—would have expected.

The subject matter of referendums falls into four main categories:

- *Constitutional issues.* After a revolution or a territorial breakup, a country needs to give legitimacy to the fresh arrangements and to the rules under which it is to operate in the future. A popular vote of endorsement is an excellent way of giving democratic authority to the new regime.

   Equally, when changes in the rules are needed—a revised electoral system, a different franchise, or a fresh distribution of power between center and periphery—those in office may be forced by constitutional provisions or by political prudence to seek specific approval from the voters.

- *Territorial issues.* After 1918, President Woodrow Wilson's principle of self-determination led to the settlement of several border questions by referendums of the inhabitants. The same thing happened during decolonization in the post-1945 period. More recently, the transfer of national powers implicit in the establishment of a European Community and the reorganization of frontiers following the breakup of the Soviet Union and of Yugoslavia have given rise to a number of referendums. These are listed in appendix B and in chapter 6, which chronicle over 100 referendums that have been conducted in subordinate territories to determine or confirm their status.

- *Moral issues.* Some questions cut across party lines and cause deep

---

2. In some cases, a 50.1 percent majority may not be enough; the precondition may be a two-thirds majority (for example, Sierra Leone), a three-quarters majority (for example, Belau), a majority of the registered electorate (for example, Weimar Germany), or a majority in a majority of cantons or regions or states (for example, Switzerland and Australia).

divisions among politicians who are normally allied in office or in opposition. Alcoholic beverage prohibition, divorce, and abortion are examples of contentious problems that several countries have sought to settle by referendums.

- *Other issues.* In some countries, citizens have the power to insist that certain matters be put to a popular vote. In Switzerland and Italy, and in a number of states in the United States, a vast diversity of questions have been referred to the electorate; these have ranged from hunting laws to property taxes and from food subsidies to traffic regulation. Some of these questions may, like moral issues, be almost apolitical—for example, driving on the left of the road or adopting daylight saving time. On occasion, elected officials have used referendums to escape from making decisions that they fear will create as many enemies as friends.

In most countries, the decision to hold a referendum has lain with the party or parties in office, and they have called referendums to suit their own political convenience. In totalitarian states, and sometimes in democracies, they have been rewarded with Yes votes of 90 percent (or even of 99 or 99.99 percent), which they have used to demonstrate to the world that the people were behind them.

The calling of a referendum, however, can prove to be a boomerang. Charles de Gaulle felt forced to resign from the presidency of France in 1969 when a referendum defeat seemed to him a vote of no confidence. In Ghana in 1978, in Chile in 1988, in Turkey in 1989, and in Malawi in 1993 the voters conspicuously failed to give governments the answer they wanted. But in a few countries, initiatives and referendums can be launched by ordinary voters. Subsequent chapters show the importance of the initiative in Switzerland and, more recently, in Italy, as well as in some American states.

The list of referendums in the appendixes refutes four common notions about referendums:

- *"Referendums are habit forming."* People who argue against holding a referendum on a particular issue often use the thin-edge-of-the-wedge argument: If you consult the people on this question, how can you refuse a referendum on a host of other issues? But in practice, there is little to indicate that one referendum leads to another. In some states in the United States, as well as in Switzerland and in Italy, the number of referendums has increased exponentially. But elsewhere in Western democracies, there is no sign of an addictive tendency. Although most countries have employed referendums once or twice to deal with particular problems, the floodgates have certainly not opened.

3

Worldwide, the use of referendums has increased—but not nearly as fast as the number of independent nations or the number of countries that have credible claims to be democracies. The countries that have never held nationwide referendums—India, Israel, Japan, the Netherlands, and the United States—seem to have little in common.

Table 1–1 shows how, in each decade of this century, the number of referendums has increased in almost every part of the world. The increases were small until the 1970s, though, when Switzerland and, to a much lesser extent, Egypt were mainly responsible for a rise. In Europe, Italy by itself caused the sharp increase in the 1980s. In the great majority of countries, there has been no significant increase in the use of referendums, although, as chapter 7 shows, since the 1970s the use of initiatives and referendums in the American states has increased considerably.

- *"Referendums are normally decided by close votes."* Despite the common assumption that this happens, remarkably few have produced Yes votes—between 49 percent and 51 percent; leaving out Switzerland and Australia, only seven have fallen in that range. Recounts seem unknown, and decisive results are the norm. The close calls in France and Denmark in 1992 were unusual. Table 1–2 shows the distribution of Yes percentages in referendums in established democracies since 1900. Table 1–2 makes plain that Australia is the exception. Two-thirds of the referendums have produced results in the 60–40 percent range, and in sixteen the Yes vote has been between 48 and 52 percent.

Of course, in the nondemocratic world the outcomes are different. Only nine out of ninety-two referendums in Africa have failed to yield a 90 percent Yes vote. In a majority (fifty-two), the outcome was, implausibly, more than 98 percent Yes.

- *"Referendums are instruments for radical change."* In fact, the verdicts of referendums have tended to be conservative. In Australia, thirty-six of forty-two referendums to change the constitution have been rejected. Nuclear power has been restricted in Italy and Austria. Scotland did not endorse devolution of power from London to Edinburgh. The record on Common Market votes has been one of caution. In the United States, as chapter 7 shows, the picture has been mixed, but conservative positions seem to have as many successes as liberal positions. At the national level in recent years, New Zealand and Italy stand out as countries where indignant populations used the referendum device to force electoral reform on reluctant politicians.

- *"The public likes referendums."* The advocates of referendums insist that the public wants to be consulted. But in fact, as chapter 2 shows,

TABLE 1-1
Nationwide Referendums, by Decade, Pre-1900–1993

	Switzerland	Rest of Europe	Near East	Asia	North and South America	Australia and New Zealand	Total
Up to 1900	57	11	—	—	3	—	71
1901–10	12	2	—	—	—	4	18
1911–20	15	6	1	—	3	5	29
1921–30	28	8	—	—	2	6	45
1931–40	23	17	—	—	7	6	53
1941–50	21	15	1	1	3	11	52
1951–60	32	6	8	5	3	5	59
1961–70	30	14	18	4	4	7	77
1971–80	87	18	36	14	8	14	177
1981–90	76	33	24	6	10	4	153
1991–93	33	19	5	—	6	2	65
Total	414	149	93	30	49	64	799

SOURCES: Appendix A and the lists in chapters 4, 5, and 6

TABLE 1-2
PERCENTAGE OF YES VOTES IN REFERENDUMS IN
ESTABLISHED DEMOCRACIES, PRE-1900–1993

	0–40	40–50	50–60	60–70	70–80	80–90	90–100
Switzerland	28	22	17	17	11	4	1
Australia	18	52	14	2	3	2	1
Rest of world	16	13	15	15	15	10	16

SOURCES: Same as for table 1-1.

turnout in referendums has been consistently lower than in general elections—and sometimes much lower.

To carry conviction, referendums have to be orderly affairs, conducted under accepted rules. But no two countries have identical electoral systems, and none have identical regulations for the conduct of referendums. The laws governing the organization and finance of Yes and No campaigns and the format of the ballot paper vary, as does the significance attached to the result.

In subsequent chapters, our contributors focus on the way referendums have evolved in the places where they have been most employed, with special attention to the past fifteen years. But three key areas fall outside the scope of those chapters. In Canada, South Africa, and Latin America, referendums have recently been used in dramatic fashion to deal with critical constitutional issues.

The Referendum in Chile, 5 October 1988

The most important of all Latin American referendums took place in Chile on 5 October 1988. It brought to an end the fifteen-year dictatorship of President Augusto Pinochet in a test of his own devising.

President Pinochet had seized power in September 1973 in a military coup against the left-wing government of President Salvador Allende. He had twice sought popular endorsement of his free-market right-wing regime. In a 1978 referendum, he won 75 percent support in a dubiously conducted referendum asking one of the most loaded questions in the history of the device:

> In the face of international aggression unleashed against the government of the fatherland, I support President Pinochet in his defense of the dignity of Chile, and I reaffirm the legitimate right of the republic to conduct the process of institutionalisation in a manner befitting its sovereignty.

In 1980, Pinochet's military regime devised a further referendum to approve a new constitution. Again, there was no international monitoring and no guarantee of free and fair campaigning and counting. Nonetheless, only 67 percent were reported to have voted Yes. This referendum, however, contained a "ticking time bomb." After eight years, a referendum was to be called to endorse Pinochet as president for another eight years or to hold a new election. As 1988 approached, the opposition groups decided to fight rather than to boycott the referendum.

Because Chile had been faring quite well economically, Pinochet's junta expected to win the referendum. They had full control of the media, and many parts of the establishment were with them. But outside pressures, above all from the United States, for a fully monitored vote created an awkward climate: if President Pinochet wanted to perpetuate his regime, he had to demonstrate that the referendum was a fair expression of public opinion. His government seems genuinely to have believed that it was popular and would secure this legitimation.

Although the opposition did not get equal air time, the referendum was generally thought to be reasonably fair and open. It resulted in a convincing defeat for Pinochet. Of the valid votes, 56 percent went to the opposition, and the military regime reluctantly accepted the verdict. Elections followed, and a center-left regime, headed by a new president, Patricio Aylwin, assumed power. Pinochet remained in command of the armed forces. Nonetheless, a dictator had accepted his removal from power by a free referendum that he himself had instituted.

The Referendum in Uruguay in 1992

Latin America provides two other significant recent examples of the use of the referendum. Uruguay holds the Western Hemisphere record for referendums: ten of the forty-two conducted in Latin American countries have been in that country. In 1973, the long-standing democratic regime in Uruguay had been toppled in a military coup. In 1980, the military regime sought approval for an authoritarian constitution but got a No vote of 57 to 43 percent. The 1967 constitution, which was then reinstituted, stipulated that, if the signatures of 25 percent of the electorate could be obtained, a referendum on a new law must be held. This provision was invoked in 1989 against an amnesty law giving immunity for acts committed under the military regime; the law survived by 57 to 43 percent on an 84 percent turnout. The referendum provision was invoked again in 1992 against a far-reaching privatization law; on a 77 percent turnout the law was disallowed by 72 to 28 percent.

7

This reversal of government policy constitutes one of the most decisive in the history of referendums.

The Referendum in Brazil, 21 April 1993

One more South American referendum is worthy of special note. In 1985, Brazil emerged from twenty years of military rule. In 1988, the Congress produced a constitution under which the ultimate nature of the regime was to be decided by a referendum in 1993. In 1992, the country was shaken by a major scandal over the behavior of President Fernando Collor, which led to his resignation. Because of the ensuing controversy in Congress, the shaping of the referendum ballot question fell to the courts. It was decided to give the electorate two choices, first between a monarchy and a republic and second between a presidential and a parliamentary system.

The result was firmly in favor of a republic over a monarchy, 87 to 13 percent. It was also clearly in favor of a presidential system, 69 to 31 percent. The presidential system survived in spite of, or perhaps because of, the successful impeachment of President Collor during the preceding months. After a troubled period, a free referendum gave unquestioned legitimacy to the Brazilian regime.

Canada's Referendum of 27 October 1992

In North America, Canada tried to settle its long-running constitutional controversies with a referendum. The desire of Quebec for full independence or at least for its Francophone interests to achieve national recognition had been debated ever since the Parti Quebecois won power in the province in 1976 and held its unsuccessful independence referendum in 1980. One byproduct of the referendum was the agreed repatriation of the Canadian Constitution in 1982 taking all amending power from London to Ottawa. An accord designed to meet Quebec's aspirations within a Canadian framework, hammered out by the ten provincial premiers and the dominion prime minister at Meech Lake in 1987, had foundered on the opposition of Canada's aboriginal population and belated resistance from Manitoba and Newfoundland. Under a threat from Quebec of unilateral action, a new arrangement was worked out to be put to the people in a referendum on 27 October 1992. The voters were asked to approve a complicated package that included a revised Senate, a recognition of Quebec as a distinct society, and a new definition of the powers of each province.

At first, a Yes majority looked likely in all, or almost all, ten provinces. But during the final month, the tide turned. Women's groups, complaining of underrepresentation, campaigned against the package. Perhaps the most influential event was a speech on 3 October by the former prime minister, Pierre Trudeau, arguing against the proposition being put before the Canadian people. Opinion changed fast, and in the end only 44 percent voted Yes. Six of the ten provinces voted No. The verdicts ranged from 74 percent Yes in Prince Edward Island to 31 percent in British Columbia. The western provinces, infuriated by the continuous concessions to Quebec, voted firmly No. The Maritimes, except for Nova Scotia, voted firmly Yes; the two big provinces were cross-pressured and closely divided—49 percent No in Ontario and 55 percent No in Quebec.

Although Canada's constitutional crisis was not ended by this vote, the decisiveness of the verdict allowed the issue to fall into abeyance—at least until new elections or initiatives in Quebec stirred it up.

The South African Referendum, 17 March 1992

Thus, in Canada a referendum was the key to stopping a constitutional revolution. In South Africa, however, as in Chile, a referendum opened the door to a fundamental change of regime. The accession to the nation's presidency of F. W. de Klerk in 1989 and the subsequent release of African National Congress (ANC) leader Nelson Mandela, together with the formal ending of apartheid, meant that the South African constitution would have to be transformed. But the prospect met bitter resistance from large sections of the dominant white population.

The Conservative party, which had broken away from the ruling Nationalists, fared well in the 1989 general election; and as constitutional talks between the government and the ANC advanced, painfully but apparently inexorably, the Conservatives began to show their strength. When their candidate won impressively in a by-election at Potchefstroom on 19 February 1992, President de Klerk concluded that he needed a clear mandate for his plans to end apartheid. He called for a referendum, in which only whites could vote, on 17 March 1992.

The government had probably intended that separate referendums among the three main segments of the population should be held to approve any new constitutional settlement (the idea was subsequently abandoned). This effort to get a preliminary endorsement of his policies outflanked President de Klerk's right-wing opposition. In a barnstorming campaign, President de Klerk argued that a No vote would produce chaos and return South Africa to international isolation. He was helped by the efficient National party machine and by the discreet quiescence of Mandela and the African National Congress.

The result was a surprisingly high 69 percent Yes verdict on an 85 percent turnout. In the English-speaking areas, affirmatives rose to 85 percent, but most Afrikaans districts also returned Yes majorities.

South Africa's constitutional troubles were certainly not solved by this tactical appeal to the (white) people. There can be no doubt, however, that it provided an outstanding example of how a referendum can enormously strengthen a government's hand in a very difficult situation.

Conclusion

The examples cited here illustrate how referendums can be employed as solutions to special problems and how they can defuse tensions that the ordinary routines of politics seem inadequate to manage. Chapters 3 and 6 give more detailed examples from Western and Eastern Europe. But first, the general arguments about the place of referendums in a democratic system must be examined.

2
Theory

David Butler and Austin Ranney

In chapter 1, we described the increased use of referendums after 1978 by many nations and by many states in the United States.[1] Not surprisingly, this increase in usage has been accompanied by a similar increase in scholarly studies of the referendum device, as evidenced by new books, articles, and conferences, several of which are listed in the bibliographies at the end of this and later chapters.

Only a handful of works on referendums appeared between 1920 and 1980, most works on the subject having been published in the early twentieth century. But the 1980s and 1990s have seen the number of such studies more than double, including works on referendums in the American states, comparative analyses of referendums and other forms of direct popular participation as ways of realizing democracy, and speculation about the possibilities of new forms of electronic communications for establishing something approaching town-meeting democracy on a national scale.

This chapter considers what new light, if any, recent writings shed on the earlier arguments both for and against referendums.

The Case for Referendums Reconsidered

What Institutions Best Realize the Principles of Democracy? While political theorists and practitioners have long used the term *democracy* in many different ways, most appear to agree that it denotes at least the principles of popular sovereignty, political equality, popular con-

This chapter draws heavily from a paper by Austin Ranney, "Referendums: New Practice and Old Theory," prepared for "Democracy and Referendums," a conference sponsored by the Societa italiana di study elettorale in Prato, Italy, 3–5 October 1991. We are grateful to Professor Pier Vincenzo Uleri and the Societa for their many kindnesses in the preparation of this chapter.
   1. See also John T. Rourke, Richard P. Hiskes, and Cyrus Ernesto Zirakzadeh, *Direct Democracy and International Politics* (London: Lynn Rienners Publishers, 1992), chap. 1.

sultation, and majority rule.[2] But since the seventeenth century, democrats have divided into two main schools of thought about the institutions required to realize those principles. One might be called the participationist or direct-democracy school, led by such classical theorists as Jean Jacques Rousseau and the English levelers and such modern theorists as Benjamin Barber, Lee Ann Osbun, and Carole Pateman. They argue that the only truly democratic way to make decisions on matters of public policy is by the full, direct, and unmediated participation of all citizens. The citizens, they declare, should set the agenda, discuss the issues, and determine the policies. Any indirect form of participation, such as decisions by elected representatives, cannot be fully democratic.

Two reasons are given. First, if the citizens' ideas and preferences are expressed only by squeezing them through the minds and mouths of representatives, they are bound to emerge distorted. Hence, the only way to achieve the ideal that political decisions be made in full accordance with the wishes of the people is to ensure that those wishes are expressed directly, not mediated or interpreted. Second, democracy, like any form of government, is not an end in itself but only a means to a higher end. The higher end that democracy seeks is the full development of each citizen's full human potential; the citizens' civic potentials can be realized only by their direct and full participation in public affairs, not by delegating their civic powers and obligations to representatives.

The model institutions for the full realization of democracy have been the face-to-face citizen meetings of the New England towns and the Swiss *Landsgemeinden* (see chapter 4 for a more detailed discussion of Swiss institutions). Benjamin R. Barber argues that modern technology makes possible several new institutions, including the regular neighborhood assemblies that he urges, a national civic information database accessible to any citizen with a personal computer, and regular, nationally televised "town meetings" of the sort organized in the 1992 American presidential campaign by candidates Bill Clinton and Ross Perot.[3]

Opposing this conception of democracy is the representationist or

---

2. For a more complete statement of this view, see Austin Ranney and Willmoore Kendall, *Democracy and the American Party System* (New York: Harcourt, Brace, Jovanovich, 1956), chaps. 1–3.

3. For discussions of these and other approaches to direct democracy through new technologies, see F. Christopher Arterton, *Teledemocracy* (Newbury Park, Calif.: Sage Publications, 1987); and Iain McLean, *Democracy and New Technology* (Cambridge, Eng.: Polity Press, 1989).

accountable elites school of democratic theory, led by such writers as John Stuart Mill, Henry Jones Ford, Joseph Schumpeter, E. E. Schattschneider, and Giovanni Sartori. They argue that the dream of direct democracy is relevant only for polities so small that all citizens can meet face-to-face in one place at one time. Even more important, the dream can be made flesh only in communities in which all citizens can spend all their time on political decisions—perhaps as in the ancient Greek city-states by using the full-time labor of slaves to liberate citizens for full-time participation in politics. In the modern nation-state, they say, not only is it impossible for all the citizens to meet face-to-face in one place, but, since slavery is prohibited, it is impossible for all but a handful to spend all their time on politics. Accordingly, to insist that full participation by every citizen in every public decision is a necessary condition for democracy is simply to make democracy irrelevant for the governing of modern nations. Such a posture, the representationists say, is both unnecessary and foolish.

In their view, the essence of democracy is locating the ultimate power to rule in all the citizens rather than in one citizen or a small oligarchy of citizens. That ideal can be realized by the citizens, at frequent intervals, electing representatives who then "re-present" their constituents in lawmaking assemblies and, at the end of their terms, are held to account by their constituents for how well or badly they have used their temporary powers. Thus, representative government not only realizes the essential principles of democracy; it does so in a way that makes those ideals reachable goals rather than irrelevant dreams.

Referendums as Useful Supplements to Representative Democracy. Some of the most extreme advocates of both the participationist and the representationist schools appear to take the position that a modern polity has only two institutional choices: full and direct participation and undiluted representation. The democrat, they seem to be saying, must choose between these two alternatives, for there is no satisfactory way in which elements of one can be grafted onto the other. Yet, as we sometimes forget, most advocates of referendums see them as supplements rather than as alternatives. They agree with the representationists that representative government must and should be the basic institutional form for democracy in any densely populated community, such as a modern nation-state. But they believe that representative democracy can be improved by permitting, under certain conditions, the direct votes of citizens to confirm, reject, or even make laws. The main benefits they expect from supplementing representative institutions with referendums are the following.

13

1. *Maximizing legitimacy.* Most democratic theorists believe that democratic regimes, far more than authoritarian regimes, rely on the consent of citizens rather than on the coercive power of governments to ensure the rule of law. Consequently, they especially value making political decisions in ways that will seem entirely legitimate to the most citizens. Advocates of the referendum device believe that one of its greater virtues is the belief of most ordinary people that decisions they make themselves are more legitimate than those made by public officials: decisions by referendums produce more unambiguous mandates than candidate elections; they are more likely than acts of legislatures to promote the public interest over special interests; and ordinary citizens are less subject than public officials to bribery, intimidation, and other forms of pressure. And, as Geoffrey Walker puts it, "The citizen is more likely to feel entitled to flout a law promoted by an elite, or procured by blackmail or corruption, than one that is seen to reflect the free and informed consent of the majority of citizens."[4] This is even more important in an era, such as our own, in which contempt for elected officials and doubts about the responsiveness of representative institutions have been growing in many democratic nations.

Recent experience and research give some support for this position, although it has not been proved beyond a reasonable doubt. New supporting evidence comes from several studies of the attitudes of American voters toward initiatives and referendums.[5] Surprisingly, majorities of the respondents in these studies did not idealize the superior wisdom and honesty of ordinary people over elected representatives; indeed, many said that laws enacted by legislatures tend to be better than those produced by popular initiatives. Even so, majorities ranging from 77 to 85 percent said that referendums are a good thing, that people should have the right to vote directly on issues, and that voting on issues is more likely than voting for candidates to produce policies the people want. Accordingly, citizens should have the right to put measures on the ballot when they wish and should not be restricted to voting only on measures that elected officials put before them. Similarly, a number of nationwide polls taken in the United States from 1977 to 1987 showed majorities of 57 to 58 percent in favor

---

4. Geoffrey deQ. Walker, *The People's Law* (Sidney: Centre for Independent Studies, 1987), p. 50. See also Harlan Hahn and Sheldon Kaminiecki, *Referendum Voting* (Westport, Conn.: Greenwood Press, 1987), p. 16.

5. The studies are summarized in David B. Magleby, *Direct Legislation: Voting on Ballot Propositions in the United States* (Baltimore, Md.: Johns Hopkins University Press, 1984), pp. 7–20.

of establishing some form of the referendum at the national level.[6]

Such recent experience and research tend to confirm the proposition that the strongest single argument for referendums as a supplement to representative institutions is the fact that most people regard them as the most authoritative, because the least mediated, of all expressions of the popular will. Therefore, in a system based on the principles of popular sovereignty, political equality, popular consultation, and majority rule, direct popular decisions made by referendums have a legitimacy that indirect decisions by elected representatives cannot match. This does not mean that all decisions should be made by direct vote of the people. It does not even mean that decisions made by referendums are wiser or more prudent than those made by representatives. It means only that when a representative democracy wishes a particular decision to be made with maximum legitimacy, it would do well to make that decision by referendum.

2. *Maximizing participation.* Many political commentators believe that popular participation in politics is a central concern, some would say *the* central concern, for democratic polities. As we have seen, they declare or assume that one of the prime goals of democracy is to maximize the potential for civic virtue of all its citizens, and they believe that direct participation in the making of public decisions is the best way to develop everyone's potential. As Barber puts it:

> Only direct political participation—activity that is explicitly public—is a completely successful form of civic education for democracy. The politically edifying influence of participation has been noted a thousand times since first Rousseau and then Mill and de Tocqueville suggested that democracy was best taught by practicing it. . . . Of course, when participation is neutered by being separated from power, then civic action will be only a game and its rewards will seem childish to women and men of the world; they will prefer to spend their time in the "real" pursuit of private interests.[7]

Participationists contend that the most important single indicator of a democratic nation's civic health is the degree to which its citizens participate in politics: high participation is a sure sign of political good health, while low participation is an unmistakable symptom of political sickness. Voting is the indispensable minimum form of participa-

---

6. The findings are summarized in Thomas E. Cronin, *Direct Democracy: The Politics of Initiative, Referendum, and Recall* (Cambridge, Mass.: Harvard University Press, 1989), pp. 4–5, 174–79.

7. Benjamin R. Barber, *Strong Democracy: Participatory Politics for a New Age* (Berkeley: University of California Press, 1984), pp. 235–36.

tion. Therefore, while the more people discuss politics, form organizations, work in campaigns, contribute money, and attend rallies the better, voting turnout is the most important single indicator of a political system's health.[8]

Most partisans of referendums contend that people are more likely to vote when they can vote directly on policy issues than when they are restricted to choosing candidates for public office. Thomas E. Cronin, for example, cites studies showing that voting turnout is generally higher in the American states that have popular initiatives on the ballot than in the states without popular initiatives, although he does not claim that the presence of initiatives causes the higher turnouts.[9]

One way to test this proposition is to compare the turnouts in referendum elections with those in candidate elections. Table 2–1 compares the mean turnouts in referendum elections with those in parliamentary general elections in twelve nations from 1945 to 1993. The data in table 2–1 show that in all twelve nations, the mean turnout in referendum elections from 1945 to 1993 was lower than the turnout in parliamentary general elections. The mean turnout rates in referendum elections since 1986 have declined even further.

These findings are matched by similar findings about the drop-off in American state elections (see David Magleby's analysis in chapter 7). Both Magleby and Cronin find that in most elections in which both candidate choices and referendum propositions are on the same ballots, the proportion of voters casting ballots on the propositions is markedly smaller than the proportion casting ballots on the candidates: the mean drop-off is fifteen percentage points. Turnout is somewhat higher on popular initiatives than on legislative referendums, but, with the exception of a few unusually controversial and highly publicized measures, such as California's popular initiatives to cut property taxes (Proposition 13, 1978) and repeal open-housing laws (Proposition 14, 1964), the turnout in referendums is consistently lower than that in candidate elections.[10]

---

8. For a modest dissent from this widely held view, see Austin Ranney, "Nonvoting Is Not a Social Disease," *Public Opinion*, vol. 6 (1983), pp. 16–19.

9. Compare Cronin, *Direct Democracy*, pp. 226–28.

10. Ibid., pp. 67–70; Magleby, *Direct Legislation*, pp. 83–87. One might think that the low and declining turnout in referendum elections would worry partisans of the device, but Geoffrey Walker, at least, is not concerned. He comments, "It would appear that [the Swiss] want the right to decide and vote, but if the matter is not one on which they have strong views, they are content to delegate its exercise to their fellow-citizens, knowing from experience that they are safe to do so" (*The People's Law*), p. 81.

TABLE 2-1
MEAN TURNOUT IN CANDIDATE AND REFERENDUM
ELECTIONS IN SELECTED COUNTRIES, 1945–1993
(percent)

Nation	Candidate Elections	Referendum Elections	Difference
Australia[a]	95	90	−5
Austria	93	64	−29
Belgium[a]	92	92	0
Denmark	86	74	−12
France	77	72	−5
Ireland	73	58	−15
Italy	90	74	−16
New Zealand	90	60	−30
Norway	81	78	−3
Sweden	85	67	−18
Switzerland	61	45	−16
United Kingdom	77	65	−12

a. Compulsory voting laws.
SOURCES: Ivor Crewe, "Electoral Participation," in David Butler, Howard R. Penniman, and Austin Ranney, eds., *Democracy at the Polls* (Washington, D.C.: American Enterprise Institute, 1981), table 10–3, pp. 234–36; David Butler and Austin Ranney, *Referendums* (Washington, D.C.: American Enterprise Institute, 1978), appendix A; John Austin, David Butler, and Austin Ranney, "Referendums, 1978–1986," *Electoral Studies*, vol. 6, pp. 139–49; and appendix A of this book.

In short, while the evidence is far from dispositive, little in recent experience supports the proposition that referendums increase voting turnout. There is no reason to suppose that the ready availability of referendums encourages other forms of participation.

The Case against Referendums Reconsidered

The main arguments against holding referendums in representative democracies include: (1) ordinary citizens have neither the analytical skills nor the information to make wise decisions; (2) decisions by elected officials involve weighing the intensity of preferences and melding the legitimate interests of many groups into policies that will give all groups something of what they want; (3) decisions made by representatives are more likely to protect the rights of minorities; and (4) by

17

allowing elected officials to be bypassed and by encouraging officials to evade divisive issues by passing them on to the voters, referendums weaken the prestige and authority of representatives and representative government. What light does recent experience shed on those arguments?

Decisions by Ignorant, Uncomprehending Voters. Since 1978, several studies on the information and understanding of voters in direct-legislation elections in the American states have been published. Magleby begins his review of those studies by noting that ballot measures are frequently worded so that a Yes vote is, in effect, a vote against a particular policy. Proposition 14, the 1964 "fair housing" referendum in California, for example, was a proposal to repeal the legislative act that prohibited discrimination in the purchase and rental of houses and apartments on the basis of race; hence, voters who favored the law had to vote No on the measure, while those who opposed it had to vote Yes.[11]

Magleby cites several studies showing that in elections in which voters had to vote Yes on a proposition to oppose a policy or No to support one, 10 to 20 percent of them cast "mistaken" votes. A particularly egregious example was California's 1980 referendum on rent control (Proposition 10), in which 23 percent of the voters wanted to preserve rent control but mistakenly voted Yes on the proposition to repeal it, while 54 percent of the voters who opposed rent control mistakenly voted No on the proposition to repeal. Magleby reports, however, that on measures on which most of the voters had strong preferences, almost all accurately perceived the policy consequences of Yes and No votes and voted accordingly.[12]

As noted, turnouts in referendum elections have averaged about 15 percent less than those in candidate elections. Recent studies of these two electorates in the United States show that, compared with candidate election voters, referendum election voters are older, have more formal education, are of higher socioeconomic status, and are more involved and active in politics: analyses of voting behavior in candidate elections show that these traits are the main correlates of political knowledge and understanding. Referendum voters, however ignorant and unsophisticated they may seem when measured against the theorists' ideal citizen, seem nevertheless to be better informed and

---

11. This is, in effect, how Italy's so-called abrogative referendum is structured. For details, see chap. 3.

12. Magleby, *Direct Legislation*, pp. 141–44.

more sophisticated than voters in candidate elections.[13]

But voters in referendums have a cognitive handicap that voters do not have in most other elections. In most elections of candidates to state offices in most states (Nebraska is the only exception), the candidates' party labels printed on the ballot provide powerful clues to voters about which alternatives are the most desirable—clues, moreover, that persist from one election to the next and thus grow more useful over time. Referendum electorates have no such clues, and so they probably find it more difficult to translate the information they receive into Yes or No votes on the measures before them.

Majority Tyranny. In assessing the argument that decisions made by popular majorities in referendums are more likely than decisions by elected representatives to abridge minority rights, we might begin by remembering that most nations' referendums are votes on measures put before the voters by legislatures, constitutional conventions, or other assemblies of elected representatives. The wording of such measures is worked out by processes similar to those by which representative assemblies receive, weigh, and accommodate the demands of different interests and ideologies. Consequently, the fears of majority tyranny sometimes expressed about decisions by referendums are relevant only to decisions made by popular initiatives, in which citizen petitioners, not elected representatives, decide the wording of measures on the ballot.

Only Switzerland and twenty-six American states allow proposals for new laws to be put on the ballot by popular initiatives without any prior action by elected representatives (and in Switzerland, as Kris Kobach shows in chapter 4, these must be in the form of constitutional amendments). Accordingly, relatively few popular initiatives on the ballot in Switzerland and in the American states since 1978 proposed radical changes or significant restrictions on minority rights, and those few had little success. In Switzerland, only a few of those initiatives sought truly radical changes, notably abolition of the army (1989) and popular approval of all military expenditures (1987); both these proposals lost, with, respectively, 36 and 40 percent of the votes. The Swiss initiative to limit the number of foreigners allowed to live in Switzerland (1988) might also be considered an attack on minority rights; that proposal too lost, with only 33 percent of the votes.

Recent popular initiatives in some American states were considered by many civil libertarians to be significant abridgments of minority rights; these proposals had some success but far from total victory.

13. Ibid., pp. 127–30; Cronin, *Direct Democracy*, pp. 70–77.

The most successful measures proposed moving the balance in criminal trials somewhat away from defendants' rights and toward victims' rights and prosecutors' powers. In 1988 and 1990, for example, six states voted on initiatives to increase the power of judges to deny bail to persons accused of crimes when judges conclude that freeing those defendants before trial would endanger the public. All six measures passed. Conversely, initiatives to restrict the use of public funds for abortions for poor women won only in Arkansas and lost in Colorado and Michigan. Moreover, the voters in Maine approved a measure to fund the rewriting of the state constitution in gender-neutral language.

While, in some instances, voters in American states used popular initiatives to restrict some minority rights in ways that state legislatures had eschewed, it is hard to point to any successful referendum that constituted a flagrant act of majority tyranny against minority rights. If elected representatives are more protective of minority rights than popular majorities voting in referendum elections, the difference is at most marginal.

Referendums as Subversive of Representative Democracy. Many opponents of referendums have argued that referendums, though intended to supplement the institutions of referendum democracy, in fact subvert them in several ways. First, referendums allow ordinary citizens to reject decisions made by elected representatives; popular initiatives enable ordinary citizens to enact laws without participation by—and even over the objections of—elected officials. Inevitably, then, referendums subvert the authority and diminish the prestige of legislatures, cabinets, and executive heads of government. Moreover, by providing a politically acceptable way in which elected representatives can evade difficult decisions by passing the buck to the voters, referendums make it easy for representatives to shirk their responsibilities and evade the consequences of doing their jobs.

Recent experience and research have not definitively confirmed or disconfirmed these propositions. Some facts, however, are worth noting. Many democratic nations have not held any national referendums since 1978, and some (for example, Australia and France) have used them less frequently than before 1978. Switzerland has continued to hold far more nationwide referendums than any other nation. Only Italy, with five measures voted on before 1978 and fifteen measures since then, has significantly increased its use of referendums.

Moreover, in the few polities with both government-controlled referendums and popular initiatives, referendum measures referred to the voters by governments have generally succeeded more than measures placed on the ballot by popular initiatives. The American states with both legislature-referred referendums and popular initiatives show similar patterns: the winning rate for referendums has been about 60 percent, while the winning rate for initiatives has been about 14 percent.[14]

In most democratic systems, then, the voters can vote only on measures that are worded and placed on the ballot by elected representatives. In the few polities that also allow the voters to word and place measures on the ballot without the approval of the representatives, measures lacking the sponsorship or endorsement of elected representatives rarely win. It is therefore hard to believe that either form of the referendum seriously subverts representative democracy.

Wanting It Both Ways

As Magleby concluded in *Direct Legislation*, people who believe in undiluted representative democracy place the highest value on the virtues of stability, compromise, moderation, and access for all segments of the community, regardless of how small, and seek institutional arrangements that insulate fundamental principles from short-term fluctuations in public opinion. People who believe in coming as close as possible to direct democracy place the highest value on the virtues of change, participation, competition, conflict, and majority rule and seek institutional arrangements that maximize rapid and full responses to what popular majorities want.[15]

Many democrats apparently want it both ways. They want stability, which allows change when it is needed, and majority rule that preserves minority rights and ensures peaceful acquiescence by the minority in public decisions. And these democrats want laws that, by giving every group something but never everything it wants, keep all groups convinced that they have a stake in maintaining the system. Such people are likely to continue to reject extreme versions of both representationism and participationism. They are also likely to continue to regard some forms of referendums as occasionally useful supplements to, but never total replacements for, the institutions of representative democracy.

Bibliography

Arterton, F. Christopher. *Teledemocracy: Can Technology Protect Democracy?* Newbury Park, Calif.: Sage Publications, 1987.

---

14. David Butler and Austin Ranney, *Referendums* (Washington, D.C.: American Enterprise Institute, 1978), table 4–6, p. 81; Austin Ranney, "Referendums, 1988," *Public Opinion* (January/February 1989), pp. 15–17. For more recent data, see chap. 7.

15. Magleby, *Direct Legislation*, pp. 180–81.

Austen, John, David Butler, and Austin Ranney. "Referendums, 1978–1986." *Electoral Studies* 6:139–48.

Barber, Benjamin R. *Strong Democracy: Participatory Politics for a New Age.* Berkeley: University of California Press, 1984.

Cronin, Thomas E. *Direct Democracy: The Politics of Initiative, Referendum, and Recall.* Cambridge, Mass.: Harvard University Press, 1989.

Dahl, Robert A. *Democracy and Its Critics.* New Haven, Conn.: Yale University Press, 1989.

Guillaume-Hofnung, Michele. *Le Referendum, Que sais-je?* Paris, 1987.

Hahn, Harlan, and Sheldon Kamieniecki. *Referendum Voting: Social Status and Policy Preferences.* Westport, Conn.: Greenwood Press, 1987.

Hine, David. "The Italian Referendum of 8/9 November 1987." *Electoral Studies* 7:163–66.

Hollander, Richard. *Video Democracy: The Vote-from-the-Home Revolution.* Mt. Airy, Md.: Lomand, 1985.

LaPalombara, Joseph. *Democracy Italian Style.* New Haven, Conn.: Yale University Press, 1987.

Magleby, David B. *Direct Legislation: Voting on Ballot Propositions in the United States.* Baltimore, Md.: Johns Hopkins University Press, 1984.

McGuigan, Patrick B. *The Politics of Direct Democracy in the 1980s: Case Studies in Popular Decision Making.* Washington, D.C.: Institute for Government and Politics, 1985.

McLean, Iain. *Democracy and New Technology.* Cambridge, Eng.: Polity Press, 1989.

Neuman, W. Russell. *The Paradox of Mass Politics.* Cambridge, Mass.: Harvard University Press, 1986.

Osbun, Lee Ann. *The Problem of Participation.* Lanham, Md.: University Press of America, 1985.

Ranney, Austin. *The Referendum Device.* Washington, D.C.: American Enterprise Institute, 1981.

———. "Nonvoting Is Not a Social Disease." *Public Opinion* 6(1983):16–19.

———. "Referendums, 1988." *Public Opinion* 11(1989):15–17.

Rourke, John T., Richard P. Hiskes, and Cyrus Ernesto Zirakzadeh, *Direct Democracy and International Politics: Deciding International Issues through Referendums.* Boulder, Colo., and London: Lynn Rienners, Publishers, 1992.

Sartori, Giovanni. *The Theory of Democracy Revisited.* Chatham, N.J.: Chatham House, 1987.

Schmidt, David D. *Citizen Lawmakers: The Ballot Initiative Revolution.* Philadelphia: Temple University Press, 1989.

Uleri, Pier Vincenzo. "The Deliberative Initiative of June 1985 in Italy." *Electoral Studies* 4(1985):271–77.

————. "The 1987 Referenda." In *Italian Politics, A Review*, edited by Roberto Leonard and Piergiorgio Corbetta, 155–77. London: Pinter, 1989.

Walker, Geoffrey deQ. *The People's Law*. Sidney: Centre for Independent Studies, 1987.

Zimmerman, Joseph F. *Participatory Democracy: Populism Revisited*. New York: Praeger, 1986.

Zisk, Betty H. *Money, Media, and the Grass Roots: State Ballot Issues and the Electoral Process*. Newbury Park, Calif.: Sage Publications, 1987.

3
Western Europe

Vernon Bogdanor

Democracy is a form of government in which ultimate power lies with the people. Yet, in almost every modern democracy, the role of the people is negative.

The Constitutional Requirements

The fundamental principle lying behind the constitutions of the West European democracies, a group of countries sharing a common historical experience and the ideological heritage of the French Revolution, is that of popular sovereignty. But the practice is very different. For in every country, with the single exception of Switzerland, the people play a strictly subordinate role in public affairs. Switzerland, the exception to almost every generalization, can be regarded indeed as a test case, illustrating the implications of taking the idea of popular sovereignty seriously. Switzerland is, indeed, the only country in Europe that Rousseau would have regarded as genuinely democratic. (For other ideas about what is genuinely democratic, see chapter 2.)

Thus, Western Europe lies squarely in the second of the "two different worlds." There "referendums are held infrequently, usually only when the government thinks they are likely to provide a useful ad hoc solution to a particular constitutional or political problem or to set the seal of legitimacy on a change of regime."[1]

The constitutional role of referendums in Western Europe is summarized in table 3–1. Western Europe includes seventeen major democracies—Austria, Belgium, Britain, Denmark, Finland, France, Germany, Greece, Iceland, Ireland, Italy, the Netherlands, Norway,

---

I should like to thank Gráinne de Burca, Jack Hayward, David Hine, Desmond King, and Barry Nicholas for their help in the preparation of this chapter.

1. David Butler and Austin Ranney, *Referendums: A Study in Practice and Theory* (Washington, D.C.: American Enterprise Institute, 1978), p. 221.

Portugal, Spain, Sweden, and Switzerland. Of these, three—Belgium, the Netherlands, and Norway—make no provision for the referendum in their constitutions. Finland has made provision for the referendum only since 1987, and Portugal since 1989. Germany provides for the referendum only to reorganize *Land* boundaries (Articles 29 and 118), and perhaps by implication to endorse a new constitution produced by a unified Germany. Article 146 declares that the Basic Law "shall cease to be in force on the day on which a constitution adopted by a free decision of the German people comes into force." But Germany has not held a national referendum during the postwar period. Britain, which has no codified constitution, was regarded until the 1970s as a representative democracy in which the referendum had no place.

The Netherlands is the only West European democracy never to have held a referendum. The referendum has been used in Belgium and Norway, although it is not mentioned in their constitutions, and it was used in Finland before constitutional provision was made for it in 1987.

Seven of the seventeen European democracies—Austria, Belgium, Britain, Finland, Germany, the Netherlands, and Portugal—have held either one or no national referendum under their current constitutions. Iceland and Norway have held only one national referendum in the postwar years. In the case of two other democracies—Greece and Spain, since they returned to democracy in the 1970s—the referendum has been used only to ratify the form of state. Spain has held one other referendum, however, on membership of NATO.

Excluding Switzerland, this leaves just five countries in which the referendum has played an important role in the postwar period— Denmark, France, Ireland, Italy, and Sweden. But the referendum has also exerted profound effects on the party system in Britain and Norway, even though these countries have used it hardly at all. Moreover, British politics has been considerably affected by two nonnational referendums: the Northern Ireland border poll in 1973 and the two devolution referendums, held in Scotland and Wales, in 1979.

Excluding Switzerland, therefore, the referendum has played an important role in seven of the seventeen democracies of Western Europe—nearly half. It is upon these seven countries that our analysis is concentrated. But first it is necessary to clarify the role of the referendum in the constitutions of those West European democracies that make provision for it.

The Constitutional Status of Referendums

If the referendum exists in "two different worlds," it is unlikely that generalizations about its effects in Switzerland will be of much rele-

TABLE 3–1
REFERENDUMS IN WESTERN EUROPEAN CONSTITUTIONS

Country	Referendums Mentioned in Constitution?	Referendums Required for Constitutional Amendments?	Constitutional Provision for Referendums in Noncon. Legislation?	Who Triggers?	Provision for Qualified Majority?	Consultative or Binding?
Austria	yes	yes[a]	yes	government or ML	no	binding
Belgium	no	no	no	government	no	consult.
Britain	no	no	no	government	yes	consult.
Denmark	yes	yes	yes	ML	yes	binding
Finland	yes	no	yes	government	no	consult.
France	yes	yes[b]	yes	government[c]	no	binding
Germany	yes	no	no	NA	no	binding
Greece	yes	no	yes	H	no	binding
Iceland	yes	no[d]	yes	H	no	binding
Ireland	yes	yes	yes	H and ML	yes	binding
Italy	yes	no[e]	yes	E[f]	yes	binding

Netherlands	no	no	NA	no	NA
Norway	no	no	government	no	binding
Portugal	no	yes	H	no	binding
Spain	yes[g]	yes	government or ML	no	binding
Sweden	no	yes	government or ML	yes	binding & consult.
Switzerland	yes	yes	E	yes	binding

NOTES: NA = not available.

E = a portion of the electorate; H = the constitutional head of state; ML = a minority of the legislature.

a. For a total revision of the constitution. A partial revision can be put to a referendum at the request of one-third of the members of either house.

b. As one alternative, the other being a joint session of the two houses and a three-fifths majority.

c. The president, who is generally head of government as well as head of state, can normally call a referendum at his or her pleasure.

d. Only for altering the position of the established Lutheran church.

e. As one alternative, if demanded by a half-million voters, one-fifth of the members of either chamber, or five regional councils. But a referendum cannot be called if the amendment in question has been passed by two-thirds majorities in both chambers.

f. Five regional councils or 500,000 voters.

g. For total revision, and for partial revision covering certain basic matters. Other matters can be put to referendums if demanded by one-tenth of the members of either house.

SOURCE: Author.

vance for other West European democracies. But even within the restricted world of those democracies that use it infrequently, the referendum is a more complex instrument than is usually assumed. It has a number of different functions that must be distinguished, one from the other, if valid generalizations are to be made.

The first use to which the referendum can be put is to ratify changes to the constitution. In Denmark and in Ireland (Articles 88 and 46, respectively), the referendum is required to ratify *any* amendment to the Constitution.

In Austria (Article 44 [2]) and in Spain (Articles 44 [2] and 168 [3], respectively), a referendum is required for a total revision of the Constitution, and in Spain also for a partial revision affecting certain basic matters. In each case, a qualified majority in Parliament is also required for constitutional change. In Austria, constitutional laws can be ratified only in the presence of at least half the members of the lower house, and a two-thirds majority is required. In Spain, a bill proposing such a total revision or a partial revision affecting basic matters must be approved by a two-thirds majority of each chamber of the Cortes twice, with a general election intervening. The amendment is then put to a referendum, after having been approved for a second time.

Both countries also contain provision for a partial revision of the Constitution (in Spain a partial revision not affecting basic matters), to be put to referendum at the request of a minority of the legislature. In Austria, partial revisions, like total revisions, require the presence of at least half the members of the lower house and a two-thirds majority. There is no compulsory referendum, but one-third of the members of either house can demand it. A further use of the referendum in Austria is provided by Article 60 (6), by which the federal president can be deposed by referendum before the expiry of his term of office. This requires a two-thirds majority in the lower house with at least half the members present and a majority in a joint public session of the two houses meeting together.

In Spain (Article 167), a partial revision of the Constitution that does not affect the basic matters to which Article 168 applies requires a three-fifths majority in each house, or an absolute majority of the members of the Senate, and a two-thirds majority in the lower house. One-tenth of the members of either house can, after such an amendment has been passed, demand a referendum. So far, no doubt because of the stringent conditions required, there have been no constitutional referendums in either Austria or Spain.[2]

---

2. The referendum has also been used in Spain to establish the first of the "Autonomous Communities" in Andalusia, the Basque country, Catalonia, and Galicia between 1979 and 1981.

Sweden also has a provision by which a minority in the legislature can secure a referendum on constitutional change. A constitutional amendment of 1988—chapter 8, Article 15 of the Instrument of Government—provides that any alteration to the Constitution requires approval by two separate Riksdags, separated by a general election. The general election must be called at least nine months after the amendment has been approved for the first time by the single-chamber Riksdag. Within fifteen days from the date on which the Riksdag first adopts the bill, a referendum can be held on a motion by at least one-tenth of the members of the Riksdag, provided that it is supported by at least one-third of the members. The referendum is held simultaneously with the general election. For a constitutional amendment to be *rejected* at this stage, not only must there be a majority against the proposal but the number of votes cast against it must exceed half the votes validly cast at the general election. No constitutional referendums have yet been called in Sweden.

In Iceland, the referendum is required to ratify any revision of the status of the Evangelical Lutheran Church, which is the state church (Article 79). But the referendum has never yet been invoked for this purpose.

In France and Italy, the referendum is one alternative method of changing the constitution. In France, Article 89 of the Fifth Republic Constitution prescribes that, after passage by both chambers, a constitutional amendment must be put either to referendum or to the two chambers sitting together as a congress, where it must secure a three-fifths majority. In Italy (Article 138), similarly, an amendment must be put either to referendum or to the two houses sitting together, where it needs a two-thirds majority. In addition, a referendum can be held on a constitutional law within three months of its publication—if either one-fifth of the members of one of the chambers, or a half-million electors, or five regional councils call for one.

So far, however, no referendums have been held in France or Italy under these provisions. In France, constitutional changes have been secured either by seeking the necessary parliamentary majority, or through an alternative route that allows the president to call a referendum without securing the support of Parliament (see the section on France, which follows).

Constitutional change in Austria, France, Ireland, and Spain requires merely a simple majority when put to referendum. In Italy, however, an absolute majority of the electorate, and not merely of those voting, must support the constitutional change for it to succeed. Sweden also has a turnout requirement. Denmark is the only other European democracy in which a qualified majority—40 percent of the electorate—is required for constitutional change. In Britain, however, the referendums on devolution to Scotland and Wales in 1979, widely regarded as providing for constitutional change, had a 40 percent qualifying majority imposed on them by backbench members of Parliament, against the wishes of the government.

It is perhaps natural for a democracy to require a referendum before its constitution can be amended. The rationale behind a codified constitution, after all, is that some matters are of such fundamental importance that they should be placed beyond the reach of transient parliamentary majorities. A general election may be said to yield a mandate to govern. But it yields no mandate to alter the framework of government, the constitution. For that, something over and above endorsement at a general election and a parliamentary majority is required. It is natural to seek the extra endorsement needed in popular approval through a referendum. The referendum is thus one method by which a constitution or parts of it may be entrenched. That entrenchment is of course all the greater if, as in Denmark, a qualified majority is required for constitutional amendments.

The referendum performs its function of entrenchment through dividing the legislative power between Parliament and the people. It helps to secure a liberal ideal—limited and constitutional government—through conservative means, by checking government. For, although commonly seen as an instrument of popular sovereignty, the constitutional referendum gives the people only the power of veto. The electorate is confined to giving a verdict on a change that has already been endorsed. The people act in effect as a third chamber—or, in unicameral Denmark and Sweden, a second chamber. The constitutional referendum is thus necessarily a conservative weapon. Like a good second chamber, it provides a check upon government. If the people approve a constitutional amendment, then it will pass. But, ex hypothesi, it would have passed if the referendum had not been required; for it already had legislative endorsement. Conversely, if the measure is rejected, it must be dropped. Thus the constitutional referendum is necessarily a weapon for protection and not for change.

The Facultative Referendum. In addition to its use in ratifying constitutional amendments, the referendum can be used to ratify ordinary, nonconstitutional legislation. With constitutional legislation, the referendum is either required, or is one of two required alternatives; with ordinary legislation, it is merely allowed.[3] In such circumstances, the referendum is often labeled facultative—that is, optional or permis-

---

3. There is one exception, described in the section on Denmark.

sive—as opposed to obligatory. Specific provision is made for the facultative referendum in the constitutions of eleven countries: Austria (Articles 41 and 43), Denmark (Articles 20, 29, and 42), Finland (Constitutional laws, III, a), France (Article 11), Greece (Article 44 [2]), Iceland (Article 26), Ireland (Article 27), Italy (Article 75), Portugal (Article 118), Spain (Articles 87 [3] and 92), and Sweden (Article 8, chapter 4). In Finland, Spain, and Sweden, the referendum is consultative only; in the other countries, it is binding.[4]

Unlike the constitutional referendum, the facultative referendum is not necessarily a conservative political weapon. In France, under the provisions of Article 11, the president can call a referendum without parliamentary approval. The referendum can thus be used, and has been used, to override the will of Parliament and strengthen the president. In Austria, Finland, Spain, and Sweden, also, the power to call a nonconstitutional referendum lies in effect in the hands of the government.

In general, where the government has discretion as to whether to call a referendum, the referendum will strengthen the government. The constitutional referendum, however, takes the decision to call a referendum out of the hands of the government, since it is *required* before the constitution can be amended.

Thus, for an evaluation of the political consequences of the referendum, it is necessary to identify which person or institution triggers the decision to call one and what discretion that person or institution has in making the decision. Where the power to call a referendum lies in the hands of government, it is likely to prove a tactical weapon in strengthening its powers.

But the government is not the only institution that can be given the authority to call a referendum. This decision can be entrusted by the constitution to some other authority. It can, for example, be entrusted to the constitutional head of state. In Greece, Iceland, Ireland, and Portugal, the president has authority to call a referendum under certain circumstances. In Greece, the 1975 Constitution, as modified by constitutional amendments passed in 1986, allows the president to call a referendum "on crucial national issues" if supported by an absolute majority of the legislature, and to call a referendum "on crucial social questions" if supported by 60 percent of the legislature. In Iceland, the president can submit any bill passed by Parliament to the people. In

---

4. In Austria, following the nuclear power referendum of 1978, a bill was passed prohibiting the starting of any nuclear power plant unless there was a two-thirds majority in Parliament or a referendum. See Anton Pelinka, "The Nuclear Power Referendum in Austria," *Electoral Studies* (1983), p. 257.

Portugal, the president can call a referendum at the request of Parliament or the government on a "question of national interest," excluding budgetary or fiscal matters. So far, however, no referendums have been called under any of these provisions.

In Ireland, a majority in the Senate, together with a minority in the Dáil (the lower house), can seek a referendum on any nonconstitutional bill that the Dáil has approved but the Senate has rejected. The president, acting at his or her discretion, then decides within ten days whether the bill contains "a proposal of such national importance that the will of the people thereon ought to be ascertained." If a referendum is called under this provision, one-third of the electorate as well as a majority of the voters must oppose the bill in question for it to be defeated.

A third means by which the legislative referendum can be triggered is through the agency of a minority of the legislature. This can be done in Ireland, as we have seen, and also in Denmark. In Denmark, one-third of the members of the single-chamber Folketing can demand a referendum on any item of legislation, with the exception of bills concerning finance, government loans, salaries and pensions, naturalization, expropriation, taxation, and bills discharging treaty obligations. For a law to be rejected in a referendum, not only must a majority of voters reject it, but this majority must constitute at least 30 percent of the electorate.

In addition, referendums must be held with a similar qualified majority requirement for any bill transferring powers to international authorities, unless a majority of five-sixths of the Folketing is obtained (Article 20); and for any bill altering the age qualification for the suffrage (Article 29).

The final form of trigger is the people themselves. This is possible in Western Europe only in Italy and in Switzerland. In Italy, provision is made for an abrogative referendum to be invoked by voters in a petition. Such a referendum can be held on any law on the statute book, however long it has been there, except for international treaties, taxation or budgetary laws, or laws dealing with amnesty, if a petition to this effect is signed by 500,000 electors or five regional councils. The referendum, however, can be used only to repeal laws, not to propose them.

Two West European Constitutions—Austria's and Spain's—make provision for submission by electors of draft legislation to the legislature, although in contrast with the Swiss initiative procedure the legislature is not bound to take action on them. Such initiatives are known in Austria as *Volksbegehren*, to distinguish them from the initiative proper, as employed in Switzerland, *Volksinitiativen*. In Austria, 100,000 voters, or one-sixth of the voters in three *Länder*, can submit *Volksbegehren;* there have been fifteen since the first one was held in 1964. In Spain, provision is made for an organic law to regulate this instrument. At least 500,000 signatures are to be required, and "matters concerning organic laws, taxation, international affairs or the prerogative of granting pardons" are excluded.

Thus Italy is the only West European democracy, apart from Switzerland, which allows the referendum to be taken entirely out of the hands of the political class. Only in Italy can a referendum be called even if every member of the political class as represented in Parliament and the executive is against it. Yet even in Italy the electorate has only a negative role, in that it can only abrogate; it cannot require a law to be put in the statute book. Only in Switzerland can electors insist that a legislative measure be passed even if government is against it. Elsewhere, electors can repair the sins of commission of their governments, vetoing or in Italy repealing laws that they do not like; they cannot repair the sins of omission by putting on the statute book laws they believe governments ought to have enacted. Excepting Switzerland, then, the referendum is employed in the democracies of Western Europe to supplement, or perhaps complement, the representative system but not to supplant it.

The United Kingdom

The United Kingdom is the only democracy in Western Europe without a codified constitution. The British Constitution, it has been said, can be summed up in eight words—whatever the Queen-in-Parliament enacts is law. Thus Parliament could, if it wished, submit any item of legislation to referendum. In the absence of a codified constitution, however, the referendum cannot ever be *required* as an instrument to ratify legislation. Moreover, there is no reason why any British government, which normally commands a majority in the House of Commons and therefore controls Parliament, should wish to call a referendum. Why should it seek to put at risk its own legislation by calling for the verdict of the people upon it?

Until the 1970s, the referendum was thought of as contrary to the British Constitution. The Constitution, it was said, knows nothing of the people. The central principle of the British Constitution—perhaps its only principle—was that of the sovereignty of Parliament, a principle developed during the seventeenth century, well before the coming of universal suffrage. From this point of view, the referendum could be seen as a threat to the sovereignty of Parliament, as a means of

33

constraining members of Parliament (MPs) in a direction they might not wish to take.

Although Britain's first and so far its only referendum was not held until 1975, nevertheless its introduction has been a subject of lively debate since the end of the nineteenth century.[5] This debate casts a great deal of light on the role the referendum might be expected to play in a representative democracy.

The referendum was first advocated in 1890 by the great jurist A. V. Dicey in an article in the *Contemporary Review*, entitled "Ought the Referendum to Be Introduced into England?" It is paradoxical that Dicey should have been the first to advocate the referendum in Britain, for he was the author of the classic work *Introduction to the Study of the Law of the Constitution* (1885). Foremost among the principles there identified as central to the British Constitution was the sovereignty of Parliament—a principle generally held to preclude the referendum.

For Dicey, however, there was a crucial weakness in the British system of government. This was "the possibility . . . which no one can dispute of a fundamental change passing into law which the mass of the nation do not desire."[6] For one of the corollaries of the doctrine of the sovereignty of Parliament was, "There is under the English Constitution no marked or clear distinction between laws which are not fundamental or constitutional and laws which are fundamental or constitutional."[7]

In particular, Dicey was concerned to combat Gladstone's policy of Irish Home Rule, a fundamental change that in any other country would be regarded as a constitutional measure. It was, moreover, a measure that Dicey believed would lead inevitably to the breakup of the United Kingdom and which he also thought was opposed by the majority of the electorate.

Britain, as much as any other democracy, required a constitutional check to ensure that fundamental legislation was not passed against the will of the people. A codified constitution with a bill of rights was, however, anathema to Dicey, since it would impose a rigid and artifi-

---

5. See part 1 of Vernon Bogdanor, *The People and the Party System: The Referendum and Electoral Reform* (Cambridge: Cambridge University Press, 1981), which seeks to analyze the historical debate. See also Vernon Bogdanor, "Grand-Bretagne," in Francis Delpérée, *Referendums* (Brussels: CRISP, 1985), for an account of the current constitutional position.

6. Albert Venn Dicey to James Bryce, 23 March 1891, Bryce Papers, Bodleian Library, MS 3 fo. 83.

7. Albert Venn Dicey, *Introduction to the Study of the Law of the Constitution*, 10th ed. (London: Macmillan, 1959), p. 89.

cial framework on the nation's constitutional development. The great advantage of the referendum lay in its being a *democratic* check on government. It was "the best, if not the only possible, check upon ill-considered alterations in the fundamental institutions of the country," and it was "the only check on the predominance of party which is at the same time democratic and conservative."[8]

The referendum was advocated, then, less to secure popular participation than as a means of circumventing the excesses of democratic government. Its motive force stemmed less from a belief in the sovereignty of the people than from distrust of the working of popular institutions, and especially the party system. The referendum, Dicey believed, was "the one available check on the recklessness of Party leaders," and it would yield "formal acknowledgment of the doctrine which lies at the basis of English democracy—that a law depends at bottom for its enactment on the consent of the nation as represented by the electors."[9] Its introduction therefore would be "an emphatic assertion of the principle that the nation stands above parties."[10]

Dicey did not succeed in securing a referendum on Irish Home Rule. But his arguments were taken up by Conservatives seeking to check Liberal legislation of which they disapproved. In 1910, the Conservative party, by then in opposition, proposed that the referendum be used to resolve any dispute between the two houses of Parliament on a nonfinancial bill. They also sought to demarcate a special category of "constitutional" legislation that would need to be ratified by referendum in the case of disagreement between the two houses. This constitutional category would comprise any legislation that affected the existence of the Crown, or Protestant succession; established any legislative body within the United Kingdom; or altered the constitution or powers of either house of Parliament or the relations between them. But the Liberal government of the day refused to accept the referendum and the issue lapsed.

The referendum, then, was advocated in an attempt to stop Irish Home Rule. It was also advocated in an attempt to reject the other main radical measure of the period, tariff reform—the policy of departing from free trade and putting customs duties on foreign imports. This policy was strongly favored by Conservative activists, but it was

---

8. Albert Venn Dicey, "Ought the Referendum to Be Introduced into England?" *Contemporary Review* (1890), pp. 505, 507.

9. Albert Venn Dicey, *A Leap in the Dark*, 2d ed. (London: John Murray, 1911), pp. 189–90.

10. Albert Venn Dicey to St. Loe Strachey, 6 May 1895. Strachey papers, House of Lords Record Office, S/5/5/2.

thought to be unpopular with the voters. Therefore, just before the December 1910 general election, the Conservative leader Arthur Balfour promised that the Conservatives, if returned, would not introduce tariff reform without holding a referendum.

Paradoxically, however, there were some advocates of tariff reform who pressed for a referendum on it, hoping to overcome the inertia of the Conservative leadership. That was the position of the main protagonists of tariff reform—Joseph Chamberlain, who called for a referendum in 1903, and Lord Beaverbrook, who in 1930 forced the Conservative leadership to promise a referendum on the issue. The Conservative commitment to the referendum soon lapsed, however.

Thus advocates of the referendum were unable to make headway. During the 1930s, the use of bogus referendums by foreign dictatorships discredited them in Britain. When Winston Churchill proposed a referendum in 1945 on whether the wartime coalition should be prolonged, Clement Attlee, the Labour leader, replied:

> I could not consent to the introduction into our national life of a device so alien to all our traditions as the referendum, which has only too often been the instrument of Nazism and Fascism. Hitler's practices in the field of referenda and plebiscites can hardly have endeared these expedients to the British heart.

The predominant motive of supporters of the referendum was negative, the desire to prevent change—whether Home Rule or tariff reform—rather than positive. It was essentially a defensive weapon, and supported on the whole by Conservatives rather than by Liberals or by the nascent Labour party. Indeed, between 1910 and 1945, three of the five Conservative leaders—Balfour, Baldwin, and Churchill—advocated it.

During the immediate postwar years, however, the referendum disappeared as an issue in British politics. For these were the years of consensus politics, when the pendulum seemed to swing fairly evenly between the two major parties, Conservative and Labour. No issues seemed to raise major constitutional concerns in the way that Irish Home Rule had done.

In postwar Britain, the issue of the referendum first arose not in the mainland but in Northern Ireland, and under highly unusual circumstances; for Northern Ireland was the only part of the United Kingdom whose membership was constitutionally guaranteed. When, in 1948, Eire decided to become an independent republic outside the Commonwealth, the British government had responded by passing the 1949 Ireland Act, which provided, *inter alia*, that Northern Ireland would not cease to be a part of the United Kingdom without the consent of the Parliament of Northern Ireland—Stormont. In 1972, however, Edward Heath's government prorogued Stormont, and it had therefore to find some other way to affirm the status of Northern Ireland. It was for this reason that a referendum in Northern Ireland—the Northern Ireland border poll—was held in 1973.

Advocates of the border poll hoped that it would "take the border out of politics" in Northern Ireland. For politics in the province was bedeviled by the dispute about the border, which polarized political opinion into a Protestant Unionist party and various Catholic Republican parties. If the issue of the border could be decided by referendum, then perhaps the party conflict could evolve away from sectarian conflict so that politics in Northern Ireland would come to resemble the politics of the rest of the United Kingdom.

Such reasoning was, however, rather simplistic. For Irish nationalists could argue that the outcome of the border poll was predetermined by the politicians who had established partition in 1920–1921. Northern Ireland had been set up as it was precisely because it was the largest area that could comfortably be carved out of the island of Ireland and dominated by a permanent Protestant majority. Therefore, republicans argued, the referendum was nothing more than a propaganda exercise. It was not needed to discover the opinion of the majority in Northern Ireland. That had been predetermined by the way the boundary had been drawn in the 1920s. Resolution of the Northern Ireland problem depended not upon displaying the obvious fact that there was a Protestant majority in the North but in devising a satisfactory relationship that could accommodate the needs of both Protestant and Catholic communities. It was by no means clear how the border poll would contribute to that aim. For this reason, the parties representing the Catholic community advised their supporters to boycott the poll, advice that seems largely to have been taken.

The border poll asked the electors of Northern Ireland two questions:

"Do you want Northern Ireland to remain a part of the United Kingdom?" ("Yes," 591, 820).

"Do you want Northern Ireland to be joined with the Irish Republic outside the United Kingdom?" ("Yes," 6,463).

The turnout was 58.6 percent. Since 98.9 percent of those voting supported the Union, it could be argued that it had the positive endorsement of 58.0 percent of the Northern Irish electorate.

When the Northern Ireland Parliament was prorogued, Edward Heath promised that "a system of regular plebiscites" scheduled at ten yearly intervals would be held.[11] No further border poll was held in 1983. The Northern Ireland Constitution Act of 1976, however, provides that Northern Ireland shall not cease to be part of the United Kingdom without the consent of the electorate of Northern Ireland. Thus the referendum serves to entrench the position of Northern Ireland within the United Kingdom.

The poll might have proved a useful propaganda exercise in convincing opinion abroad that Northern Ireland remained a part of the United Kingdom entirely voluntarily, but it did nothing to resolve the basic problem of the province, which well illustrates Henry Maine's dictum:

> Democracies are quite paralysed by the plea of Nationality. There is no more effective way of attacking them than by admitting the right of the majority to govern, but denying that the majority so entitled is the particular majority which claims the right.[12]

In such a situation, the referendum has little to offer.

The Referendum on European Community Membership. Not until Britain's entry into the European Community (EC) in the early 1970s did the question of a national referendum come again to be raised in British politics. This occurred less as a result of constitutional doctrine than for quite accidental reasons.

The question of whether Britain should enter the European Community was, like Irish Home Rule, one that transcended party loyalties. The issue split both major parties. During the 1970s, most of Labour's left wing was hostile to entering what it saw as a capitalist cartel, but the majority of the right wing, including most of the leading figures in the party, favored entry. Most Conservative MPs also favored entry, but some who belonged to the old imperialist wing of the party opposed it. Others, led by Enoch Powell, also opposed entry, believing that the EC required an unacceptable curtailment of national sovereignty. Opinion was divided in the country also, nor did the divisions in popular opinion follow party lines.

By 1971, Edward Heath, the Conservative prime minister, had secured agreement among the other members of the European Community on the terms of British entry. In the preceding general election of 1970, however, all three parties had supported British entry. This meant that there was no way of telling whether the electorate sup-

---

11. House of Commons, 24 March 1972, *Hansard*, col. 1862.
12. Henry Maine, *Popular Government*, 5th ed. (London: John Murray, 1897), p. 28.

ported what seemed to many the most important constitutional issue of the century, involving in effect a permanent transfer of legislative power away from Westminster. At a press conference on 2 June 1970, Heath claimed that a referendum would not be needed to ratify Britain's entry, arguing:

> I always said that you could not possibly take this country into the Common Market [as the European Community was then known in Britain] if the majority of the people were against it, but this is handled through the Parliamentary system.[13]

He did not explain, however, how "the Parliamentary system" would reflect public opinion when all three major parties favored entry.

The Labour party had also been opposed to a referendum; but, in opposition after 1970, the leadership was being pressed by the left wing and by constituency activists to oppose entry. There seemed a real possibility that, acting in concert with Conservative opponents of the European Community, Labour might be able to defeat the government on the issue. Fearing a split, the leadership espoused the referendum, in James Callaghan's words "a rubber life raft into which the party may one day have to climb"[14] as a device to avoid a split.

The Labour leaders accepted the referendum both to avoid having to commit a future Labour government to withdrawal from the European Community and to maintain the unity of the party. This decision was in accordance with feeling in the country. Survey evidence from February 1971 indicated that a large majority of the electorate favored a referendum.[15]

In opposition, Labour was unable to secure a referendum to ratify Britain's entry into the European Community, which took place in January 1973. Having returned to power in the general election of February 1974, however, Labour renegotiated the terms of British entry. It put these renegotiated terms to the people on 5 June 1975, the date of Britain's only national referendum, with a recommendation that they be accepted. To maintain Labour's unity, however, the referendum was accompanied by another constitutional innovation, the suspension of collective cabinet responsibility. This had occurred only once before, in 1932, under the special circumstances of a coalition government.

---

13. Edward Heath, quoted in Vernon Bogdanor, *The People and the Party System*, p. 38.

14. Quoted in David Butler and Uwe Kitzinger, *The 1975 Referendum* (London: Macmillan, 1976), p. 12.

15. See Stanley Alderson, *Yea or Nay? The Referendum in the United Kingdom* (London: Cassell, 1975), p. 2.

Seven cabinet ministers, including Michael Foot, a future leader of the party, and Tony Benn, the leader of the Left, took advantage of the suspension of collective responsibility to argue for withdrawal from the European Community, against the majority of their cabinet colleagues.

The referendum endorsed Britain's membership in the EC by a majority of 67 percent to 33 percent on a 65 percent turnout. The Yes vote was spread fairly evenly across the country, varying in mainland Britain between 55 percent and 76 percent. In Northern Ireland, the Yes vote was a bare majority, 52 percent, but the Western Isles and Shetland were the only counting areas to yield a No majority.

In the short run at least, it therefore seemed as if Harold Wilson had secured his two main aims: to make Britain's membership in the European Community legitimate and to preserve the unity of the Labour party. "It means," claimed Wilson when the result was announced, "that fourteen years of national argument are over."

It would, however, be misleading to see the outcome of the referendum as evidence of Britain's commitment to the EC. In their book on the referendum, published shortly after the event, David Butler and Uwe Kitzinger warned presciently that the verdict was "unequivocal, but it was also unenthusiastic. Support for membership was wide but it did not run deep."[16] The referendum result owed as much to the fact that the political leaders most respected by the electorate advocated remaining in the EC as it did to enthusiasm for it. A "leadership effect" was noticed by Humphrey Taylor, leader of a survey research organization conducting polls for the promarketeers. "One strong card in our hands now is that the major public figures advocating EEC membership are relatively popular while those advocating leaving the EEC are relatively unpopular," he declared.[17] The campaign took the character of a struggle between "moderates," who included the leaders of all three parties and who were in favor of the European Community, and "extremists," such as Enoch Powell; the Rev. Ian Paisley, the Northern Ireland Protestant leader; the Labour left wing; and the trade union leaders. In such a struggle, there could be little doubt where the allegiance of the British electorate would lie.

Moreover, to attract the support of the electorate, the implications of EC membership had to be understated by its supporters. Voters were assured that membership involved no loss of sovereignty. The commitment of the European Community to securing, in the words of the preamble to the Treaty of Rome, "an ever closer union" was never

---

16. Butler and Kitzinger, *1975 Referendum*, p. 280.
17. Ibid., p. 259.

mentioned. The EC was presented as little more than a commercial arrangement, and one that could in a short time yield considerable economic benefits to Britain. Perhaps for this reason, disillusionment with the EC set in very rapidly.

In the parliamentary debates on the Maastricht Treaty in 1992–1993, all three parties were once again in favor of the treaty, as they had been during the general election of 1992. Thus the elector opposed to the treaty had no means of expressing his opinion. Conservative Prime Minister John Major was opposed to a referendum, as Edward Heath had been, but so also was John Smith, the Labour leader, unlike his predecessor, Harold Wilson. The referendum, however, was advocated by Paddy Ashdown, the Liberal Democrat leader, who favored the treaty, and by Margaret Thatcher, John Major's predecessor as prime minister, who was opposed to the treaty. But, with both front benches opposed to a referendum, amendments proposing it were comfortably defeated both in the Commons and in the Lords.[18] Nevertheless, Britain remains an awkward member of the Community.

Harold Wilson's second aim in holding the referendum of 1975 had been to preserve the unity of the Labour party. But this too was secured only in the short run. The Labour government held together until its election defeat in May 1979, and the device of suspending collective responsibility meant that ministers with incompatible beliefs could stay together within the same cabinet. It was a loveless marriage, however, since the Labour promarketeers had found themselves working together with those of other parties during the referendum campaign. They began to believe that they might have more in common with the Liberals than with their own colleagues on the Left. The referendum of 1975 was one of the factors predisposing leading figures on Labour's right—such as Roy Jenkins, David Owen, and Shirley Williams—to lead a breakaway from the Labour party in 1981 and form a new party, the Social Democratic party, in alliance with the Liberals. In the long run, therefore, far from preserving traditional party alignments, the referendum may have helped to undermine them.

Britain's first and only national referendum was held less because of a principled commitment than for reasons of internal party politics. Dicey had perhaps foreseen that this would happen when he commented in 1909, a time when it seemed the Conservative party would come to favor a referendum:

> It is singular and not perhaps very fortunate that in accordance with English habits, a reform good in itself, should be

---

18. The relevant debates occurred in the House of Commons on 21 and 22 April 1993, and in the House of Lords on 14 July 1993.

proposed by men who probably do not believe in it, and who want to meet a party difficulty. Still, I hail it with satisfaction.[19]

Fifteen years earlier, Dicey had predicted that "once established, the Referendum would never be got rid of by anything short of a revolution."[20]

The 1975 referendum was an ad hoc response to what was thought of as a unique issue. It was not intended to create a precedent. "It is not just that it is more important," declared a Labour junior minister, Gerald Fowler; "it is of a different order. There is, and there can be, no issue that is on all fours with it. That is why we say that this issue is the sole exception, and there can be no other exception, to the principle that we normally operate through parliamentary democracy."[21] The difficulty was, however, that once the principle had been conceded, it would be difficult to prevent it from being invoked again.

The Devolution Referendums. Within just eighteen months of the European Community referendum, the Labour government was forced by backbench pressure to concede referendums on devolution in Scotland and Wales. The devolution referendums, like the European Community referendum, were proposed to avoid a split in the Labour party. But whereas the European Community referendum had been proposed by the Labour leadership, the devolution referendums were forced on the Labour government in December 1976 by dissident backbenchers. These dissidents were anxious to defeat a major item of legislation without forcing the government out of office or condemning it to loss of face. Thus, while a separate parliamentary bill was proposed by the government in 1975 to provide for the referendum, in 1976 it was tabled as an amendment by backbench MPs to a government bill.

The referendum was accepted by the government as part of the bill since otherwise it might well have been defeated in the House of Commons. The referendum was a device that would enable Labour backbenchers opposed to devolution nevertheless to vote for it in the House of Commons while campaigning against it in the referendum. One of the few Conservative supporters of devolution drew attention to what he called "a unique constitutional matter that this Parliament is likely to put on the statute book—a Bill in which it does not be-

---

19. Dicey to Leo Maxse, 12 October 1909, cited in Richard A. Cosgrove, *The Rule of Law: Albert Venn Dicey, Victorian Jurist* (London: Macmillan, 1980), p. 108.

20. Dicey to Maxse, 2 February 1894, cited in ibid., p. 107.

21. *Hansard,* House of Commons, 22 November 1974, col. 1743.

lieve."[22] Enoch Powell, an opponent both of devolution and of the referendum, called it:

> an event without precedent in the long history of Parliament
> . . . that members openly and publicly declaring themselves
> opposed to the legislation and bringing forward in debate
> what seemed to them cogent reasons why it must prove disastrous, voted nevertheless for the legislation and for a guillotine, with the express intention that after the minimum of
> debate the Bill should be submitted to a referendum of the
> electorate, in which they would hope and strive to secure its
> rejection.[23]

The referendum, in the words of S. E. Finer, had become "the Pontius Pilate of British politics,"[24] enabling MPs to vote for a bill while washing their hands of it.

The concession of the referendum, however, was not sufficient to secure passage of the devolution legislation, which had to be withdrawn in March 1977. Following the government's pact with the Liberals, which began shortly afterward, new bills were introduced during the 1977–1978 parliamentary session. This time, a damaging amendment was passed, against the wishes of the government, requiring 40 percent of the electorate to vote Yes in the referendum to ensure that devolution came into force. This amendment was proposed by a Labour backbench opponent of devolution, George Cunningham, and it has some claim to be regarded as the most significant backbench initiative in postwar British politics. With cruel irony, it was passed on 25 January 1978, the anniversary of the birth of Scotland's national poet, Robert Burns. It was to shatter Scottish nationalist hopes.

The devolution referendums were held on 1 March 1979. The Welsh referendum resulted in a devastating defeat for devolution by an 80–20 vote on a 59 percent turnout.

In Scotland, the result was more equivocal. Devolution won 52–48, but since the turnout was only 64 percent, only 32 percent of the electorate had supported it—far short of the 40 percent of the electorate required for implementation. Thus the Conservative government elected shortly after the referendum, in May 1979, was able to repeal both the Scotland and the Wales Acts, and devolution did not come into force.

The 40 percent rule raises important and interesting constitutional

---

22. *Hansard,* House of Commons, 15 February 1978, col. 595.

23. Cited in Bogdanor, *The People and the Party System,* p. 50.

24. S. E. Finer, ed., *Adversary Politics and Electoral Reform* (London: Anthony Wigram, 1975), p. 18.

questions,[25] since it subtly combined two different requirements. The first was that a minimum percentage of the electorate should turn out to vote; the second was that there should be a decisive majority in favor of devolution for the legislation to come into force. The lower the turnout, the higher the majority that would be needed. On a turnout of 80 percent, a simple majority would be sufficient to satisfy the 40 percent requirement. But, if the turnout were 70 percent, the Yes vote would have to reach 57 percent to satisfy it. With a 60 percent turnout, a 67 percent Yes vote would be needed.

Even so, the failure of the Yes vote to satisfy the 40 percent requirement would not necessarily defeat devolution. For in the absence of a codified constitution, the referendum in Britain cannot bind Parliament; it can only be advisory. The relevant provision in the devolution legislation required the government, in the event of the 40 percent hurdle not being met, merely to "lay before Parliament the draft of an Order-in-Council for the repeal of this Act." Parliament, however, could be asked to vote down the draft order, and might well have been asked to do so had there been a large Yes majority, even if the Yes vote did not reach 40 percent. Suppose, for example, that 39 percent of the Scottish electorate had voted for devolution and only 20 percent against. In such circumstances, there can be little doubt that the government could have secured the rejection of the draft Order, and Scottish devolution would have come into force. Thus, it was the combination of the two factors—the smallness of the total Yes vote, more than 7 percent below the 40 percent requirement, together with the narrow Yes majority—and not simply the 40 percent rule that doomed the Scotland Act.

When the 40 percent amendment was passed, some commentators drew the conclusion that, in effect, it would allow abstainers to be treated as No voters. But that is not strictly correct; for it would be Parliament that decided whether to allow devolution to proceed or not, and its decision would be based principally on the size of the gap between the Yes and No votes. The situation would, of course, have been very different if the referendum had been mandatory. In 1939, a referendum was held in Denmark on a proposal to reform the upper house. Forty-five percent of the electorate was required to vote Yes for the referendum to succeed. Ninety-two percent of those voting supported this proposal, but since only 44.5 percent of the electorate supported it, the proposal failed. Such an outcome could have been avoided with an advisory referendum, and perhaps the experience of

---

25. See Vernon Bogdanor, "The 40 Per Cent Rule," *Parliamentary Affairs* (1980), pp. 249–63.

the 40 percent rule shows one of the advantages of a flexible constitution and a flexible use of the referendum.

Like the referendum on the European Community, the devolution referendums did not finally resolve the issue. Devolution to Scotland and Wales remains the policy of the Labour party, while the Liberal Democrats are committed to a fully federal scheme of government for the United Kingdom. The fact that the referendum cannot finally resolve an issue is not, however, a conclusive argument against it. For finality, as Benjamin Disraeli once insisted, is not the language of politics. One should not expect to find in a democracy, therefore, any political instrument that can settle an issue with absolute finality.

What the referendum can and did achieve in the devolution referendums was to defuse an issue. After all, an important part of the case for devolution was that it met a powerful demand in Scotland and Wales. The referendums and the 40 percent requirement were a means of testing this case. They did so by showing that, contrary to claims made by the Scottish National party, the Scottish electorate was not fundamentally hostile toward remaining within the United Kingdom, and felt lukewarm toward devolution, and that, in Wales, Plaid Cymru (the Welsh nationalist party) enjoyed only limited support, while devolution was extremely unpopular. Both the devolution referendums and the referendum on the European Community helped to isolate extremists by showing that they did not enjoy majority support. A similar function was performed by de Gaulle's referendums on Algeria in 1961 and 1962, which served to isolate the extreme right and to deny it democratic legitimacy. Moreover, in Britain the referendum was the *only* instrument that could have succeeded in isolating opponents. For had the European Community not been put to referendum, opponents would have argued from survey evidence that Parliament was flouting the will of the people; and Scottish devolution could not have been rejected in a predominantly English Parliament without provoking separatist feeling. For in Scotland, as in Northern Ireland, there were no representative institutions capable of speaking for the people. That was the basic case for the referendum. By defusing the potential for conflict, the referendum has proved to be of considerable benefit to the democratic process in Britain.

Where, however, as in Northern Ireland, the will to agreement does not exist, the referendum cannot bring it into being. It can articulate a submerged consensus, but it cannot create one. It will only succeed in resolving a contentious dispute when there is some common ground between the parties. That common ground is almost wholly absent in Northern Ireland.

Fundamental Change without a Codified Constitution. The introduction of the referendum in Britain provides a striking illustration of how a barrier to fundamental change can be introduced in a country lacking a codified constitution. Since the referendums held in Britain have all been advisory, parliamentary sovereignty has remained formally intact. In practice, however, a referendum that produces a decisive result clearly limits the power of Parliament. In practice if not in theory, then, the referendum constitutes a method of demarcating some laws from others as fundamental, such that they require ratification by the people.

Precisely because Britain lacks a codified constitution, however, and because the referendum was introduced in an unplanned way, there has been hardly any discussion of what its scope should be. For there is no clear method of demarcating those laws that *are* fundamental and require the special protection of the referendum from laws that are not fundamental. Dicey's friend, James Bryce, asked him in 1915:

(1) What is to be the authority to decide when a Bill should be referred?
(2) How can "constitutional changes" be defined in a country that has no [rigid] constitution?[26]

Without a codified constitution, these questions cannot be satisfactorily answered. Since Britain has an elastic Constitution, so also use of the referendum must be elastic.

So far, the referendums that have been held in Britain have all been concerned with the legitimacy of transferring the powers of Parliament, either by excluding an area from Parliament's jurisdiction—the Northern Ireland border poll—by the transfer of powers to the European Community, or by limiting the power of Parliament to legislate for Scotland and Wales—devolution referendums. Such transfers of the powers of Parliament are likely to be in practice irreversible. It may seem, therefore, as if a persuasive constitutional convention has been built up that the powers of Parliament should not be transferred without popular endorsement.[27]

---

26. Bryce to Dicey, 6 April 1915: Bryce papers, Bodleian Library, MS 4 fo. 84.

27. In 1993, however, the Labour opposition declared that, if returned to power, it would put the issue of electoral reform to referendum. John Smith, the Labour leader, declared that, while personally opposed to any change in the electoral system, he thought that this was an issue that ought to be settled by referendum. Electoral reform, like entry into the European Community and devolution in the 1970s, was an issue on which Labour was deeply divided; and so here too the referendum was being advocated to preserve party unity.

There is a clear rationale for such a convention. For proposals to transfer the powers of Parliament involve the machinery by which laws are made, the framework within which legislation is enacted. The electorate, it might be said, entrusts its MPs as agents with legislative power, but it gives them no authority to transfer that power. Such authority, it may be argued, can be obtained only through a specific mandate—that is, a referendum. The idea that power is entrusted to the nation's representatives only for specific purposes reflects one of the most enduring themes of liberal constitutionalism, whose origins lie in the political thought of John Locke. "The Legislative," Locke claimed, "cannot transfer the power of making laws to any other hands. For it being but a delegated power from the People, they who have it cannot pass it to others."[28] So it is that the introduction of the referendum into British politics has served to emphasize the commitment to liberal constitutionalism that lies at the heart of the British system of government. The accidental and quite unintended way in which this has come about bears some resemblance perhaps to what Hegel would have called the Cunning of Reason.

France

The constitutional history of France contrasts with that of Britain in that it has been dominated by the search for a stable constitutional structure. During that search, France has veered between two alternative conceptions of government. The first is the *"régime d'assemblée,"* characteristic of the Third and Fourth Republics, in which the will of the people is identified with Parliament, and any limitations on the power of Parliament are seen as limitations on democracy itself. This conception of government allows hardly any place for the referendum. The Third Republic found no use for the referendum at all, while in the Fourth Republic, the referendum made only "a timid and ineffectual appearance"[29] as one method of amending the Constitution, and it was never used. Thus the political systems of the Third and Fourth Republics are perhaps best characterized by the phrase *"le peuple absent."*[30]

The second conception of government has been called the "directorial,"[31] after the Directory of 1975, a structure in which the executive

---

28. John Locke, *Second Treatise of Government*, para. 141.

29. Philip M. Williams, *Crisis and Compromise: Politics in the Fourth Republic*, Anchor Books ed. (New York: Doubleday, 1966), p. 309.

30. Williams, *Crisis and Compromise*, p. 460.

31. By Guy Carcassonne. See his chapter, "The Fifth Republic after Thirty years," in Vernon Bogdanor, ed., *Constitutions in Democratic Politics* (London: Gower, 1988), pp. 241–56.

power was separated from the legislature. The directors themselves were chosen from the legislature, but it seemed natural to suggest that if a strong executive were needed to curb the ambitions of the legislature, that executive should be given its strength through popular election. Thus, under a constitution of the directorial type, the referendum would have a major role to play in legitimizing government. From the time of Napoleon, however, the referendum had been used to provide popular legitimacy not for democratic government, but for dictatorship. In 1800, it was used to make Napoleon first consul; in 1802, to make him consul for life; and in 1804, hereditary emperor. Napoleon's nephew, Louis Napoleon, used the referendum in December 1851, after his coup d'état, to secure ratification of his new Constitution, which replaced the Second Republic and made him president for ten years. He used it again in 1852 to establish the empire in which he became Napoleon III. In 1940, Marshal Pétain's proposed constitution would also have found a place for the referendum.

It is hardly surprising, then, that the referendum was regarded by many French democrats with suspicion. They saw de Gaulle's advocacy of it during the Fifth Republic as confirmation of his undemocratic leanings. In October 1962 de Gaulle submitted to referendum his proposal to elect the president directly instead of, as hitherto, through an electoral college composed of local notables. Gaston Monerville, president of the Senate, said that de Gaulle was establishing "not democracy, but at best a sort of enlightened Bonapartism" that was "the negation of democracy." The former Fourth Republic president, Vincent Auriol, declared that "the referendum is an act of absolute power. . . . While ostensibly making obeisance to the sovereignty of the people, it is, in fact, an attempt to deprive the people of its sovereignty, for the benefit of one man."[32] Not least among de Gaulle's achievements is his showing that these fears were groundless. He domesticated the referendum, so that it was no longer associated with dictatorship.

De Gaulle ensured that the Fourth Republic Constitution would be ratified by referendum. Pondering on the future of his country in 1945, after the Liberation, "with an eye to the future" he "introduced the referendum system, made the people decide that henceforward its direct approval would be necessary for a Constitution to be valid, and thus created the democratic means of one day founding a good one [himself], to replace the bad one [that is, the Fourth Republic], which was about to be concocted by and for the parties."[33] Thus de Gaulle

---

32. Quoted in Charles de Gaulle, *Memoirs of Hope: Renewal and Endeavor* (New York: Simon and Schuster, 1971), p. 325.

33. Ibid., pp. 6–7.

created a precedent that, by contrast with the Third Republic, future constitutions would require ratification by referendum. Both the Fourth Republic in 1946 and the Fifth in 1958 were ratified in this way.

The Constitution of the Fifth Republic was a conscious attempt to break away from the *régime d'assemblée* that Gaullists argued had paralyzed France and to replace it with a system of the directorial type, based on a strong executive, the separation of powers, and a direct line of responsibility between government and the people.

Article 3 of the Fifth Republic Constitution declares: "National sovereignty belongs to the people, which shall exercise it through its representatives and by means of referendums." By contrast, Article 3 of the Fourth Republic Constitution had restricted use of the referendum to "constitutional matters," declaring that "in all other matters, [the people] shall exercise it [that is, their sovereignty] through their deputies in the National Assembly." In the Fifth Republic, scope is provided for the referendum to be used not only for constitutional amendments but also for certain ordinary, nonconstitutional bills. Provision for the popular referendum is something quite new in modern French constitutional experience, although it was part of the stillborn Jacobin Constitution of 1793, which contained a provision for a popular vote on laws, and the Bonapartist Constitutions of 1800 and 1851.

The main provisions regulating the referendum lie in two articles of the Fifth Republic Constitution. The first is Article 11:

> The President of the Republic may, on the proposal of the Government during the sessions of Parliament or on the joint motion of its two Houses, . . . submit to a referendum any bill dealing with the organisation of the public authorities, entailing approval of a Community agreement, or providing for authorisation to ratify a treaty which, without being contrary to the Constitution, would affect the function of institutions.
>
> Should the referendum have decided in favour of the Bill, the President of the Republic shall promulgate it within the time limit stipulated in the preceding Article.

The other is Article 89, dealing with the amendment of the Constitution:

> The initiative for amending the Constitution shall pertain both to the President of the Republic, on the proposal of the Prime Minister, and to the members of Parliament.
>
> The Government's or the Private Member's Bill for amendment must be passed by the two Houses in identical terms. The amendment shall become effective after approval by referendum.

Nevertheless, the proposed amendment shall not be submitted to a referendum should the President of the Republic decide to submit it to Parliament convened as Congress; in this case, the proposed amendment shall be approved only if it is adopted by a three-fifths majority of the votes cast. . . .

No amendment procedure may be undertaken or followed when the integrity of the territory is in jeopardy.

The Republican form of government shall not be subject to amendment.

In addition, there is an implicit reference to the referendum in Article 53, where it is declared that "no cession, no exchange, no addition of territory shall be valid without the consent of the populations concerned," while Article 86 declares that a change of status of a member-state of the French Community requires confirmation by means of a local referendum in the member-state concerned.

The crucial difference between Article 89, dealing with amendment of the Constitution, and Article 11 is that under Article 89, the electorate ratifies or rejects a measure that the legislature has already accepted. Under Article 11, the legislature has no role, but is bypassed through the referendum. Thus Article 11 allows laws to be passed to which the legislature might well be opposed. Admittedly, the legislature must be in session when the referendum is proposed. That need not be a serious restriction, however, since nothing prevents the president from calling an extraordinary session of Parliament for the purpose of submitting a measure to referendum.

Three-Phase Amending Procedure. Article 89 provides for a three-phase procedure for amending the Constitution: the first is the decision to amend; the second is the vote by the two houses; and the third is approval by referendum or by Congress. The first stage can be taken either by the president, on the proposal of the prime minister, or by members of Parliament. The wording of the amendment indicates that the president is not required to accept the prime minister's proposal. In practice, since the president and the prime minister will normally be of the same political complexion, conflict is unlikely. During a period of cohabitation, however, when the Élysée and the Hôtel Matignon are occupied by politicians of different political complexions—as occurred between 1986 and 1988, and after 1993—this provision gives the president a veto over a constitutional referendum. He need not call one unless he wishes to do so.

Parliament is unlikely of its own accord to propose a constitutional amendment, although in 1985 Valéry Giscard d'Estaing, speaking for the opposition, put forward a motion in the National Assembly urging that President François Mitterrand's proposal to change the electoral system for the National Assembly from the two-ballot system to proportional representation be put to referendum. Giscard's motion, predictably, was rejected by the National Assembly. Indeed, when the Right won control of the assembly and formed a government, following the legislative elections of 1986, it proceeded to change the electoral system back to the two-ballot system, without considering for one moment that this change should be referred to the voters.[34]

The second phase is the vote by the two houses, each of which must pass the bill in identical terms. By contrast with other legislation, governed by Article 45 of the Constitution, there is no provision for a joint committee in case of disagreement between the two houses, nor for the National Assembly to have the final word. Since the government will normally enjoy a majority in the assembly, the political effect of this provision is to give the Senate a veto on constitutional reform; for the government has no way of overcoming its opposition. That was the basic reason why, as president, de Gaulle used Article 11 rather than Article 89 to revise the Constitution.

The third phase is either the referendum or the Congress. It is for the president to choose which of these two methods to adopt, except in the case of a proposal initiated by Parliament, when the president can use only the method of ratification by referendum.

It was, no doubt, assumed when the Constitution was drawn up that the main method of amendment would be a referendum under the provisions of Article 89. But in fact no Article 89 referendum has ever been held, although the Constitution has, on a number of occasions, been amended through the alternative Congress method. The main reason for this is that the Senate, and in 1962 the assembly also, was unwilling to pass the necessary legislation. Thus, all seven of the referendums so far held under the Fifth Republic have been held under the provisions of Article 11, whose use for amending the Constitution seems now to have become a broadly acceptable convention of the Fifth Republic Constitution.

Article 11, however, is by no means as unambiguous as Article 89. It provides for a referendum to be held at the discretion of the president for any of three purposes. The second of these, approval of a French Community agreement, is now of little relevance; the third, concerning the ratification of treaties, followed from the abortive struggle to ratify the European Defense Community in 1954, a treaty that

---

34. Bernard Tricot and Raphaël Hadas-Lebel, *Les Institutions Politiques Françaises* (Paris: Presses de la Fondation Nationale des Sciences Politiques and Dalloz, 1985), p. 235.

the Gaullists hotly opposed. But the first purpose, "dealing with the organization of the public authorities," has caused many problems. The "public authorities" may reasonably be interpreted to mean the authorities established by the Constitution. But what does the word *organization* mean in this context?

The first two referendums held under the Fifth Republic, those of January 1961 and April 1962, were concerned with self-determination and independence in Algeria. It would be difficult to argue that these were matters of the "organization" of the public authorities, unless organization is considered to include territorial competence.

It was the third referendum, however, held in October 1962 to ratify direct election of the president, that aroused the most violent controversy. For almost all the leading non-Gaullist politicians, and most of the leading jurists, argued that it was unconstitutional to amend the Constitution by this route rather than by Article 89.

De Gaulle replied to this criticism by arguing that as Article 11 referred to "any Bill dealing with the organisation of the public authorities"—*"tout projet"*—he was entitled to refer a constitutional bill to the people. If the framers of the Constitution had intended to exclude constitutional legislation from the ambit of Article 11, this should have been specified in the Constitution. There were therefore, in de Gaulle's view, two alternative methods of amending the Constitution: the Article 89 route, "operative when the public authorities deemed it preferable to use parliamentary channels,"[35] and the Article 11 route.

To this, his critics replied that Article 89 provided for a special method to be used for amending the Constitution, which implicitly excluded any alternative method. But that was by no means a conclusive argument. Article 46 specified a special method of legislating organic laws, but no one had suggested that organic laws were excluded from the ambit of Article 11; and Article 34 and the articles following specified methods of legislating ordinary laws, which of course were not excluded from the ambit of Article 11. Moreover, the phrase "organization of the public powers" had a certain constitutional resonance since it echoed the official title of the first of the three constitutional laws of 1875, establishing the Third Republic, which designated it as a "law concerning the organization of public powers." Thus, such a law could, in the light of French history, be regarded as a constitutional law.

Whether de Gaulle was or was not justified on juridical grounds in using Article 11 to amend the Constitution, he was certainly acting in the spirit of the Constitution he had promulgated. For the essence

---

35. De Gaulle, *Memoirs of Hope*, p. 314.

of de Gaulle's interpretation of the Fifth Republic Constitution lay in the proposition that, in the last resort, the government should be insulated from, so as not to be dependent on, the legislature. The legislature was for de Gaulle the arena for political parties and pressure groups, and as such an object of suspicion, since these bodies distorted rather than reflected the popular will. Thus the president's tenure of office was not to be dependent on the legislature, and it could not be affected by elections to the National Assembly. Moreover, the president enjoyed the power of dissolving the legislature, a power that could not be effectively exercised by governments in the Third or Fourth Republics. Thus, wherever a conflict arose between the institutions of the state, this conflict could be resolved through an appeal to the people; for, in the Gaullist view, it was the people who were the supreme court of France.[36]

In terms of this conception of government, it was surely anomalous that Parliament was able in 1962 to block what has been called the most popular constitutional reform for a hundred years.[37] To prevent Article 11 from being used for constitutional amendment would be to give the Senate an absolute veto over the process of amendment; and it would be difficult to argue that such a veto is in the spirit of the Fifth Republic. The principle of the sovereignty of the people was, for Gaullists, of a higher priority than that of parliamentary government.

The controversy over Article 11 was, moreover, one that agitated the political class rather than the electorate as a whole. "For most Frenchmen," as André Malraux put it, "the violation of the Constitution means a coup d'état, not an electoral consultation."[38] In 1969, when de Gaulle once again used Article 11 to secure a constitutional amendment, there was little criticism of the method. The amendment was defeated, and de Gaulle in consequence resigned; but there is no suggestion that his defeat was due to qualms concerning the constitutionality of the method used.

Since Article 11 has been used for purposes of constitutional revision by two of de Gaulle's successors, from both Right (Georges Pompidou) and Left (Mitterrand), it may be accepted that this is now the normal route by which the Constitution is to be amended by referendum. Article 89, by contrast, is likely to be used only when the method

36. Carcassonne, "The Fifth Republic," p. 248.

37. Maurice Duverger, *Le System Politique Français: Droit Constitutionnel et Systemes Politiques*, 19th ed. (Paris: Presses Universitaires de France, 1987), p. 336.

38. Cited by Vincent Wright in "France," in Butler and Ranney, *Referendums*, p. 155.

of ratification by Congress is chosen.

The Referendum and the European Community. The referendum, however, has played a much more peripheral role in France since de Gaulle's departure. Indeed, after the fifth referendum, held in 1972, it was widely believed that it had fallen into desuetude. In that year, President Pompidou held a referendum to secure approval of the amendment to the Treaty of Rome providing for Britain, Denmark, and Ireland to join the European Community. Such a referendum was not strictly needed under the Constitution, since the treaty amendment could hardly be said to "affect the functioning of institutions." Pompidou called it for essentially tactical reasons. He sought to prove to his EC partners that, by contrast with de Gaulle, he was a "good European," and that he had the full support of the French people for this role. By receiving the endorsement of the electorate, he would strengthen his domestic position, while the Left opposition would be divided, since the Socialists favored the European Community but the Communists were hostile.

But although 67 percent of those voting supported the EC treaty, only 60 percent of the electorate bothered to vote. Thus, only around 40 percent of the electorate gave Pompidou the endorsement he needed. Because many voters could not understand why it had been called, the referendum backfired and yielded no advantage to the president. In 1973, Pompidou sought once again to revise the Constitution so as to shorten the presidential term from seven years to five. Significantly, he now proposed the Congress route under Article 89; but although he secured majorities in both houses, these majorities fell short of the three-fifths needed. Pompidou, perhaps bearing in mind the outcome in 1972, thought it too risky to put the bill to referendum. He instead decided to postpone it until the presidential elections, due in 1976. Pompidou's death in 1974, however, marked the end of this proposal for the time being.

Giscard d'Estaing is the only Fifth Republic president not to have used the referendum, fearing that it would prevent his achieving the consensus he sought. In 1977, he declared before the Constitutional Council that the Constitution should be modified only by Parliament: that is, by the Congress method.[39] But, in 1979, in his *Discours de Hoerdt*, he suggested that any further extension of the powers of the

---

39. Léo Hamon, "Du Référendum à la Démocratie Continué," in Olivier Duhamel and Jean-Luc Parodi, eds., *La Constitution de la Cinquieme République* (Paris: Presses de la Fondation Nationale de Sciences Politiques, 1985), p. 511.

European Parliament should require ratification under Article 89.[40]

In 1984, the Senate, objecting to President Mitterrand's recommended education reforms, proposed a referendum on the right to private education. Mitterrand countered by an alternative proposal of a referendum under the Congress procedure of Article 89 to expand the scope of Article 11 so that it could include "the protection of political liberties" in addition to the organization of the public authorities. The Senate blocked this initiative, but Mitterrand did not resort to a referendum under Article 11, fearing that his political unpopularity would lead to the defeat of the project. This intricate tactical maneuvering, the so-called referendum on the referendum, did nothing to enhance the legitimacy of the referendum as a constitutional weapon.

In 1988, a referendum was held on self-determination in the overseas *département* of New Caledonia.[41] Like the 1961 referendum on self-determination in Algeria, this did not strictly require a referendum, since Article 86 of the Constitution requires only a local referendum—that is, a referendum in the *département* concerned—in such a situation. The 1988 referendum was unique in the Fifth Republic in that it was less an initiative of the president than of the prime minister, Michel Rocard. Although 80 percent endorsed the government's policy with regard to New Caledonia, the turnout in the referendum was only 37 percent. As in 1972, the electorate could not understand why it was being asked to vote and decided to stay at home in even greater numbers.

The September 1992 referendum was designed to ratify the Maastricht Treaty, providing for a more integrated European Community. The Constitutional Council had declared that three amendments to the Constitution were needed before Maastricht could be ratified. These amendments were to provide for the transfer of economic competences, the right of citizens of other member states of the European Community to vote and stand for election in municipal elections in France, and the right of citizens of other EC member-states to be allocated visas enabling them to enter France.

President Mitterrand decided to call a referendum under Article 11, despite having already achieved ratification under Article 89, using the Congress method, and easily achieving the three-fifths majority. No doubt there was a good reason in terms of democratic principle for calling a referendum. For it could be argued that Maastricht marked

---

40. Matthew Dodd, "The Political Constraints on the Referendum in France" (Oxford M. Phil. thesis, 1993), p. 65.

41. See Marie-Luce Pavia, "Le Référendum du 6 November 1988," in *Revue du Droit Public* (1989), pp. 1699–1734.

such an important step forward for France's commitment to the European Community that it ought to be endorsed by the electorate. But it is difficult all the same to ignore the tactical considerations that seem to have lain behind Mitterrand's decision.

Like Pompidou in 1972, Mitterrand hoped to show himself a "good European," since the only parties whose leaders opposed Maastricht were the Communists and the Front Nationale. Like Pompidou, he hoped to reinforce presidential authority and to divide his political opponents. Just as the Left was split on Europe in 1972, so the Right was similarly split on closer ties to Europe in 1992. The majority of Giscard's Union pour la Démocratie Française were in favor of Maastricht, but many, probably the majority, of the Gaullist Rassemblement pour la République were unwilling to follow their leader, Jacques Chirac, in supporting it. Indeed, Chirac himself had, in his *Appel de Cochin* in 1978, lambasted the UDF as "the party of the foreigner," and many in the RPR sought to distinguish their party from the UDF, precisely through its appeal to French national feeling.[42] Thus Mitterrand could look forward happily to splits and faction fights among his opponents on the Right.

But like Pompidou in 1992, Mitterrand was to discover that the referendum was a boomerang that could damage the man who called it. At the time when he announced the referendum, it appeared that Maastricht would be comfortably endorsed. But the opponents of Maastricht made considerable headway during the referendum campaign; and indeed, at one stage, it appeared that the treaty might actually be rejected. In the end, on a turnout of nearly 70 percent, the treaty scraped through, receiving the support of 51 percent of the voters. This was far from the popular endorsement for which Mitterrand had hoped.

Referendums before and after de Gaulle. Analysis of the referendum during the Fifth Republic reveals a fundamental discontinuity between its use under de Gaulle and under his successors. For de Gaulle, the referendum was part of the regular system of government, one of the methods by which he sought to maintain his rapport with those who had elected him. During his presidency, de Gaulle never allowed a period of longer than three and a half years to pass before appealing to the people either through a referendum or through a presidential election.

Moreover, the referendum took on the function of a presidential election in that, on each occasion when he called one, de Gaulle made

---

42. Dodd, *Political Constraints*, p. 86.

it clear that rejection of his proposal would mean his resignation. The first three referendums of the years 1961 and 1962 were in the nature of plebiscites on the Fifth Republic, which could hardly, at that early stage, have survived the departure of its founder. Each of de Gaulle's referendums took on the character of another instrument of direct democracy, the recall; for, as well as enabling electors to pronounce on the proposal in question, they could also if they wished recall from office the man who was proposing them, as in fact they did in 1969. Thus, during the first eleven years of the Fifth Republic the referendum, through this mechanism of recall, may be seen as the equivalent in a presidential regime of the vote of confidence under a parliamentary system.

De Gaulle's use of the referendum as a plebiscitary weapon was in a sense accentuated by his habit of yoking together two separate questions and seeking one answer to both. He used this tactic in three of the four referendums held during his presidency. In 1961, he asked, "Do you approve of self-determination and the proposed provisional institutions of Algeria?" This discomfited the Communists and the Left Socialists, who supported Algerian self-determination but disapproved of the second part of the question, since it did not provide for direct negotiations with the main Algerian nationalist movement, the FLN.[43] In the referendum of April 1962, de Gaulle asked voters whether they approved of the Evian agreement with the FLN and also with the giving of full powers to the president to bring them into force. In 1969, de Gaulle asked voters whether they favored both his proposed regional reforms and the reform of the Senate. A third part of the bill that was being put to referendum, concerning the conferment of the interim presidency on the prime minister rather than the president of the Senate, was not put on the ballot paper at all.[44] A member of the Conseil d'Etat declared that the bill was "the worst drafted bill it has ever considered."[45] The yoking together of separate proposals is far more open to criticism than the use of Article 11 for constitutional amendment; for it devalued the very instrument that Gaullists claimed was necessary to ensure the legitimacy of the regime.

Since de Gaulle's departure from office in 1969, the referendum has been used infrequently, and never on an issue central to the future of the state. On each occasion, moreover—in 1972, 1988, and 1992—the

---

43. Philip M. Williams and Martin Harrison, *Politics and Society in de Gaulle's Republic* (London: Longman, 1971), p. 69.

44. Wright, "France," p. 156.

45. Quoted in J. E. S. Hayward, "Presidential Suicide by Plebiscite: de Gaulle's Exit," *Parliamentary Affairs* (1969), p. 293.

president made clear that his responsibility was in no way engaged and that defeat in the referendum would not entail his resignation. In 1992, President Mitterrand went to some lengths to dissociate his future as president from the outcome of the referendum, declaring, "I am not at stake in this business, either with a 'yes' or with a 'no.' "[46] At the time, his personal rating lay at around 26 percent.[47] Mitterrand's unpopularity was so great that, had he staked his personal position on the ratification of Maastricht, the electorate might well have rejected it in order to remove him from office.

The first three referendums—in 1961 and 1962—played a vital role in the establishment of the Fifth Republic and in the formation of the modern French party system. The referendums on Algeria defused the extremists of the far Right by showing that they lacked support among the wider electorate. Indeed, de Gaulle's Algerian policy could probably not have been legitimized in any way other than by referendum.

If the referendums of 1961 and April 1962 legitimized de Gaulle's Algerian policy, the referendum of October 1962 legitimized a presidential Constitution. For the Fifth Republic Constitution, like the constitutional laws of the Third Republic drawn up in 1875, represented a compromise between opposing viewpoints. In 1875, the compromise had been between republicans and supporters of a strong government that could restore the monarchy. In 1958, it was between those like Michel Debré, first prime minister in the Fifth Republic, who looked with favor on the British cabinet system, and those who favored a full-fledged presidential model.

It was by no means inevitable that the Fifth Republic would in fact develop as a presidential system. Many Fourth Republic politicians regarded de Gaulle as an interim president, brought in to resolve the Algerian problem but then disposable just as former president Gaston Doumergue had been recalled in 1934 following the February riots to form a temporary cabinet of national union, and he was then dispensed with. The October 1962 referendum, however, by providing for direct election of the president, ensured that the presidential form of government would be permanent. It reversed the verdict of 1877, when President MacMahon had been forced by the legislative elections to accept a republican government against his wishes, so ensuring that the Third Republic would be a *régime d'assemblée*. The 1962 referendum showed that there would be no going back to such a regime.

In 1962, together with direct election of the president, France was to enjoy its first government resting on a single-party majority in mod-

---

46. Dodd, *Political Constraints*, pp. 81, 83.
47. Ibid., p. 83.

ern times. These developments meant that the importance of the referendum was bound to decline. For the referendum would no longer
be needed to confirm support for a regime that was becoming firmly
established or to endorse a president who had been elected by popular
suffrage. The legitimacy of the government would now be secured not
through referendum but through the presidential election and the election of a legislative majority prepared to support the president.

The referendums of 1961 and 1962 played their part in creating
such a majority and more generally in helping to create a bipolar party
system. They served as a means to detach from their traditional parties
those voters who favored the new Constitution and wished to support
a party that would sustain it. As de Gaulle put it in November 1962,
"The referendum has demonstrated beyond the shadow of a doubt a
fundamental principle of our time: the fact that the parties of yesterday
do not represent the nation."[48] This was confirmed by the defeat of the
cartel des nons, the Fourth Republic parties opposed to direct election
of the president in the 1962 legislative elections. This gave a clear signal
that no opposition to the Gaullists could be successful until it had accepted the basic premises of the Fifth Republic Constitution.

The referendums held between 1958 and 1962 did more than help
to establish a new structure of government and a new party system.
They undermined the political class that had been accustomed to rule
France from the beginning of the Fourth Republic. In 1969, the political
class gained its revenge and de Gaulle resigned. De Gaulle's successors, however, were part of a new political class. In both 1972 and 1992,
Presidents Pompidou and Mitterrand used the referendum, in complete contrast with de Gaulle, on issues that were important to the
political class but not to the electorate. This was done in an attempt to
gain short-term political advantage. For this reason, instead of reinforcing presidential authority, they undermined it.

The 1992 referendum clearly revealed that Maastricht was an issue
that could polarize the electorate against the leaders of all the major
parties. It gave evidence of the existence of that most dangerous of all
cleavages, the one that had helped to destroy the Fourth Republic: that
of the people versus the politicians. The division of voting choices in
the 1992 referendum, shown in table 3–2, pointed to basic divisions
among moderate France, Social-Christian France, and a nationalist
France of the extremes.

In France, the referendum remains a weapon to be held in re-
serve—or, as President Pompidou put it, "in exceptional circum-

---

48. De Gaulle, *Memoirs of Hope,* p. 333.

TABLE 3–2
PREFERENCES OF FRENCH GROUPS IN THE 1992 REFERENDUM

Group	Percent Yes	Group	Percent No
Socialists	74	*Le Pen* supporters	95
Génération Écologie	69	Communists	92
UDF	58	RPR	67
Center-Left	72	Extreme Left	82
Left	57	Right	68
Neither Left nor Right	53	Extreme Right	83

SOURCE: SOFRES poll, quoted in *Le Monde*, 25 September 1992; *Modern and Contemporary France, 1993: Documents & Resources*, p. 126. See also, on the Maastricht referendum, Byron Criddle, "The French Referendum on Maastricht," *Parliamentary Affairs* (1993), pp. 228–38.

stances, or when an essential matter of policy is involved."[49] It has not been entirely abandoned, but it is no longer used as it was in the days of de Gaulle as a regular part of the machinery of government, nor is it ever likely to be used in this way again. That perhaps is just as well, for France remains the only West European democracy in which the referendum can be used without requiring parliamentary approval at all. Were the referendum to become in reality what de Gaulle hoped it would be, a regular form of communion between the president and the electorate, it would increase the power of the president to an unacceptable degree.

The referendum has fallen into desuetude because the Fifth Republic, inevitably, has evolved in a different direction from that which de Gaulle envisioned. De Gaulle saw the president as being in essence a sovereign power. In the words of his press conference of 31 January 1964, "It must of course be understood that the entire indivisible authority of the State is confided to the President—that no other authority exists, neither ministerial nor civil nor military nor judicial, which is not conferred and sustained by him."[50] Such a sovereign power had to have his authority directly conferred by the people, not by the majority in a legislature. "I did not return to become a leader of the majority," de Gaulle is supposed to have told René Mayer.[51] For de Gaulle, direct election consecrated the president as an elective monarch who

49. Georges Pompidou, *Le Noeud Gordien*, cited in Hamon, "Référendum," pp. 510–11.
50. Quoted in Williams and Harrison, p. 272.
51. Hamon, "Référendum," p. 505.

would owe nothing to any political party.

Such a conception, however, is unrealistic in the modern world, where democratic government can hardly exist except as party government. The president of France is no longer an elective monarch, but the leader of a majority, and the Fifth Republic is as much a *régime des partis* as the despised Fourth Republic. With the parties having reconquered the political system, it is natural that the referendum, conceived of as a weapon against parties, should fall into disuse. With a parliamentary majority, the referendum becomes both less necessary, since the president can govern without it, and more dangerous, since it allows the opposition to humiliate him in midterm. For if the president does not link his own future with the referendum, the voters can form an electoral coalition against him without risk, as occurs, for example, with by-elections in Britain. For these reasons, the referendum is unlikely to regain its former importance in France.

Thus the referendum has fallen into disuse, not for contingent reasons, but because of the path taken by French constitutional evolution and the development of the French party system. But there is an even deeper reason for the decline of the referendum. For the first decade of the Fifth Republic saw the working out of a profound and fundamental conflict between de Gaulle's conception of the president as an elective monarch and the reality of a president who was becoming, like the prime minister of Britain or the Federal German chancellor, not so much the leader of the nation as the leader of just one part of it: that represented by the majority party. By the time of de Gaulle's departure in 1969, the prosaic reality of party government had replaced the romantic dream of a president above party; the logic of majoritarianism had replaced that of *rassemblement*, a rallying of the French people.[52] In France, the referendum, as an instrument of regular communion between president and people, had always belonged primarily to the world of romance rather than to the world of political reality.

Italy

While the French Constitution of 1958 was established in reaction to a parliamentary regime thought to have caused paralysis and *immobilisme*, the Italian Constitution of 1947 was reacting against the Fascist conception of strong leadership. Therefore, while the French Fifth Republic Constitution found a place for the referendum to legitimize strong leadership, the Italian Constitution created a parliamentary re-

---

52. Jean-Louis Quermonne, "Le Référendum: Essai du Typologie Prospective," *Revue de Droit Public* (1985), p. 601.

public in which the legislature was to enjoy a central role. Provision was made for the referendum, but it was to be used only under exceptional circumstances, since it was essentially an appeal by the people *against* Parliament.[53]

Paradoxically, however, Italy has become the West European democracy that has used the referendum most frequently, next to Switzerland. This is because Italy is the only West European democracy (excepting Switzerland) in which the people can themselves trigger a referendum. Italy exemplifies the thesis that referendums are likely to be held more frequently in such circumstances than when they remain under the control of government.

Article 138 of the Italian Constitution allows for either half a million voters, one-fifth of the members of either legislative chamber, or five regional councils to demand a referendum on a constitutional law, unless the law in question has been passed by a two-thirds majority in both chambers of the Italian Parliament. So far, however, no referendum has been held under this provision.

Article 132 provides for a referendum on modifying the borders of the Italian region. This provision, too, has never been used. There have, however, been numerous regional referendums under Article 123 to ratify regional laws.

Italy held a consultative and largely symbolic referendum in April 1989, at the time of the elections to the European Parliament, asking the electorate whether it was willing to give the European Parliament authority to draft a text for a Treaty on European Union. Eighty-eight percent of those voting said they were so prepared.

The other twenty-six referendums held in Italy under the 1947 Constitution have all been held under Article 75, which provides for the popular veto or abrogative referendum on all laws, except for those dealing with financial legislation, pardons, and treaty ratification. Under the provisions of Article 75, laws not falling into the above categories must be put to referendum if there is a demand from 500,000 voters or five regional councils. By contrast with the American states and Switzerland, a proposal to abrogate need not specify the whole of a statute; it can specify a part of it or even individual articles or clauses.[54]

---

53. Giulio Andreotti, "Intervention," in G. Andreotti et al., eds., *Deux Constitutions: Le Ve République et la République Italienne: Parallele et Commentaires* (Rome: Ecole Française de Rome, 1988), pp. 71–73.

54. For an overview of the Italian referendums, see David Hine, *Governing Italy: The Politics of Bargained Pluralism* (Oxford: Clarendon Press, 1993), pp. 154–57.

For referendums held under Article 75, unlike those under Articles 123, 132, or 138, there is a qualifying requirement. The turnout must equal 50 percent-plus-one of the total electorate for the result to be binding. In 1990, three referendums—two on field sports and one on pesticides—failed. Although there were majorities for abrogating the laws in question, the turnout was below 50 percent.

A referendum under the provisions of Article 75 is abrogative—that is, it seeks the repeal of a law. Thus a Yes vote is a vote to repeal the law; a No vote one to maintain it on the statute book. By contrast with Switzerland and the American states, which also use this instrument, the abrogative referendum can be applied not only to laws just passed but to any law on the statute book, whenever it was passed. Thus, when in the 1970s voters sought to make abortion legal, they needed to abrogate a law passed by Mussolini in 1930 "for the protection of the race," which made abortion a "crime against the health and integrity of the race."

This example shows that, although the abrogative referendum seems to be purely negative in its effect—it can repeal a law, but not propose a new law—nevertheless, in practice it can be used for the purposes of reform, for putting a new issue on the agenda. Thus, the referendum in 1993 that abrogated the electoral law of 1948 requiring that nearly all the senators be elected by proportional representation also put on the agenda the adoption of the first-past-the-post electoral system on the British model. Admittedly, the abrogative referendum is a blunt weapon for proposing new laws, but the absence of the initiative on the American or Swiss model is perhaps not so great a handicap to reformers as it might appear.

Restrictions on the Abrogative Referendum. There are, however, a number of restrictions on the use of the abrogative referendum in Italy. The first is that a proposal to use this instrument must receive the approval of the Constitutional Court. The court has not only sought to ensure that a request does not include the excluded items—finance, pardons, or ratification of treaties. It has interpreted its role much more widely. Indeed, it has been argued that the court has on occasion been influenced by explicitly political considerations.[55]

The court has decided that it will, for example, exclude any proposal containing "such a plurality of heterogeneous demands that there was a lack of a rational, unitary matrix that would bring it under

---

55. For the role of the court, see Jean-Claude Escarras, "Après le 'big bang' référendaire de la Cour Constitutionelle," *Revue Française de Droit Constitutionelle* (1993), pp. 183–95.

the logic of Article 75 of the Constitution." This was to prevent the abrogative referendum being "transformed without possibility of appeal into a distorted instrument of representative democracy, whereby essentially plebiscites or votes of confidence are proposed with regard to complex, inseparable political choices of parties or of organized groups that have adopted or supported the referendum initiatives."[56]

In 1991, with regard to electoral reform, the court made it clear that it would refuse to accept a proposal abrogating all the existing electoral laws. For this reason, reformers secured first, in 1991, a referendum repealing the law providing for preference voting; and then, in 1993, of the law providing for proportional representation for the Senate.[57] The wide view taken by the court of its remit has led to a significant proportion of referendums being declared inadmissible. Between 1970 and 1987, fourteen of thirty-three proposals were declared inadmissible by the court.[58]

After a request has been declared admissible by the court, the government still has two methods available by which it can postpone or deter a referendum. The first is to dissolve Parliament, which has the effect of postponing a referendum. This occurred in 1972, postponing the divorce referendum, and in 1976, postponing the abortion referendum. An early dissolution has, however, occurred only once since then. Every other referendum has been held within the timetable laid down for it.

Second, Parliament can intervene by amending the law within four months (two months, until 1987), so that it corresponds to the intentions of the promoters of the referendum. This occurred five times between 1970 and 1987, on issues involving abortions (1978), investigating committees (1978), insane asylums (1978), military justice (1981), and cost-of-living bonuses (1982).

Thus, as in Switzerland and the American states, the existence of an instrument that can be initiated by the people does not entirely take away the possibility of government action. One might compare the action of Italian governments in the case of the five laws listed above with that of Swiss governments in putting forward *contre-projets* so as to head off demands for referendums. Thus even the abrogative

---

56. Pier Vincenzo Uleri, "The 1987 Referenda," in Robert Leonardi and Piergiorgio Corbetta, eds., *Italian Politics: A Review*, vol. 3 (London: Frances Pinter, 1989), p. 176.

57. Gianfranco Pasquino, "The Electoral Reform Referendums," in Robert Leonardi and Fausto Anderlini, eds., *Italian Politics: A Review*, vol. 6 (London: Frances Pinter, 1992), p. 14.

58. Uleri, "1987 Referenda," p. 159.

referendum, which is initiated by electors, does not exclude the action of representative institutions, showing that in this case also the instruments of direct democracy serve to supplement rather than to replace representative government.

Until 1987, every referendum resulted in a No vote—that is, a vote not to repeal the law in question. It was often suggested before 1987 that the introduction of the abrogative referendum into the Italian Constitution had been without effect. But that suggestion ignores the fact that the threat of the abrogative referendum made governments enact the five laws listed above, which otherwise they might not have done. And perhaps, as in Switzerland, the most important referendums in Italy have been those that have not been held, the threat of the referendum having persuaded governments to put forward, or to refrain from putting forward, particular bills.

Article 75, providing for the abrogative referendum, was part of the 1947 Constitution, but it could not come into effect until the necessary implementing laws had been enacted. This was not done until 1970, since the dominant Christian Democrats saw no reason to promote an instrument whose effect would be to deprive them of their control over the legislative process.

In 1970, however, the Christian Democrats were in a minority in Parliament and could not prevent the passage of a divorce law. Catholic groups opposed to divorce then pressed for the introduction of the legislation implementing the abrogative referendum so that they could repeal the law. Thus it was not until twenty-two years after the Constitution came into force that the law providing for the abrogative referendum was enacted.

The divorce referendum finally occurred, after numerous postponements, in 1974, but it resulted in a defeat for those who sought to repeal the law.[59] This was a defeat not only for the Christian Democrats and other Catholic groups that supported them but also for the Italian Communist party, whose position on divorce had become highly equivocal.[60] Thus the referendum undermined the authority of the two main parties sustaining the political system. This pattern was to be repeated in later referendums, making the referendum an important weapon in the reform of the Italian political system.

---

59. Martin Clark, David Hine, and R. E. M. Irving, "Divorce—Italian Style," *Parliamentary Affairs* (1974), pp. 333–68; and Alberto Ferradi, "Italy's Referendum on Divorce: Survey and Ecological Evidence Analyzed," *European Journal of Political Research* (1976), pp. 115–39.

60. Paul Ginsborg, *A History of Contemporary Italy, Society and Politics 1943–1988* (London: Penguin, Harmondsworth, 1990), pp. 350–51.

The second and third referendums, held in 1978, concerned the possible repeal of the laws providing for the public funding of political parties and measures against terrorism. Both resulted in No votes, so the legislation remained on the statute book. In 1981, five further referendums were called. Three of them—on antiterrorist legislation, arms licensing, and life sentencing—were relatively uncontentious: each resulted in a defeat for the proponents of the referendum and retention of the laws.

The fourth and fifth referendums held in 1981, however, were on the abortion issue and were extremely controversial. As we have seen, the threat of the referendum had persuaded the government to pass a law liberalizing abortion in 1978. It was on this law that the two referendums were held, one seeking to delete the law and so render abortion illegal once more, the other seeking to liberalize the law by removing the age limit of eighteen and by making other reforms. Both proposals were defeated, however, so the 1978 law remained on the statute book unchanged.

The main effect of the divorce and abortion referendums was to reveal the Italian electorate as both more secular and more liberal than had been generally suspected. The outcome of the referendums threatened the hegemony of the Christian Democrats over the political system. For many in the church, the result of the abortion referendum was "psychologically comparable to the fall of Rome in 1870."[61]

The next referendum, in 1985, undermined the other main pillar of the Italian republic: the Communist party. This was the first occasion on which the party had sponsored a referendum. It sought to abrogate a decree of February, sponsored by the government of Bettino Craxi, Italy's first postwar Socialist prime minister, and the centerpiece of the government's economic policy. The referendum was in effect a method by which the Communists could put forward a vote of censure against Craxi, and the prime minister indicated that he would resign if it were to be carried. In the event, however, voters refused to abrogate the decree and so the policy was sustained. The resort to the referendum on the part of the Communists was a sign of weakness, precisely because the party had hitherto been so suspicious of this instrument. Also, it showed that the Communists were losing their place in the corporate structure of Italian politics, being no longer able to veto policies of which they disapproved. Their defeat in the referendum, in which the Communists were supported by none of the mainstream parties of Italian politics but only by the neo-Fascist Movimento Sociale

---

61. Frederic Spotts and Theodor Wieser, *Italy: A Difficult Democracy* (Cambridge: Cambridge University Press, 1986), p. 248.

Italiana, served but to emphasize the growing isolation of the party.[62]

The first referendums to succeed were held in 1987. They were a series of five on disparate subjects, three being concerned with nuclear energy, one with the liability of magistrates, and one with a law regulating the conditions under which ministers could be brought to trial.[63] Of these five referendums, it was the one on the civil liability of magistrates that "took on heated tones and assumed such broad dimensions as to almost completely obscure discussion of four other referendums which were held simultaneously."[64] This was despite the fact that the three referendums concerned with nuclear energy were being held in the aftermath of Chernobyl. It led to the quip that Italians felt more threatened by the corruption of their judges and public prosecutors than by nuclear contamination.

The abrogative referendum on the civil liability of magistrates was proposed by the Socialist party and the small lay parties—Social Democrats, Republicans, and Liberals. It was opposed by the Christian Democrats and Communists, although once the referendum had been secured, the Communists altered their viewpoint and advised a Yes vote. This referendum had great symbolic importance, showing that the faults of the judicial system, and therefore by implication of the political system, could be remedied by the abrogative referendum.

The referendum of 1987 thus opened the way to the 1991 referendum abolishing the preference vote for elections to the Chamber of Deputies,[65] and then to the package of eight referendums in 1993, providing for a wholesale reform of the political system. These referendums, by contrast with the earlier ones, were sponsored by members of all parties who sought to break the hold of their leaders on Italian politics. The main promoter was Mario Segni, a leading Christian Democrat, opposed to the "historic compromise" with the Left and favoring instead a bipolar political structure based on the first-past-the-post electoral system.

The 1991 referendum on preference voting, on a 62.5 percent turnout, led to the largest victory ever secured for the proponents of a refer-

---

62. On this referendum, see Peter Lange, "The End of an Era: The Wage Indexation Referendum of 1985," in Robert Leonardi and Raffaela Y. Nanetti, eds., *Italian Politics: A Review*, vol. 1 (London: Frances Pinter, 1986), pp. 29–46.

63. David Hine, "The Italian Referendums of 8–9 November 1987," *Electoral Studies* (1988), pp. 163–67.

64. Giuseppe Di Federico, "The Crisis of the Justice System and the Referendum on the Judiciary," in Leonardi and Corbetta, vol. 3, p. 25.

65. See Patrick McCarthy, "The Referendum of 9 June," in Stephen Hellman and Gianfranco Pasquino, *Italian Politics: A Review*, vol. 7 (London: Frances Pinter, 1992), pp. 11–28.

endum; 95.6 percent supported abrogation and only 4.4 percent voted against it. This result occurred despite the fact that neither the Christian Democrats nor the Socialists endorsed a Yes vote. The Christian Democrats offered no advice at all to their supporters, while the Socialists told their supporters to "go to the seaside." Seen in this light, the outcome of the 1991 referendum revealed a massive demand for reforming the political system. It exerted a considerable psychological effect on the 1993 referendums, which resulted in Yes majorities that were nearly as large. When the law of 1970 was enacted, there was

> probably an implicit, undeclared agreement among the parties to use the referendum instrument only for exceptional matters and, at any rate, to maintain control over the instrument by the parties of the "constitutional arch"—that is, those parties which had founded the constitutional pact after the collapse of the fascist regime.[66]

But the referendum offered the electorate a new weapon. It did not lie in the hands of the political parties to determine how it would be used, nor how often it would be used.

The first referendum on divorce, as we have seen, was promoted by Catholic organizations. After that, however, a new party, the Radical party, at that time unrepresented in Parliament, perceived that it could use the referendum systematically to secure the secularization and liberalization of Italian society. Between 1970 and 1987, the Radicals promoted twenty-seven of the thirty-three referendums,[67] and they were, in particular, the moving force behind the referendums seeking to liberalize abortion and to abolish the public funding of parties. From the mid-1980s, however, single-issue groups also sought to use the referendum, and it is now used by any party or group that seeks to bring public pressure to bear on Parliament. For the abrogative referendum has been shown to be a powerful tool of reform, allowing the electorate to help determine the political agenda by putting onto it such matters as the funding of political parties, abortion, and electoral reform, which the political class would rather were kept off. Moreover, the legitimacy of using the referendum has come rapidly to be accepted. Whereas parliamentary decisions on such matters as divorce and abortion would not have been accepted by important groups in the country, the referendum has been able to settle them.

An Italian commentator has argued:

---

66. Uleri, "1987 Referenda," p. 158.
67. Ibid.

A referendum [on whether the monarchy should be preserved] resulted in the foundation of the Italian Republic in June 1946. Another referendum has been the stepping-stone towards the Second Republic. . . . The prevalent aim of the angry voters was to eliminate the existing political class, smash the proportional method in favour of one in which one party or a coalition of parties alternate in government.[68]

The Constitution of the postwar Italian Republic was a reactive one, designed to ensure that a one-party dictatorship such as that of Mussolini could not be repeated. Fear of fascism and communism led to the political system being so structured that it diffused the power of veto and ensured a fragmented two-chamber system based on proportional representation. The central motif was the politics of agreement, of "bargained pluralism,"[69] to be secured through special majorities and oversized coalitions.

Such a system, however, had lost its rationale with the disappearance of the Soviet Union and the removal of the Communist threat, while the widespread corruption it engendered lost it the respect of most Italians. The system came to be dominated by the political parties who governed in their own interests rather than in the interests of those they claimed to represent. Italy had become a *partitocrazia*—a "partyocracy." As the parties lost their authority, with deference disappearing and a desire on the part of the electorate for greater participation, use of the referendum gathered pace. So the referendum is both cause and consequence of the transformation of the Italian political system.

The referendums of 1991 and 1993 were an essential part of this transformation. The slogans of the reformers were "from partyocracy to democracy" and "vote for a person, a majority, a program."[70] The Italian political system, hitherto based on consensual government, is now being transformed into a more majoritarian model. As in France between 1958 and 1962, so also in Italy, the referendum has played a fundamental role in paving the way for a new political system of a more majoritarian kind. Many would argue that in doing so, the referendum has done much to serve the long-term interests of the Italian people.

Scandinavia

The Scandinavian countries are among the world's most advanced democracies, and they place a high priority on values such as commu-

---

68. Francesco Didoti, "The Italian Political Class," *Government and Opposition* (1993), p. 348.

69. I owe this phrase to David Hine. See note 54, above.

70. Hellman and Pasquino, *Italian Politics*, p. 15.

69

nity, participation, and the accountability of political leaders to the people they represent. An important role in their progress toward democracy has been played by grass-roots popular movements. It is a paradox, then, that the referendum plays so minor a role in the Scandinavian countries. With the exception of Denmark, it is used extremely infrequently—indeed, until the 1980s, Denmark and Sweden were the only Scandinavian countries that made constitutional provision for the referendum. In Denmark, the referendum was required for constitutional change, but in Sweden, the sole provision was a constitutional amendment of 1922 allowing for optional advisory referendums at the discretion of the government.

In the 1980s, however, both Finland and Sweden amended their Constitutions. Finland in 1987 made provision for consultative referendums, while Sweden in 1988 provided for the use of the referendum to amend the Constitution. So far, however, no referendum has been held either in Finland or in Sweden under the new procedures.

Not only has the referendum been hardly recognized in the Scandinavian countries, but when it has been used, it has not always yielded the beneficial results claimed for it by its advocates. Sometimes it has resolved political problems, but on other occasions it has exacerbated them. Far from enabling public opinion to be expressed, it has on occasion been a means for the parties to manipulate it. Thus the referendum has not always succeeded in fulfilling its legitimizing function, and its use in Scandinavia remains a last resort.

Until the 1980s, referendums in the Scandinavian countries, apart from Denmark, were held on a consultative and ad hoc basis. They were held for two types of issue. The first was to mark a change of constitutional status, a new beginning: when Norway in 1905 separated from Sweden, but decided to remain a monarchy, and when Iceland in 1918 decided to end the union with Denmark, and in 1994 decided to separate entirely from Denmark and become a republic.

Second, the referendum has been used for issues that threatened to split political parties or coalition partners. The aim of the referendum in such circumstances was to remove a threatening issue from the political agenda. That was the origin of the prohibition referendums in Norway in 1919 and 1926, in Sweden in 1922, in Finland in 1931, and in Iceland in 1933. It was the origin of the other three referendums held in Sweden—driving on the right of the road in 1955, supplementary pensions in 1957, and nuclear energy in 1980.[71]

The European Community referendum in Norway in 1972, per-

---

71. See Tor Bjørklund, "The Demand for Referendum: When Does It Arise and When Does It Succeed?" *Scandinavian Political Studies* (1982), pp. 237–59.

haps the most important of all in its political consequences, lies, however, slightly outside these two categories. For the decision to submit the issue to the electorate was in part constrained by the Norwegian Constitution, since Article 93 of the Constitution requires a three-fourths majority in the Storting for the transfer of powers to an international organization, and it was very doubtful if this would have been secured in 1972.[72]

Denmark is the only Scandinavian country in which the referendum was required for constitutional change before the 1980s. The referendum was first introduced in the 1915 Constitution, Article 93 of which provided for all constitutional amendments to be submitted to the people after being passed by the then two-chamber Parliament. This became Article 94 in the Constitution of 1920, and it was adapted, with modifications, as Article 88 in the current Constitution of 1953.[73] The 1915 and 1920 Constitutions provided for a qualifying majority of 45 percent for constitutional amendment—that is, in addition to securing a majority, at least 45 percent of the electorate had to vote Yes for the amendment to be approved. In 1953, the requirement was reduced to 40 percent, but the constitutional referendum has not been used since that date.

One of the main provisions of the 1953 referendum was the abolition of Denmark's second chamber. In exchange for abolition, the Danish Right secured the passage of Article 42, providing for a referendum on nonconstitutional legislation. Under this provision, one-third of the members of the single-chamber Folketing can demand a referendum on any item of legislation (with the exception of bills concerning finance, government loans, salaries and pensions, naturalization, expropriation, taxation, and bills discharging treaty obligations) within three days of the bill in question having been passed. For the law to be rejected, there is also a qualified majority requirement: in addition to

---

72. Henry Valen, "Norway 'No' to EEC," *Scandinavian Political Studies* (1973), pp. 214–26; Ottar Hellevik and Nils Peter Gleditsch, "The Common Market Decision in Norway: A Clash between Direct and Indirect Democracy," *Scandinavian Political Studies* (1973), pp. 227–35; and Henry Valen, "National Conflict Structure and Foreign Politics: The Impact of the EC Issue on Perceived Cleavages on Norwegian Politics," *European Journal of Political Research* (1976), pp. 47–82. For Norwegian referendums in general, see Tor Bjørklund, *Referendums in Norway* (Oslo: Institute for Social Research, 1992). For the Danish European Community referendum of 1972, see Jorgen Elklit and Nikolaj Petersen, "Denmark Enters the European Communities," *Scandinavian Political Studies* (1973), pp. 198–213.

73. Henrik Zahle, "Danemark," in Francis Delpérée, ed., *Référendums* (Brussels: CRISP, 1985), p. 97.

there being a No majority, at least 30 percent of the electorate must vote No.

In addition, referendums *must* be held under the provisions of Article 42, with a 30 percent qualifying requirement to reject, for two specific types of bills. The first type, provided for under Article 29, alters the age qualification for the suffrage. So far, four referendums have been held under this provision, and these have progressively lowered the voting age from twenty-three in 1953 to eighteen in 1978.[74]

The second type of bill, provided for under Article 20, transfers powers to international authorities unless there is a five-sixths majority of the Folketing, when the referendum need not be held. So far, two referendums have been held under this provision—in 1972 to ratify Denmark's entry into the European Community and in 1992 to ratify the Maastricht Treaty. The 1986 referendum that ratified the Single European Act, however, was *not* held under Article 20. It was a consultative and advisory referendum to which the provisions of Article 42 did not apply. A referendum of this kind is provided for under Article 19 of the Constitution, and the 1986 referendum is so far the only advisory referendum to have been held since the 1953 Constitution came into force.

It may seem a paradox that the Single European Act, which could not have gained a majority in the Folketing, received a majority in the country, while Maastricht, which enjoyed the support of parties with 80 percent of the seats in the Folketing, was rejected by the voters in 1992. But the paradox is not difficult to explain. The Danish electorate has always been hostile to political union but fearful of being economically disadvantaged if it is excluded from EC markets.[75] In 1986, Danish Prime Minister Poul Schluter assured voters that "the political union is stone-dead,"[76] and this assurance was accepted.

By 1992, however, it seemed that Denmark was being asked to

---

74. See H. Jorgen Nielsen, "Voting Age of Eighteen Years Adopted by the Danish Folketing, Rejected by Popular Referendum," *Scandinavian Political Studies* (1979), pp. 301–5; and Palle Svensson, "The Lowering of the Voting Age in Denmark," *Scandinavian Political Studies* (1979), pp. 65–72.

75. Nikolaj Petersen, "Attitudes towards European Integration and the Danish Common Market Referendum," *Scandinavian Political Studies* (1978), pp. 23–42. On the 1986 referendum, see Ole Borre, "The Danish Referendum on the EC Common Act," *Electoral Studies* (1986), pp. 189–93.

76. Quoted in Karen Siune, "The Danes Said No to the Maastricht Treaty: The Danish European Community Referendum of June 1992," *Scandinavian Political Studies* (1993), p. 94. See also Karen Siune and Palle Svensson, "The Danes and the Maastricht Treaty: The Danish EC Referendum of June 1992," *Electoral Studies* (1993), pp. 99–111.

transfer further competences to a rapidly evolving federal Europe. It was not until they were given assurances at the European Council summit at Edinburgh in December 1992 that the Danes were prepared to endorse Maastricht in a second referendum in 1993. This second referendum was *not* held under Article 20 but under specific legislation passed by the Folketing in March 1993. Unlike the 1986 referendum, the 1993 referendum was to be binding. Rejection was to require, as under the Article 42 procedure, 30 percent of the electorate to vote against it as well as a majority of those voting.

One of the features of the Edinburgh Declaration was that Denmark emphasized that it could not, under the terms of its Constitution, participate in the third stage of monetary union without a further referendum. Thus the referendums on the European Community have been of value to Denmark in enabling it to define to its partners the limits of its commitments to the European Community. They were also the first indication that a vision of the future that had been widely endorsed in the chancelleries of Europe was supported much less enthusiastically by the voters.

The provision by which ordinary laws can be put to referendum at the behest of one-third of the members of the Folketing has been used only once so far. That was in 1963, when four land-planning laws proposed by the Social Democratic government were rejected. On other occasions, it has been both difficult and unnecessary to invoke it: difficult since, in a fragmented Folketing, it is not easy to secure the support of parliamentarians from a wide range of political parties; and unnecessary because Denmark, whose governments are often minority administrations, is characterized by a search for agreement between the parties of government and opposition.

Thus the significance of Article 42 is not to be measured solely by this single occasion when it was brought into use. Rather, it serves to emphasize and encourage the search for consensus in Danish politics. Danish governments will be under an incentive to seek the support of opposition parties so as to disarm the threat of the referendum. Indeed, the referendum was held in 1963 precisely because the normal Danish search for consensus had broken down, and the Social Democrats were determined to push through their legislation against the opposition of the parties of the Right. Thus, Article 42 prevents a Danish government, even if it enjoys a secure majority in the Folketing, from passing legislation that is unattractive both to a minority in Parliament and to the electorate. The provision gives a minority in the Folketing a strong position to challenge legislation it believes is unpopular in the country. But were the opposition in the Folketing to seek to use Article 42 in an aggressive manner, it would be endangering the convention that parties outside the government ought to be consulted on legislation before it is brought to Parliament.

The referendum in Denmark, then, has performed a valuable function. But the same cannot be said of its use in the other Scandinavian countries, where it has been employed in an ad hoc and consultative way at the behest of governments. Precisely for this reason, its two most striking political effects in Scandinavia, by contrast with many other democracies, have been to split parties and to exacerbate rather than resolve the issues it has been called on to settle.

For the Scandinavian countries are consensual democracies, in which it is usually possible to resolve issues within the parliamentary arena. Putting an issue to referendum is often a sign that the normal consensual mechanisms have broken down. The referendum may be used not for reasons of democratic principle but in the desperate hope that the people can resolve a question when the politicians have failed. It is not surprising if this hope is rarely fulfilled. And since use of the referendum is unconstrained by the Constitution (except in Denmark), it can be used by the political class in its own interest. The results, however, are often unexpected. In Scandinavia, referendums have revealed cleavages that the party system has hidden, and this has been a potent force in breaking up seemingly united parties. Only in Denmark has the referendum succeeded in resolving differences within parties; only in Denmark has it performed a healing function.

The Norwegian and Swedish prohibition referendums of 1919 and 1922 split their countries' Liberal parties, as did the 1972 European Community referendum in Norway. All these referendums brought to the fore a core-periphery cleavage that was obscured by the party system and that the Norwegian and Swedish Liberal parties had seemed able to transcend for as long as politics could be confined to the parliamentary arena. In the 1972 EC referendum in Norway, the electorate unexpectedly rejected the advice of the government to endorse entry into the European Community. Trygve Bratteli, the Labour prime minister, had declared that he would resign if Norway rejected entry, and he was succeeded by a minority government led by the Christian Peoples' party leader, Lars Korvald. These events put in train the steps needed to disentangle Norway from the European Community, following which a general election was called. In Sweden, the 1957 supplementary pensions referendum broke up a government composed of a coalition between the Social Democrat and Centre parties, and it caused an early general election in 1958.

In Sweden, indeed, none of the four referendums that have been held have succeeded in their supposed function of problem solving. The 1922 and 1980 referendums on prohibition and nuclear energy both failed to remove their respective issues from the political agenda; the issues in the 1955 and 1957 referendums were settled despite, not because of, the referendums. The 1955 referendum resulted in an 83 percent vote to continue driving on the left side of the road. This outcome was ignored by the politicians who, by 1967, had achieved a consensus favoring driving on the right side of the road, which was duly implemented. The 1957 referendum on supplementary benefits was so ambiguous that it took a general election in 1958 and several close votes in the Folketing before the issue was finally resolved.

The Swedish referendums of 1957 on supplementary benefits and of 1980 on nuclear energy, along with the Danish referendum of 1953 on changing the voting age, are the only postwar democratic referendums in Western Europe in which three alternatives were offered to the voters. In 1953, a majority favored lowering the voting age to twenty-three in Denmark, the middle alternative of the three. In 1957 and 1980, however, none of the three alternative supplementary pension plans or proposals for nuclear energy achieved an overall majority. This left considerable scope for dispute concerning the significance of the result.

The 1957 supplementary benefits referendum was the first held in Sweden, where the divisions lay between rather than within the parties. It was held because the Riksdag was deadlocked, since no proposal enjoyed the support of an overall majority. The Centre, although in coalition with the Social Democrats, did not support its coalition partner's proposal, and it sought to differentiate itself from them. The Centre party insisted upon including in the referendum its own separate proposal, so the electorate was confronted with three alternatives.

The 1980 referendum on nuclear power was, once again, held on an issue that divided both parties and coalition partners, cutting as it did across the normal Left/Right politics of Sweden. The three-party, non-Socialist government comprised Conservatives (broadly sympathetic to nuclear power), Liberals (moderately sympathetic), and the Centre party (fundamentally hostile). A referendum seemed the only way to contain a split that threatened to break up the coalition. The opposition Social Democrats, the largest single party, became converted to the referendum, since it too was split, and it sought to keep the nuclear power issue out of the 1979 general election. Moreover, after the accident at Three Mile Island in 1979, the referendum was almost forced on the Riksdag by the pressures of public opinion.

Nevertheless, the parties were determined to retain control of the nuclear issue in their own hands. The referendum contained three alternatives, since the Social Democrats and Liberals agreed with the Conservatives in supporting the use, for the time being, of the twelve nuclear reactors already in operation, although neither party wished to be seen publicly to align itself with the Conservatives. The Social Democrats were in opposition: the Liberals, although in coalition with the Conservatives, found themselves under pressure on the nuclear issue from their youth wing and so thought it politic to lean to the Left in the referendum. Therefore, in effect there were two pronuclear energy options, the Conservative and the Social Democrat–Liberal, against one antinuclear option, supported by the Centre and the Communist parties. Thus the referendum seemed slanted against the antinuclear option. The ambiguous outcome of the referendum allowed the pronuclear power parties, who had a majority in the Riksdag, to settle the issue. But some believed that the antinuclear option would have been victorious in a straight fight with just one pronuclear option. The 1980 referendum, therefore, has been regarded by one commentator as:

> essentially meaningless as far as the actual issue was concerned, serving primarily as a delaying tactic. . . . The only lasting effect of the 1980 referendum in Sweden is liable to be the further devaluation of referenda as an institution in modern Swedish politics.[77]

Thus, both in 1957 and in 1980, tactical considerations were dominant in the calling of the referendum in Sweden. The referendum, supposedly a weapon to allow the people to decide against the political parties, was manipulated by the parties to serve their own interests.[78] Of course, this is highly likely to occur when use of the referendum is purely discretionary and in the hands of the government. It will be used by the political parties to suit their own interests, which are not necessarily the same as those of the electors.

Normally, however, Scandinavia has no need to use the referendum because the Scandinavian democracies, although in form majoritarian on the British model, operate in a consensual manner. Not only are the ideological differences between the parties small as compared with Britain or France (although they have been widening in recent years), but it is customary for governments to consult opposition parties about forthcoming legislation rather than to proceed where legislation would be divisive. This is the case even when there is a majority in the legislature that would wish to do so. Thus the referendum, es-

---

77. P. Mark Little, "The Nuclear Power Issue in Swedish Politics, March 1979–March 1980," Hull Papers in Politics, no. 27 (1982), p. 28.

78. Sten Berglund and Joseph Board, "Managing Public Opinion: The Referendums in Sweden" (Paper presented at the European Consortium for Political Research Workshop, Aarhus, 1982).

sentially a majoritarian instrument, seems incompatible with a basic value in Scandinavian political culture: that of compromise.[79] Only when compromise breaks down—as in Sweden over supplementary pensions and nuclear energy or in Denmark over the Single European Act—is there resort to the referendum. The referendum is often a sign of the failure of the Scandinavian political system, not of the health of democracy, as might be the case elsewhere in Western Europe.

There is a second reason why the referendum is used so rarely in Scandinavia. It is incompatible with the culture of social democracy, which has been so dominant since the war. For many Social Democrats have seen the referendum as essentially a conservative weapon, a weapon against progress. This attitude was beautifully expressed by Tage Erlander, Sweden's Social Democratic prime minister, in 1948:

> Referendums go together with a different form of government than the parliamentary system. Under a coalition government of the Swiss type, no objections can be aimed at the referendum system. On the other hand, it is obvious that referendums are a strongly conservative force. It becomes much harder to pursue an effective reform policy if reactionaries are offered the opportunity to appeal to people's natural Conservatism and natural resistance to change. The enthusiasm of Conservative parties for the referendum system is thus certainly related more or less consciously to the fact that it provides an instrument for blocking a radical progressive policy.[80]

Social democratic dominance in Scandinavia largely explains the infrequency of the referendum in countries otherwise characterized by a strong adherence to the tenets of grass-roots democracy. It is perhaps significant that Denmark, in which the Social Democrats have always been weaker than their Norwegian and Swedish counterparts, has been the most willing of the Scandinavian countries to embrace the referendum. Finland, where social democracy has been weaker than in Denmark, is a seeming exception to this generalization: but until the postwar years, Finland was a painfully divided society on the verge of civil war. It had to search for consensual instruments designed to bring the divergent elements of Finnish society together. The referendum,

---

79. Kenneth E. Miller, "Policy-Making by Referendum: The Danish Experience," *Parliamentary Affairs* (1982), p. 63, uses this argument to explain the sparing use of the legislative referendum in Denmark. It can, surely, be adapted to Scandinavia as a whole.

80. Quoted in Leif Lewin, *Ideology and Strategy: A Century of Swedish Politics* (Cambridge: Cambridge University Press, 1988), p. 235.

therefore, would naturally appear as a deeply divisive element. It is perhaps significant, however, that as Finland has become less divided, so has fear of the referendum abated. It is now recognized in the Finnish Constitution.

Use of the referendum is thus found in Scandinavia to be incompatible with two powerful elements in the political culture of the area—the zeal for compromise and the social democratic framework. As long as these two elements help to shape the political culture, the referendum is unlikely to play a more important role in the Scandinavian democracies.

Ireland

"If there is one thing more than another that is clear and shining through this whole Constitution," declared Eamon De Valera, on recommending Ireland's 1937 Constitution to the electorate, "it is the fact that the people are the masters."[81] De Valera's Constitution sought to supplement the British principles of responsible cabinet government with a very un-British acknowledgment of the sovereignty of the people. For this very reason, it was to be ratified, unlike the 1922 Constitution of the Irish Free State that it superseded, not through an act of the Dáil but by referendum. It was believed that this would symbolize that the Irish people, for the first time, were giving themselves a constitution and no longer owed allegiance to any foreign power.

The 1922 Constitution had itself, however, paid obeisance to the idea of direct democracy. It not only offered, in principle, more scope for the referendum than the 1937 Constitution was to do but also provided, unlike its successor, for the initiative. But as a result of the vicissitudes of Irish politics in the turbulent early years of independence, provision for these instruments of direct democracy was to be rapidly abolished.

It is not wholly clear why the 1922 Constitution made provision for the referendum and the initiative. The most likely explanation is that it was conceived after the First World War, at a time when many of the new democratic constitutions throughout Europe followed the Weimar example in giving an important role to the instruments of direct democracy.[82] The 1922 Constitution provided that constitutional

---

81. Quoted in Basil Chubb, "Government and Dáil: Constitutional Myth and Political Practice," in Brian Farrell, ed., *DeValera's Constitution and Ours* (Dublin: Gill and Macmillan, 1988), p. 98.

82. Leo Kohn, *The Constitution of the Irish Free State* (London: Allen and Unwin, 1932), p. 238; and Agnes Headlam-Morley, *The New Democratic Constitutions of Europe* (London: Oxford University Press, 1928), chapter VIII.

amendments had to be put to the voters and had to secure the support of either a majority of the electorate or two-thirds of those voting. In addition, it provided for a referendum on nonconstitutional legislation at the request of three-fifths of the Senate or a petition of one-twentieth of the electorate—at that time, approximately 100,000 voters. The Constitution also provided for the initiative to be established either by Parliament or by a petition of 75,000 registered voters.

The provision for constitutional amendment, however, was not to be operative for eight years, when the Constitution was to be entirely flexible and amendable by Parliament. In 1929, the period of flexible amendment was extended by Parliament for a further eight years, and in 1937 a new Constitution was drawn up. So in practice, the Constitution, although amended sixteen times during its short life, was an entirely flexible one.

The provisions for the legislative referendum and the initiative were abolished in 1928 to frustrate the attempt of De Valera's Fianna Fail party to secure a referendum on the oath to the king, which had been part of the treaty with Britain in 1921. Retention of the oath was perhaps the main reason why De Valera had refused to accept the treaty settlement, and he was determined to remove it at the earliest opportunity. He had indeed obtained the requisite number of signatures to secure an initiative, but in order to avoid calling the treaty into question, the government introduced a bill abolishing the referendum and the initiative. It declared the bill providing for their abolition "urgent" so that it could not itself be submitted to referendum, a move that De Valera dubbed "sharp practice."[83]

The truth was, however, that in a deeply divided society such as post–civil war Ireland, the referendum and initiative could have no role to play. There would always be the danger that the outcome of a referendum or initiative would not be accepted as legitimate by the losing side, and so the use of either weapon could have led to a renewal of the civil war. For the referendum to be a viable adjunct to government, there had to be a basic consensus on the framework of the state. This did not develop until after 1937.

Despite De Valera's claim that the people were to be the masters, the 1937 Constitution in fact severely limited the use of the referendum. It abolished the provision of 1922 for a qualified majority of the electorate to make a constitutional change, and it abolished entirely the 1922 provision for the initiative. Almost the sole use of the referendum is for the purpose of constitutional amendment. Article 46 of the

---

83. For details, see Maurice Manning, "Ireland," in Butler and Ranney, *Referendums*, pp. 194–97.

Irish Constitution declares that the only method of amending it is by referendum. In Ireland, moreover, unlike France or Germany, the Constitution provides that there are no unamendable provisions, except the referendum requirement itself (Article 51). Any other part of the Constitution can be altered by the passage of a bill through Parliament, followed by a referendum.

There is also provision for a legislative referendum under Article 27, but this has never been used. Since it needs to be triggered by a majority of the Senate, it is never likely to be; for the Senate hardly ever opposes the government of the day.

Including the referendum on the new Constitution itself, there have been seventeen referendums since 1937. Of these, twelve have been accepted and five rejected.[84] These referendums can be divided into four groups:

- four referendums on the Constitution and the proportional representation electoral system, held in 1937, 1959, and 1968 (when two referendums were held, one on the electoral system and one on the tolerance of constituency boundaries)
- three referendums relating to the European Community, held in 1972, 1987, and 1992
- six referendums on moral and ecclesiastical issues held in 1972 (special position of the Roman Catholic Church), 1983 (abortion), 1986 (divorce), and 1992 (three referendums on abortion)
- four relatively noncontentious referendums: 1972 on lowering the voting age, 1979 on adoption and reorganizing graduate representation in the Senate (the second reform has not yet been implemented), and 1984 on giving the right to vote in Dáil and presidential elections (though not in constitutional referendums) to resident noncitizens

The rejected referendums were all in the first and third categories. Abolition of proportional representation (1959) and abolition of proportional representation and increasing tolerance of constituency boundaries (1968) were in the first category. And the losing referendums in the third category were on permitting divorce (1986) and amending the constitutional ban on abortion (1992).

The referendum in Ireland has thus had the effect of preserving the status quo with regard to the electoral system and ensuring that the conservative moral values of the Irish electorate rather than the liberal values of the legislature have been enshrined in the Constitution.

---

84. In addition, two constitutional amendments were passed between 1937 and 1941, before the referendum provision actually came into effect.

It is ironic that in 1959 De Valera's Constitution was the means of defeating a reform on which he had set his heart: abolition of the single-transferable-vote method of proportional representation in favor of the British voting system. The political effect of abolition, it was generally believed, would have been to benefit Fianna Fáil as the majority party. Largely for this reason, it was opposed by the bulk of the Fine Gael opposition, although not by its leaders, Liam Cosgrave, John A. Costello, and James Dillon. Dillon, indeed, had in 1947 dismissed proportional representation in far stronger terms than De Valera had ever used, calling it "a fraud and a cod" and "the child of the brains of all the cranks in creation." He doubted whether "any other sane country in the world has put it into operation in regard to its parliament." During the 1968 referendum campaign, however, Dillon was to claim rather unconvincingly that his 1947 comments had been intended as an argument for an alternative form of proportional representation "adapted to suit our circumstances in Ireland."[85]

In 1959, De Valera held the referendum on the abolition of proportional representation on the same day as the presidential election for which he was the Fianna Fáil candidate. He hoped the constitutional amendment would benefit from being tied to his coattails. While De Valera comfortably won the presidential election, however, voters narrowly defeated the proposed constitutional amendment. A second attempt proposed by a later Fianna Fáil government in 1968 was defeated much more heavily (61–39), and it is unlikely that the issue will be raised again in the foreseeable future.

The referendums that have aroused the most bitterness in Ireland have been those on moral issues. The referendum of 1972 deleting those parts of the Constitution's Article 44 that provided for the special position of the Catholic church was the least contentious of the six referendums in category three. For the "special position" was largely symbolic, since there is no established church in Ireland. It was widely felt that abolition of Article 44 would be a symbol to Northern Ireland that the Republic was not, as Unionists believed, a country in thrall to clericalism. Indeed, Cardinal Conway, the Irish primate, had himself said in September 1969 that he

> personally would not shed a single tear if the relevant subsections of Article 44 were to disappear. It confers no legal privilege whatever on the Catholic Church and, if the way to convince our fellow Christians in the North about this is to

85. John Coakley, "The Referendum and Popular Participation in the Irish Political System" (Paper delivered to the European Consortium for Political Research Workshop, Lancaster, 1981), p. 39.

remove it, then it might be worth the expense of a referendum.[86]

Under the circumstances, it is hardly surprising that the referendum raised little controversy, winning 84–16.

The Abortion Referendum. Quite different, however, was the referendum on abortion in 1983. Unlike the Italian referendums of 1978, this one was not concerned with the legality or illegality of abortion. Abortion has been illegal in Ireland since the passage of an act of the United Kingdom Parliament in 1861, and there was never any prospect of the Irish Parliament's agreeing to legalize it. What disturbed many opponents of abortion, however, was that the prohibition of abortion was embodied only in ordinary law and not in the Constitution. It could thus be repealed at any time by Parliament; or, alternatively, the Irish Supreme Court could declare the ban on abortion unconstitutional because it restricted personal freedoms. That was what the United States Supreme Court had done in the landmark antiabortion decision in *Roe v. Wade* in 1973. Neither of these possibilities was likely to occur in Ireland. But noticing the move to liberalize abortion in many other parts of the world, Irish antiabortionists began to campaign for the prohibition to be inserted into the Constitution to preempt any removal of the restrictions. "Attack," declared one adherent of this viewpoint, "is the best form of defense."[87]

The 1983 referendum on abortion came about through the activities of an extraparliamentary pressure group, the Pro-Life Amendment campaign.[88] The campaign's original intention had been to collect so many signatures that the politicians could not ignore it; but, by a stroke of good fortune, the launch of the campaign occurred shortly before the February 1982 general election. Both of the major party leaders— Garret FitzGerald of Fine Gael and Charles Haughey of Fianna Fáil— were fearful of losing votes on such a deeply emotional issue, and they agreed to support a constitutional amendment prohibiting abortion.

---

86. Quoted in Basil Chubb, *The Constitution and Constitutional Change in Ireland* (Dublin: Institute of Public Administration, 1978), p. 61.

87. Quoted in Tom Hesketh, *The Second Partitioning of Ireland: The Abortion Referendum of 1983* (Dublin: Brandsma Books, 1990), p. 4. See also Brian Girvin, "Social Change and Moral Politics: The Irish Constitutional Referendum of 1983," *Political Studies* (1986), pp. 61–68; and J. P. O'Carroll, "Bishops, Knights—and Pawns? Traditional Thought and the Irish Abortion Referendum Debate of 1983," *Irish Political Studies* (1991), pp. 53–71.

88. The activities of this campaign are described in Tom Hesketh, *The Second Partitioning of Ireland*. Hesketh was himself an activist in the campaign.

After a further general election in November 1982, the second FitzGerald government proposed an amendment. Its wording was determined by the Fianna Fáil opposition, however, who were able to secure the support of Fine Gael dissidents during the parliamentary battle over the bill.

The amendment put to the electorate was worded as follows: "The State acknowledges the right to life of the unborn and, with due regard to the equal right to life of the mother, guarantees in its laws to respect, and, as far as practicable, by its laws to defend and vindicate that right." FitzGerald, although opposed to abortion, was disturbed at the wording, since his legal advisers told him that the term "unborn" was ambiguous. It could mean either "that which comes into existence at the moment of fertilization" or "a foetus implanted in the womb" or "a child capable of being born." On this last interpretation, the amendment would allow abortion in the early stages of pregnancy, something to which both major parties and the vast majority of the Irish electorate were opposed.

Moreover, by providing for the "equal right to life of the mother," the amendment was in danger of excluding preservation of the life of a mother with an ectopic pregnancy, or suffering from cancer of the womb, although these were circumstances in which the Catholic church itself permitted abortion.[89]

On a turnout of only 54 percent, however, the abortion amendment was passed, 67–33. It may well be that those who were worried by the terms of the amendment were unwilling, nevertheless, to vote against it, in case they seemed to be condoning abortion.

The ambiguities in the new constitutional provision came back to haunt Irish politics again in 1992, when, in the case of *Attorney General v. X*, it became clear that the amendment did not in fact absolutely prohibit abortion. X was a fourteen-year-old girl who had allegedly been raped and who sought to travel to Britain for an abortion. She had threatened to commit suicide if she was not allowed to do so. The Supreme Court declared that in these circumstances, the Constitution permitted her to go abroad for the purpose of obtaining an abortion, since there was a real and substantial risk to the life of the mother that could be avoided only by terminating the pregnancy. An abortion could also be performed in Ireland in such circumstances. In the absence of such a risk, however, the constitutional right to travel abroad was subordinate to the principle of protecting the rights of the unborn.[90]

---

89. Garret FitzGerald, *All in a Life* (London: Macmillan, 1991), pp. 440–41.

90. James Casey, *Constitutional Law in Ireland* (London: Sweet and Maxwell, 1992), p. 348.

This decision offended both supporters of the 1983 constitutional amendment who had sought an absolute ban on abortion and those who sought to remove an amendment that restricted the right to travel. Partisans on both sides therefore sought a new referendum: Catholic and anti-abortion groups seeking an absolute ban on abortion and their opponents seeking to enshrine in the Constitution the right to freedom of travel. The matter was even further complicated by the fact that the Irish electorate was shortly to be called on to ratify the Maastricht Treaty. There was a danger that opponents of the treaty would argue that Maastricht would make it impossible to restrict the freedom to travel, and impossible, therefore, to prohibit abortion.

The Taoiseach (Irish prime minister), Albert Reynolds, was mindful of how in 1981 the agenda had slipped from the government into the hands of a pressure group. He therefore skillfully retained control of the issue in his own hands. He succeeded in decoupling the abortion question from the Maastricht Treaty by pointing out that Protocol 17 to the treaty, which he had negotiated, declared that nothing in the treaty could overrule the 1983 constitutional amendment. The government's White Paper on Maastricht insisted that the treaty "is *not* about introducing abortion into Ireland."[91] Reynolds then promised to hold another referendum on abortion after Maastricht had been ratified.

Maastricht was safely ratified in June 1993, and in November the Irish electorate was faced with three abortion referendums.[92] The first proposed a new wording to replace that embodied in the Constitution in 1983. It provided that a termination of pregnancy should be allowed only when necessary "to save the life as distinct from the health of the mother where there is an illness or disorder of the mother giving rise to a real and substantial risk to her life, not being a risk of self-destruction." Thus the Supreme Court's decision in the *X* case would be overturned and abortion made more restrictive, since the threat of suicide would no longer provide grounds for it. This was thought to be too restrictive, even by those opposed to abortion, and the first referendum was rejected, 66–34.

The second referendum sought to ensure the right to information about abortion, and the third the right to travel. Both of these were passed, with 64 and 67 percent Yes votes. This left the law on abortion in a highly confused state. By contrast with 1983, however, the politicians had at least preserved their autonomy from the depredations of the pressure groups.

---

91. Michael Holmes, "The Maastricht Treaty Referendum of June 1992," *Irish Political Studies* (1993), p. 106.

92. See Brian Girvin, "The Referendums on Abortion, 1992," *Irish Political Studies* (1992), pp. 118–24.

Following the first abortion referendum in 1983, the Pro-Life Amendment campaign had gained a second success. Emboldened by its victory, the campaign regrouped to oppose the 1986 referendum on divorce.[93] This had been introduced as part of Garret FitzGerald's "constitutional crusade" to make the laws and Constitution of the Republic more palatable to the Protestants of Northern Ireland. Since the Catholic church did not explicitly oppose the amendment and the parliamentary opposition was neutral, the amendment was generally expected to pass. Opponents of the divorce referendum claimed a religious sanction for their viewpoint, however, one emotive poster declaring "God says vote No." The referendum was defeated, 53–37.[94]

In 1959 and 1968, the government had been beaten on referendums that were seen as partisan and that were opposed by all parties except Fianna Fáil. It was generally believed at that time that the only referendums likely to succeed were those with a significant degree of cross-party support. In 1983, however, the government was coerced and in 1986 defeated, not by politicians but by well-organized pressure groups. The political parties naturally sought to distance themselves from the referendums on moral issues, but these referendums can be seen to perform the function of mirrors, reflecting as they do the deepest aspirations of a society. Thus the success of antiabortion and antidivorce groups in Ireland can be contrasted with their failure in Italy. In Italy, voters in the divorce and abortion referendums proved *more* liberal than expected, while in Ireland they proved *less* liberal than expected. In Ireland, the political class had no desire to insert the prohibition of abortion in the Constitution, and it sought to legalize divorce. It was defeated by the popular pressure of groups and grassroots politicians who refused to follow the lead of the political class and who succeeded in persuading Irish voters not to follow their leaders either. "As long as simplistic attitudes to complex moral issues persist in Ireland," Garret FitzGerald has argued, "and as long as unscrupulous politicians are prepared to exploit religious feeling, our society will remain vulnerable to the 'crawthumpers.' "[95]

---

93. Cornelius O'Leary and Tom Hesketh, "The Irish Abortion and Divorce Referendum Campaigns," *Irish Political Studies* (1988), pp. 43–62.

94. R. Darcy and Michael Laver, "Referendum Dynamics and the Irish Divorce Amendment," *Public Opinion Quarterly* (1990), pp. 1–20. This article is also of some general interest, in seeking to establish comparative propositions relating party cues and public opinion in referendums. See also Cornelius O'Leary, "The Irish Referendum on Divorce, 1986," *Electoral Studies* (1987), pp. 69–74.

95. FitzGerald, *All in a Life*, p. 446. A "crawthumper" is defined in the *Oxford English Dictionary*, vol. III, p. 1125, as "one who beats his breast (at confession)."

The most important referendum in Ireland, however, is one that has not been held, and indeed one that the politicians hardly dare hold—a referendum to remove Articles 2 and 3 from the Constitution. These articles define the national territory as consisting of "the whole island of Ireland, its islands and the territorial seas," and speak of "the re-integration of the national territory" together with "the right of the Parliament and Government . . . to exercise jurisdiction over the whole of that territory." They thus make an implicit claim to the territory of Northern Ireland. Irish courts have held that these articles have the legal effect of precluding any acknowledgment that the Irish Republic is not as of right entitled to exercise jurisdiction over Northern Ireland. In other words, they prevent the Irish government from recognizing Northern Ireland de jure; it has long recognized Northern Ireland de facto.[96] Articles 2 and 3 thus feed on the fears of the Protestant community in Northern Ireland, and they allow these fears to be exploited by extremists within the Unionist parties. Successive British governments have regarded these articles as an obstacle to reconciliation in Northern Ireland, and the biconfessional Alliance party of Northern Ireland has sought their removal in exchange for giving the Catholic community in Northern Ireland a guaranteed share in the government of the province.

In the Republic, Fine Gael leaders have never been enamored of Articles 2 and 3. Liam Cosgrave, Taoiseach from 1973 to 1977, declared in 1972 that they "should never have been in the constitution," while Garret FitzGerald declared that "we are hamstrung by Articles 2 and 3." In 1974, the Fine Gael minister of justice advocated their deletion, as did Conor Cruise O'Brien, a Labour minister in the 1973–1977 coalition government.[97] But Fianna Fáil declared that it would oppose deletion, and the government felt that it could not proceed. The more moderate element of Fianna Fáil may now agree that deletion would be of value for relations with Northern Ireland, but it is different for a Taoiseach to propose a referendum on Articles 2 and 3, since it might not succeed and could all too easily resurrect the ghosts of the civil war era.

The people, although hardly the "masters" of the Irish Constitution, as De Valera claimed, nevertheless enjoy a considerable amount of power, since their assent is required for any amendment to the Constitution. The people may not always have used their power in ways that De Valera would have approved. They refused to abolish propor-

---

96. J. M. Kelly, *The Irish Constitution*, 3rd ed. (Dublin: Jurist Publishing Company, 1984), pp. 10–12.

97. Quoted in Chubb, *The Constitution and Constitutional Change in Ireland*, pp. 69, 99.

tional representation and decided to join the European Community and ratify the Maastricht Treaty, decisions De Valera might well not have supported. But in the last resort, the people have indeed used their power under the Constitution to entrench De Valera's Ireland. They have used it, in particular, to preserve their identity in the face of the powerful secularizing trends that they see all around them. Because they are thought likely to veto the removal of Articles 2 and 3, they have made it impossible for any Irish government to recognize de jure the partition of Ireland, something De Valera fought all his life to prevent. From this point of view, the referendum has indeed played a crucial role in ensuring that the 1937 Constitution has remained De Valera's Constitution. Whether that has been for the benefit of Ireland is a matter on which opinions will legitimately differ.

Conclusion

The referendum has been used most frequently in four countries of Western Europe other than Switzerland—Denmark, France, Ireland, and Italy. They have little in common except that they are all fairly homogeneous societies. None is pluralistic—that is, a society divided along religious, ethnic, or cultural lines. Other homogeneous societies, however, such as Iceland and Norway, have used the referendum hardly ever or not at all. While homogeneity may be a necessary condition, then, it cannot be a sufficient one to explain the frequency of using referendums. Perhaps, therefore, Arend Lijphart was right to "admit defeat in the search for general propositions and theories" to explain why some countries used the referendum and others did not. For, "Constitutions express certain philosophies of government,"[98] and those philosophies of government will owe so much to history and to divergent national patterns that generalization may not be possible. As David Butler and Austin Ranney have noted, "Each seems to have a special history, rooted in an individual national tradition."[99]

Much of our pattern of explanation in this chapter has been concerned with the effects of different national traditions on democratic practice and the holding of referendums. Two types of democracy hardly ever use the referendum, however. The first such society is a pluralistic one such as Belgium, or a consociational democracy such as Austria or the Netherlands. Belgium's one national referendum in 1950 was traumatic in exposing the hostility between the two main commu-

---

98. Arend Lijphart, *Democracies* (New Haven: Yale University Press, 1984), p. 206.

99. Butler and Ranney, *Referendums*, p. 18.

nities—the Flemings and the Walloons. Although there was a majority for retaining the monarchy, that majority was concentrated in the Flemish part of the country. It was unacceptable to the Walloons, and after communal riots, the king was forced to abdicate, despite having won the referendum. In the 1980s, the Belgian constitutional commission considering the reform of the country's institutions pronounced against the referendum. The commission argued that it "risked provoking and entrenching the deep conflicts between the communities."[100]

The referendum is not suited to a divided society for an obvious reason. Such a society, in order to obtain stability, needs to employ strategies that depart from the majoritarian model. The basic motif of such a society is not majority rule but power sharing. All the main pillars, *lagers*, or *zuilen* find themselves represented in government. Power sharing is, of course, the solution sought for Northern Ireland by successive British governments since the 1970s. Because Northern Ireland is a plural society divided by religion, the referendum—a weapon far more suited to a society based on majority rule—failed to do anything to resolve the problems of the province in the border poll of 1973.

Switzerland, of course, is the great exception to this generalization. It is a remarkable example of a plural society, divided by language, religion, and nationality, in which the referendum has functioned effectively. Far from being an instrument of majority rule, the referendum has helped to establish a political system in which the very notions of majority and minority have ceased to have much meaning. It is in fact the exception to the generalization that divided societies can find no prominent place for the referendum. For Switzerland has used the referendum, together with federalism and a coalition government embracing all the main political parties, precisely to *defuse* the conflicts that might otherwise arise in a divided society. The referendum is sometimes seen as an attack on party government. From this point of view, the Swiss have carried the logic of the referendum to its extreme. They have abandoned party government and instead employ instruments of direct democracy to replace Her Majesty's Opposition.

The second type of democracy in which the referendum will not be given a prominent place is one that has just emerged from dictatorship, since the referendum is likely to be regarded as an instrument to legitimize the dictator rather than as a constitutional check. No doubt for this reason the referendum plays a very small role in the constitu-

---

100. Quoted in L. Morel, "Le Référendum: État des Recherches," *Revue Française de Science Politique* (1992), p. 858.

tions of the new postwar democracies—West Germany, Greece, Portugal, and Spain. (The aspiring democracies in Eastern Europe and the former Soviet Union, however, may be a major exception.) Their constitutions were "reactive," in that they sought to create a constellation of power as different as possible from that which obtained under fascism.[101] Significantly, Greece, Portugal, and Spain did not seek to validate their entry into the European Community in 1981 and 1986 through referendums. But it is highly likely that the new aspirants for membership to the European Community—Austria, Finland, Norway, and Sweden—will hold referendums before entry.

Italy is a seeming exception to the generalization that former dictatorships dislike the referendum, but it appears that the political class was unaware in 1947 that the abrogative referendum would prove to be so powerful an instrument. Giulio Andreotti, the former Italian prime minister and, in 1947, the confidant of De Gasperi, father of the Italian Constitution, has confirmed that the intention of the Constitution was to give Parliament a central role. The referendum was to be used only in exceptional circumstances, since it was in essence an appeal *against* Parliament.[102]

Use of the referendum in the democracies of Western Europe, with the exception of Switzerland, has largely been confined to two types of issue: (1) constitutional, including territorial issues, and (2) "moral" issues, such as abortion or the prohibition of alcohol.

The referendum acts in Western Europe to supplement representative government. It does this by seeking to repair its main defects. The first such defect was pointed out by Dicey as long ago as 1890 in the context of Britain and is relevant to every democracy. It is the possibility of a fundamental change passing into law of which the majority disapproves. One democratic method of preventing this is to require any change in a country's constitution to be ratified by a referendum. That is the most important use of the referendum in the democracies of Western Europe.

Territorial sovereignty issues—separation, devolution, or the transfer of powers to a supranational organization such as the European Community—are also unlikely to be successfully handled by party systems. Most West European party systems are based on socioeconomic cleavages. In Britain, Denmark, and Norway, entry into the European Community cut across party lines, as did devolution to Scotland and Wales in Britain. In France, Algerian independence divided

---

101. See Vernon Bogdanor, ed., *Constitutions in Democratic Politics* (Aldershot: Gower, 1988).

102. Giulio Andreotti, "Intervention," in *Deux Constitutions*, pp. 71, 73.

the Right, while in Spain the issue of self-determination for the autonomous communities threatened to disrupt the political system. Moreover, like other constitutional changes, territorial changes are usually irreversible. So here, too, is a case for requiring changes to be ratified by a referendum. Both constitutional and territorial issues arguably go beyond the mandate that legislators are given at a general election, in that they involve altering the very framework of the political system.

Finally, moral issues and issues of conscience, such as abortion or nuclear energy, cut across the party system. For although they arouse deep feelings among many voters, they are not generally the most salient issues in general elections—the issues that determine voting behavior. Moral issues have proved especially difficult for governing parties to resolve. As the Swedish example of 1980 shows, they have a tendency to disrupt otherwise harmonious coalition governments. They pose problems that the political class finds itself unable to resolve, and so it is natural for such issues to be put to the electorate for resolution. This ensures that governing parties and coalitions are not disrupted. In a society in which it is used very rarely—for example, in Austria and Sweden over nuclear energy, or in Britain and Norway over the more constitutional issues of the European Community—use of the referendum is a sign of the breakdown of consociationalism or consensus. The Austrian nuclear energy referendum of 1978 showed, according to Anton Pelinka, that the corporate and consensual method of settling issues was breaking down. The Socialist government sought the support of the opposition for nuclear power, but this was refused, and the government did not want to take sole responsibility for this important development.[103] In such a situation, when the political class is no longer able to handle a difficult issue and it is no longer possible to defuse conflict within the governmental or parliamentary arena, the referendum may prove to be an invaluable alternative for the political class to deploy.

For constitutional, territorial, and moral issues, then, the referendum can provide a form of legitimacy that cannot be given by the normal processes of party politics. Thus use of the referendum, far from subverting the party system, actually helps to make representative government work more smoothly.

The referendum, it is generally argued, is not addictive. Yet its use has undoubtedly increased since the 1970s. In Italy, where the popular veto was not used until 1974, no fewer than twenty-seven referendums have been held on nine separate occasions since then. Thirteen of Ire-

---

103. Pelinka, "The Nuclear Power Referendum in Austria," pp. 255, 258.

land's seventeen referendums have been held since 1970. Britain's three referendums were held in the 1970s. Austria had its only referendum in 1978. Spain, of course, has had all its referendums since returning to democracy in 1975. This development is paralleled in countries where the referendum, together with the initiative, is used as part of the regular machinery of government. In Switzerland, as Kris Kobach shows, the number of initiatives rose very markedly in the 1970s, a result in part of the growth of new political movements. In the American states also, as Magleby shows, the use of referendums and initiatives has grown since the 1970s.

It seems then as if some general cause may be at work in the advanced democracies that leads to increasing use of the referendum. That common cause is likely to be the unfreezing of the political alignments and institutions formed after the achievement of universal suffrage in the first two decades of the twentieth century.

In their seminal work on party systems, Seymour Martin Lipset and Stein Rokkan put forward the famous "freezing hypothesis," according to which there had been a "freezing of the major party alternatives in the wake of the extension of the suffrage and the mobilization of major sections of the new reservoirs of political supporters." Writing in 1967, Lipset and Rokkan concluded that in Europe "the party systems of the 1960s reflect with few significant exceptions the cleavage structure of the 1920s."[104]

What has been less noticed is that, accompanying this freezing of the major party alternatives, there was also a freezing of institutions so that the liberal and radical program of democratic reform came to an end. By the beginning of the century, radicals and liberal democrats were confident that they were about to achieve universal suffrage. They proceeded to concern themselves therefore with improving the *quality* of democratic life. This was to be done by widening the opportunities available to voters. It was for this reason that proposals for constitutional reform designed to increase citizen control of government played so important a part in many European democracies at the beginning of the century. This involved, among other proposals, the introduction of the referendum. In Britain, as we have seen, the debate on the referendum began in the 1890s and continued until World War I. "Swiss experiments in direct legislation," one commentator noted in 1898, "have during the last ten years excited much interest in the United Kingdom."[105] By 1910, Dicey could write that "the name of the

---

104. Seymour Martin Lipset and Stein Rokkan, eds., *Party Systems and Voter Alignments: Cross-National Perspectives* (New York: Free Press, 1967), p. 50.

105. Simon Deploige, *The Referendum in Switzerland*, published in 1898 and quoted in Michael Steed, "Participation through Western Democratic Institu-

Referendum is now on the lips of every person interested in political theory."[106]

In Switzerland, the initiative was introduced in 1891. In Ireland, the Free State Constitution of 1922 provided for use of the initiative and the referendum in conscious reaction against the British system of cabinet government, which, Irish nationalists believed, gave too much weight to the executive over the Parliament and people. The postwar constitutions of a number of the new democracies of Central and Eastern Europe, and in particular the Weimar German Constitution of 1919, made considerable provision for use of the referendum and initiative;[107] and it was largely during the first twenty years of the century that the direct primary, the referendum, and the initiative were introduced in the United States. "Proposals for new electoral systems or for the referendum," it has been argued, "were current in all countries at the beginning of the century."[108]

After 1920, however, with the achievement of universal suffrage, the newly mobilized electorate found itself interested less in the completion of the liberal democratic program than in the improvement of social and economic conditions; and constitutional questions came to be eclipsed by socioeconomic issues that replaced them at the center of the political agenda. In most European democracies, politics became the politics of the democratic class struggle, and the party of opinion, of which liberal parties were the paradigm, found itself eclipsed by mass parties of Left and Right. At the level of democratic thought, there was some disenchantment with the possibilities of liberal democracy as the works of the founding fathers of political science—men such as Robert Michels, Vilfredo Pareto, and Max Weber—came to be more widely disseminated. "The tendency to groups is a deadly bacillus in modern legislatures," James Bryce told his friend Dicey in 1919. "When one re-reads Mill's 'Representative Government' are you not struck by the fact that he did not anticipate the development things have taken and the discredit into which legislatures have fallen?"[109] Switzerland, which before 1914 had been seen as one of the basic mod-

tions," in Geraint Parry, ed., *Participation in Politics* (Manchester: Manchester University Press, 1972), p. 95.

106. Albert Venn Dicey, "The Referendum and Its Critics," *Quarterly Review* (1910), p. 538.

107. See Agnes Headlam-Morley, *The New Democratic Constitutions of Europe*, chap. VIII.

108. Steed, "Participation through Western Democratic Institutions," p. 95.

109. Bryce to Dicey, 29 August 1919, Bryce Papers, Bodleian Library, UB 4, f 223.

els of democratic government and had been regarded by democratic theorists of the nineteenth century as the direction in which all democracies had been moving, was almost forgotten. When remembered, it was seen as but a quaint anomaly. The sovereignty of the people was seen not only as an unattainable ideal, but also as an undesirable one.

So it was that political structures came to be frozen, and constitutional change ceased to play so prominent a part in political affairs. The liberal and radical movement seemed to have played itself out. The crucial reason for this is that measures such as the referendum, designed to increase participation and the popular control of government, would threaten the very interests of the parties themselves.[110] As Michael Steed has pointed out, the development of tightly organized mass political parties was largely responsible for fossilizing the movement for constitutional change.[111] Yet tightly organized mass parties were thought to provide the best vehicle for the stability of democratic government, because parties could rely on solid blocks of electoral support based primarily on class and religion.

In a number of countries, attempts were made to narrow the scope of participation. In Ireland, provision for the referendum and initiative was abolished in 1928; the 1937 Constitution gave much less scope for the instruments of direct democracy than the 1922 Constitution had done. In Britain, the debate on the referendum and electoral reform came to an end, except for a brief flurry of interest in the years 1929–1931. Most of the new democracies of Central and Eastern Europe succumbed either to executive–dominated government or to dictatorship, as of course did Weimar Germany; and the new German Constitution of 1949 had no place for direct democracy. For the experience of fascism and national socialism aroused great fear of populism and suspicion of the plebiscitary techniques that had supposedly assisted it to power.

Thus the referendum came to be exploited and misused by the dictators, while in those countries that retained democratic government, interest in direct democracy was superseded by the growth of the mass party whose role the referendum threatened to undermine. The *International Encyclopedia of the Social Sciences* of 1968, unlike its predecessor of 1932, did not even have an entry under "Referendum."

---

110. For an example of how the interests of the two major parties came to smother the movement for the referendum in Britain, see parts 1 and 2 of Vernon Bogdanor, *The People and the Party System: The Referendum and Electoral Reform in British Politics* (Cambridge: Cambridge University Press, 1981).

111. Michael Steed, "Participation through Western Democratic Institutions," p. 96.

Lipset and Rokkan published *Party Systems and Voter Alignments* in 1967. The next year, however, the first signs of the unfreezing of political institutions became visible. The year 1968 was marked by widespread student revolt in the democracies of Western Europe and in the United States. The rhetoric of the revolt was neo-Marxist, and the students believed themselves to be pursuing new doctrines derived from modern interpreters of Marx such as Herbert Marcuse. In reality, however, the rebels of 1968 were rediscovering the old doctrines of liberal and radical reformers at the beginning of the century. For the main catchword of the students was *participation,* and its basic message was a distrust of the mass party and the other mediating institutions that had come to dominate modern representative democracies.

In place of such institutions, the rebels favored direct election, party primaries, party reform, the recall, the initiative—all weapons of direct democracy, which, so the rebels believed, enabled the people to control their leaders. These weapons, however, had nothing whatever to do with Marxism. Rather, they were part of the armory of the radical populists of the first part of the twentieth century. Their aim was to secure "what is seen as a fuller, and more genuine, version of the old democratic ideal."[112] The rebels of 1968 sought a more participatory individualism, not a more humane collectivism. They owed little to Marx, but a great deal to Rousseau, and even to Ostrogorski.

Since the 1960s, many European democracies have showed signs of a glacially slow but nonetheless perceptible unfreezing of old political alignments. In particular, the importance of social-structural determinants of voting behavior, whether religion or class, has declined. In the 1950s and 1960s, the German-American political scientist Otto Kirchheimer predicted that the party of mass integration would gradually come to be replaced by the catchall party, which would seek to appeal to as many different groups of voters as possible, not just those within its own *famille spirituelle.* "Continental European parties," he declared, "are the remnants of intellectual and social movements of the nineteenth century. They have remained glued to the spots where the ebbing energy of such movements deposited them some decades ago."[113]

This implies a decline in the authority of the political party as a source of mass loyalty. Kirchheimer believed that electors, since they

---

112. Anthony Arblaster, "Participation: Context and Conflict," in Parry, *Participation in Politics,* p. 55.

113. Otto Kirchheimer, "The Waning of Opposition in Parliamentary Regimes," in Roy Macridis and Bernard E. Brown, eds., *Comparative Politics* (Homewood, Ill.: Dorsey Press, 1964), p. 286.

no longer "belong" to a political party by virtue of their social class or religion, will no longer be willing to accept the unquestioning authority of party leaders. In addition, wider social changes in Western democracies—the spread of ownership of property, shares, and other assets—have helped to diffuse power and to undermine attitudes of deference. There has been an increasing emphasis on consumerism and choice in both public and private services. It would be unrealistic to expect that these changes would not have their consequences in the political sphere. Thus, in place of disciplined leadership, one would expect the demand for greater popular accountability and participation to increase. So it has in the democracies of Western Europe.

Although the referendum is in essence a conservative weapon, pressure for its use in Western Europe has come from radical groups seeking change: for example, antinuclear protesters in Austria, Italy, and Sweden. In Italy, where the abrogative referendum gives radical reformers considerable leverage, pressure from radical groups has been a prime factor in compelling reform of what had become a corrupt *partitocrazia*.

Indeed, Italy, where use of the referendum has been most strikingly addictive, is once again the exception that proves the rule. For Italy's abrogative referendum is a weapon that takes control of the referendum away not only from the government but also from the political class. Apart from Switzerland, Italy is the only country in Western Europe where the political class has no means of controlling the referendum. The abrogative referendum in Italy is to some extent what the referendum and initiative are in Switzerland—a replacement for a genuine opposition in the legislature. The abrogative referendum has become addictive because the electorate, and in particular various pressure groups, has gained a taste for it. In democracies where the political class can control the use of the referendum, there is no reason for it to admit issues to referendum unless it is required to do so or unless it believes that only through the referendum can a difficult political problem be solved. Such situations are likely to be few and far between. For this reason, in most democracies the referendum has not become addictive.

A striking illustration of the danger the referendum holds for the political class was provided by the referendums on the Maastricht Treaty held in 1992.[114] Three countries held referendums: Denmark,

---

114. An account of earlier referendums on the European Community is given in Anthony King, "Referendums and the European Community," in Austin Ranney, ed., *The Referendum Device* (Washington, D.C.: American Enterprise Institute, 1981).

France, and Ireland. In Denmark (in the absence of a five-sixths majority in the Folketing) and Ireland the referendum was obligatory; in
France it was not. Interestingly, Jacques Delors, president of the Commission of the European Community, gave the French referendum the
character of a recall when he declared that, in the event of a No victory,
he would not seek reappointment as president of the commission in
January 1993.

Maastricht was defeated in Denmark in 1992, despite the fact that
six of the eight parties represented in the Folketing were in favor of it,
comprising 80 percent of the members. Along with the narrowness of
the majority in France, a country that sees itself at the heart of Europe,
this was a clear sign that the European Community was losing support
among electors in the member states. In Britain, the government refused to allow a referendum, and survey evidence indicated that Maastricht would be defeated if put to the people. In Germany, where there
was no provision for a referendum, survey evidence indicated uncertainty about Maastricht's ratification. The unwillingness of electors to
endorse Maastricht when contrasted with the large majorities for it in
the legislatures of the member states showed that the European Community was beginning to give rise to that deepest and most intractable
of all political conflicts—that between the electorate and the political
class. The referendum is an instrument peculiarly well equipped to
expose such a conflict.

It is understandable, however, that where the referendum remains
under the control of the political class, that class does not have much
of a taste for it. That is why the referendum has played so limited a
role in the democracies of Western Europe.

In some countries, however, although the referendum remains formally under the control of the political class, those outside that class
are able to put pressure on those inside to grant it. That was what
happened in Britain over both the European Community in 1975 and
devolution in 1979, when groups in the Labour party, opposed by the
leadership, were able to force the party to accept the referendum as a
lesser evil. It happened also in Ireland, where pressure groups were
able to secure acceptance of their demand for a referendum on abortion in 1983; and in Austria on the nuclear energy issue in 1978. It is
possible therefore that the political class may come gradually to lose
its control over the referendum process and that what happened in
Britain and in Ireland in the 1970s will prove to be the pattern of the
future.

Popular attitudes to political participation reflect generational
changes. The generation of the 1950s grew to maturity during the era
of universal suffrage, and it was deeply scarred by the traumas of fas-

cism and communism. It is hardly surprising if it displayed a cautious attitude toward proposals for increasing participation. The current political generation, however, takes universal suffrage and political stability for granted. It is perhaps more skeptical of the pretensions of political parties to represent opinion effectively.

The referendum, as we have seen, undermines and disrupts party systems, as it did in France between 1958 and 1962, Denmark and Norway in 1972, and, arguably, Britain after 1975. Some would suggest that this disruption damages representative government by breaking up established parties, but others would claim that the referendum has played an important role in enabling otherwise fossilized political systems to adapt to new conditions by stimulating realignment.

The future of the referendum in the democracies of Western Europe is bound up with the future of the mass party that developed in the early years of the twentieth century. For as A. V. Dicey, advocate of the referendum in Britain, wrote in 1915, "It is certain that no man who is really satisfied with the working of our party system will ever look with favour on an institution which aims at correcting the vices of party government."[115]

It is of course far too early to tell whether the increasing incidence of the referendum since the 1970s signals a genuine turning point in democratic politics or whether the referendum will remain a subordinate instrument in West European political systems. But as we reach the end of the twentieth century, signs indicate that the mass party as we have known it since the beginning of the century, far from being inherent to any democratic system of government, may represent merely a phase of democratic development that is passing away. If that is so, we may confidently expect a more widespread use of the referendum in the twenty-first century than we have seen in the twentieth.

---

115. Albert Venn Dicey, "Introduction," *Law of the Constitution*, 8th ed. (London: Macmillan, 1915), p. c.

4
Switzerland

Kris W. Kobach

Switzerland is the only nation in the world where political life truly revolves around the referendum. The country of 6¹/₂ million shuns popular leaders, and the division of executive authority among the seven members of its Federal Council further discourages the politics of personality. When individual political figures do happen to rise above the multitude, it is almost always on the shoulders of a referendum campaign. Legislating in the Federal Assembly is an intricate dance of avoiding or winning a popular vote. The great political moments of modern Switzerland have occurred not in the following of bold statesmen but in the national debates that have drawn the masses to the polls to decide their country's future.

Switzerland has held more nationwide referendums since it introduced the institution in 1848 than all other countries combined, since the emergence of the modern nation-state. Among democracies in the postwar period, it accounts for more than two-thirds of the total. In fact, no other state in the world even comes close to Switzerland in applying direct democracy to national political questions.[1] By the end of 1993, Switzerland had held a total of 414 nationwide referendums, covering virtually every sphere of government activity. Australia, in a distant second place, had held only 44.[2] In most years, Swiss voters are

---

1. I use the phrase *direct democracy* to mean *referendums and initiatives,* even though, technically, the Swiss devices exemplify semidirect democracy. This practice of referring to referendums and initiatives as direct democracy is fairly common (see, for example, chap. 7). Some writers also intend the term to include recall elections and primary elections. In this chapter, the term is not meant to encompass these devices.

2. There is one other polity not mentioned here. That is, of course, the tiny Alpine principality of Liechtenstein, which shares Switzerland's obsession with referendums. With a population of 29,900 and an eligible electorate of 14,000, it is comparable in size to the smallest Swiss cantons. The principality uses both constitutional and statutory referendums, in most years presenting 0–2 questions to the voters. On average, Liechtenstein has held approximately one referendum per year since 1918. The votes cover a wide range of subject matters, limited somewhat by the fact that Switzerland conducts foreign relations on behalf of Liechtenstein, Swiss troops provide its defense, and the

called on to decide six to twelve national questions, which are typically spread over two to four separate ballots. In addition, they are asked to vote in numerous cantonal and communal referendums. When elections of national, cantonal, and communal representatives are added to these referendums, it is no exaggeration to say that Swiss citizens are called to the polls more times in one year than most Europeans are in a lifetime. Only in California and a few other Western American states are voters presented with such a volume of referendums. Ballot issues in America, however, concern only subnational matters and operate in the long shadow of national politics, where referendums are absent. Thus, the Swiss can fairly claim to be more thoroughly immersed in direct democracy than citizens of any other nation.

The Origins of the Federal Referendum

Direct democracy is a deeply rooted and definitive element of Swiss political culture. The modern federal referendum and initiative devices descended from traditional cantonal institutions. In 1991, the Helvetian Confederation celebrated its 700th birthday. Swiss direct democracy is almost as old, the first direct vote of citizens on policy occurring in 1294 in the canton of Schwyz. The vote was the first recorded decision of the canton's Landsgemeinde, an annual, sovereign assembly of all male citizens possessing the requisite status to vote. By the early fourteenth century, the Landsgemeinde was a well-established tradition in the central mountain cantons. In size, the Landsgemeinden were impressive, the smallest consisting of less than 1,000 and the largest involving more than 10,000 people. Found only in German-speaking Switzerland, the Landsgemeinde cantons included Uri, Schwyz, Obwalden and Nidwalden (the two components of Unterwalden), Glarus, Zug, Appenzell-Inner Rhodes, and Appenzell-Outer Rhodes. Five retain the practice today, usually convening the assembly on the last Sunday in April or the first Sunday in May each year. It is difficult to overstate how extraordinary the Landsgemeinde was, particularly in the early centuries of its existence. While the rest of Europe was laboring under feudal or absolutist rule, an undiluted form of direct democracy was flourishing in the mountain valleys of these Swiss cantons. In directness of participation on a relatively large scale, the Landsgem-

---

Swiss franc is its national currency. In December 1992, however, Liechtenstein's voters chose rather dramatically to break ranks with their larger neighbor by joining the European Economic Area (EEA). A record 87 percent of the electorate turned out for the vote, in which 56 percent voted for membership in the EEA.

einde has yet to be rivaled seven centuries later.

Shortly after the introduction of the Landsgemeinde in the central mountain cantons, a parallel development occurred to the east in the Raetian Republic of the Three Leagues (in what is now the canton of Graubünden). By the start of the fifteenth century, an early form of referendum was instituted in the republic. This procedure allowed for discussion and deliberation by citizens of each commune before policies could be adopted at the league or republic level. Participation was not as direct as in the Landsgemeinde, but the procedure was based on the same notion that the legitimacy of decisions rested in the assent of the people. This mutual commitment to direct democracy fostered unity among the three leagues despite linguistic differences and formidable geographic barriers.

The city cantons followed a different path of political development. In the thirteenth and fourteenth centuries, most were governed by oligarchic ruling councils. In the fifteenth and sixteenth centuries, however, most notably in Bern, an early form of referendum was put into practice in which all free men assented to cantonal decisions. Unfortunately, this procedure was eventually terminated by absolutist patriciates.

Switzerland saw its first nationwide referendum in 1802, when a constitution imposed by Napoleon was submitted to the Swiss people for approval. The cards were heavily stacked in favor of Napoleon's preferred outcome. It was announced beforehand that abstentions would be considered affirmative ballots. The constitution was accepted with 92,500 votes against and only 72,500 in favor, because there were 167,000 abstentions. This political framework collapsed, however, with defeat of the French army in 1815.

The next major development in Swiss direct democracy occurred in the 1830s, when reform-oriented Liberals in a number of cantons engineered successful coups. A wave of democratic changes ensued in the so-called Liberal Regeneration. Following every Liberal takeover except that in Fribourg, the new leadership established the constitutional referendum at the cantonal level. The same period also witnessed the introduction of the optional legislative referendum (or "facultative referendum"), which allowed citizens to challenge routine laws by petition, thereby bringing the questions before the electorate. In addition, a number of cantons proclaimed the right of their citizens to call a constitutional initiative for total revision. This institution enabled the people of a canton to demand a fundamental revision of the cantonal basic law. In many cantons, the referendum and initiative devices were viewed as an acceptable replacement for communal direct assemblies and cantonal Landsgemeinden. Population growth was making such meetings impractical. In Schwyz and Zug in 1848, the substitution was immediate and direct, with the referendum introduced as the Landsgemeinde was withdrawn.

In 1847–1848, the Sonderbund conflict, Switzerland's civil war, culminated in a settlement that finally instituted the referendum securely at the federal level. The 1848 Constitution, which embraced the obligatory constitutional referendum for all proposed amendments, also provided for a constitutional initiative for total revision, by which citizens could petition for a referendum on a proposed rewriting of the document. In the Constitution of 1874, the optional legislative referendum was introduced; and in 1891, Switzerland adopted the constitutional initiative for partial revision, by which citizens could propose and adopt amendments to the Constitution. The optional treaty referendum was introduced in 1921.

Of course, direct democracy is not the only definitive element of the Swiss political system. Today, Switzerland is also known for its consociational politics. Since the introduction of the "magic formula" in 1959, the seven seats on the Federal Council have been distributed in a continuous 2:2:2:1 seat distribution among the four largest parties: the Radicals (FDP), the Christian Democrats (CVP), the Social Democrats (SPS), and the agrarian Swiss People's Party (SVP), which is allotted the single seat. This grand coalition, combined with a pervasive ethos of compromise, has prompted many an observer to label Swiss government a textbook case of *Konkordanz-Demokratie*. This was not always the case, however. At the time of the Sonderbund War, Switzerland was the Ulster of nineteenth-century Europe, riven by an explosive religious conflict that had been smoldering for centuries. Consociational behavior and institutions grew by degrees, beginning in the 1880s and culminating in the formula of 1959. At every stage, the referendum was the primary engine behind the change.

It is difficult to overstate the importance of direct democracy in bringing about this facet of Swiss politics. In the aftermath of the Sonderbund War, the Radicals enjoyed virtually complete hegemony in the federal government. Not only did they control large majorities in both houses of the Federal Assembly, but also the seven-member Federal Council was drawn exclusively from their ranks.[3] The referendum, however, afforded Catholic and conservative opposition groups (which represented mainly the defeated Sonderbund cantons) a powerful means of blocking Radical programs. In a January 1866 referen-

---

3. The two houses of the Federal Assembly are the National Council, currently with 200 members, in which representation is based on population, and the Council of States, in which the cantons are represented equally.

dum, their vociferous opposition sparked the defeat of eight of nine constitutional amendments proposed by the Radicals. With the introduction of the facultative referendum in 1874, the Catholic-conservative alliance (later to form the Catholic Conservative party, which in turn evolved into the Christian Democrats) was given an even more potent weapon of opposition. Threatening to bring federal political life to a standstill, they engineered the popular rejection of eleven federal laws between 1875 and 1884. In 1884, the Radicals finally gave in and elected a conservative Catholic to the Federal Council. They elected another in 1891. The nascent Catholic Conservative party had won itself admittance to the national executive by employing direct democracy. The Social Democrats repeated this pattern, making frequent use of the referendum and initiative between 1900 and 1937 to harry the *bürgerliche* government. In 1943, they were finally brought on board the Federal Council. In 1959, this sharing of power became a seemingly permanent arrangement.

The Mechanisms of Direct Democracy at the Federal Level

There are no controlled or consultative referendums in Switzerland. The government may not call referendums at will. The only sense in which this is possible is through the passage of a constitutional amendment, which necessarily triggers a referendum for its enactment. All referendums represent sovereign and binding decisions, in that they cannot be overruled except by another referendum. The government, however, is free to attempt to pass a law or constitutional amendment again after it has been rejected in a referendum. With all acts of legislation except those designated as matters of urgency, direct democracy has a slight delaying effect. That is, the law in question cannot take effect until the referendum procedure has been carried out. At a minimum, this entails a delay of ninety days during which citizens may circulate petitions to demand a referendum on the law. If the effort successfully amasses the required number of signatures, then there will usually be another six months of delay before the issue can be placed on a national ballot. With decrees designated as "urgent," the measures take effect immediately but can be canceled by referendum after one year. There are four basic types of federal referendums in Switzerland:

- the constitutional referendum
- the constitutional initiative
- the optional or facultative referendum on legislation
- the optional treaty referendum

The rules governing these various devices are as follows.

All constitutional amendments must be submitted to a popular vote in an obligatory constitutional referendum. The same rules that apply to total revisions of the constitution apply to partial amendments as well. Calls for total revision have been extremely rare, occurring only in 1872 and 1874. On all constitutional questions, a double majority is required for the change to be approved; that is, it must receive both a majority of votes nationally and a majority of votes in more than half of the twenty-three cantons.[4] The double majority provision was adopted in 1848 as a concession to the smaller cantons, most of whom were in the defeated Sonderbund alliance. Envisioned as a means of safeguarding cantonal prerogatives, it has had exactly that effect. There have been only six obligatory referendums in which the people said Yes and the cantons said No (in 1866, 1955, 1970, 1973, 1975, and 1983) and two in which the cantons said Yes and the people said No (in 1910 and 1957). In each of the six cases where the cantons prevented a constitutional measure from being accepted, the change involved giving new powers to the federal government. Thus, the double majority provision has served to reinforce federalist arrangements in Switzerland.

The constitutional initiative process can be triggered when any seven voters submit a request for an initiative and a description of the desired change in the Constitution. They then have eighteen months to collect 100,000 signatures in support of their petition.[5] There are two types of constitutional revision that may be pursued via the initiative: total or partial. Total revisions are sent directly to the people after the signatures are submitted. If a majority of the nation votes in favor of revision, then the Federal Assembly (the bicameral Swiss Parliament) is dissolved, and new elections are held to elect a constitutional assembly to undertake the revision. The subsequent document must then achieve a double majority in a referendum. The only two attempts at a total revision of the Constitution via initiative were made in 1880 and 1935, although the first case was merely a partial revision in the guise of a total revision. Both failed.

---

4. The total of twenty-three may be somewhat misleading. There are actually twenty-six separate cantonal entities in Switzerland. Six of these are "half-cantons," however, which have half the weight of normal cantons in calculating referendum totals. They also send only one representative (rather than two) to the Council of States.

5. Before the constitutional amendment was approved by obligatory referendum in 1977, the required number of signatures for a constitutional initiative was 50,000.

Partial revisions can take one of two forms: either they can suggest a change in general terms, or they can present the exact text of a proposed amendment. In the generally worded case, if the Federal Assembly agrees with the suggestion, it drafts a specific amendment, which is submitted to the people. The amendment takes effect if a double majority is achieved. If, however, the legislature disagrees (which is more likely), the proposal must pass a preliminary referendum in which a double majority is not required. Then the legislature must draft an appropriate text and send it to the people again. The second time around, a double majority is required. A specifically worded initiative need go to the people only once. Not surprisingly, the overwhelming majority of initiatives take this form.

Before an initiative is placed on a ballot, the government can either endorse it, recommend rejection, or recommend rejection and submit a counterproposal of its own. Typically, such counterproposals include some of the petitioners' demands while omitting others. Before 1987, the voter was only allowed to vote Yes on either the original initiative or the counterproposal, but not on both. This procedure often led to confusion and ambiguous results. It also enabled the government to defeat an initiative by diverting some of its votes to a decoy proposition. When a majority of the electorate desired reform but was divided in its support for the original initiative and the counterproposal, it was not uncommon for both ballot issues to fail. This ploy succeeded in foiling several twentieth-century initiatives. Finally in 1987, after the presence of a counterproposal led to the defeat of a widely accepted initiative to subsidize the arts, the government gave in to demands for reform. It proposed a constitutional amendment to allow double-Yes voting for both an initiative and its counterproposal. This new rule has considerably improved the odds for initiatives pitted against government counterproposals. It is no coincidence that the counterproposal has lost its popularity as a government tactic in the years since.

Any law or decree passed by the Federal Assembly is susceptible to challenge by facultative referendum. A referendum is called if, within ninety days after the law's publication, 50,000 voters or eight cantons demand one.[6] The question is then placed on an upcoming ballot, typically alongside other unrelated referendums or initiatives. Quite often, the referendum can be held within nine months of the law's passage. Nonetheless, nine months' delay is still considerable. The government is therefore permitted to designate vital legislation as "urgent" if both houses of the Federal Assembly agree. A law classified

---

6. Before 1977, the required number of signatures for an optional legislative referendum was 30,000.

as such goes into effect immediately. It may be challenged in the same way as a normal law, but if it is rejected by the people it remains in effect until the end of a year. In cases of urgency, the Federal Assembly can also adopt unconstitutional decrees. If the decree has effect for more than a year, a referendum must then take place; and the measure must be approved by a double majority. Otherwise, it lapses after a year.

The optional treaty referendum arose from the widely held presumption in Switzerland that the country's long-established tradition of neutrality ought to be as difficult to alter as any clause in the Constitution, if not more so. Therefore, the people should be allowed to veto any agreement that might impinge on this hallowed aspect of Swiss foreign policy. The question of exactly how to treat foreign agreements first arose in 1920 with the decision to join the League of Nations. The government decided to require a double majority of people and cantons to approve League of Nations membership, rather than just a popular majority. In effect, the issue was treated as a constitutional amendment. Curiously, it was not treated as such when Switzerland left the organization. Over the next fifty years, similar ambiguities emerged in the treatment of foreign agreements.

In a 1977 constitutional amendment, the rules were finally spelled out precisely. Any agreement involving a collective security organization or a supranational community is treated as a constitutional amendment and must win a double majority in an obligatory referendum. All other treaty arrangements are subject to a referendum if one is demanded by 50,000 voters. Only a popular majority is required. Three international agreements have faced referendums under these rules. In 1986, the government's attempt to join the United Nations was treated as a constitutional amendment and was rejected overwhelmingly. In 1992, the decision to join the International Monetary Fund and the World Bank came under the provisions governing the optional treaty referendum. The decision was challenged by petition and put to a referendum, in which it was approved by 55.8 percent of the voters. Later the same year, the government sought to join the European Economic Area with the other member states of the European Free Trade Association. The proposal was treated as a constitutional amendment and failed narrowly, with 49.7 percent of the vote.

Areas of Potential Reform

Generally, the mechanisms of direct democracy have enjoyed broad acceptance among the Swiss. Several specific problems of the initiative, however, have drawn criticism of late. Most recently, the length of the initiative process has come under fire. With some proposals, the potential for delay has proved an effective weapon in the hands of government opponents. The Federal Assembly and the Federal Council (Switzerland's seven-member collegial executive) are free to spend up to four years considering an initiative. And this generous deliberation period is not all. After the government position is determined, the Federal Council is obliged to fix a date for the vote. It may, however, wait as long as it wishes to announce a date and may then choose any date it likes. Although the Federal Council has never flaunted this prerogative so brazenly as to push a voting date ridiculously far into the future, it has effectively killed initiatives through delay on numerous occasions. The executive can deflate an initiative's buoyancy by choosing a date that will arrive long after all momentum is lost. In 1977, for example, Switzerland's Social Democratic party (SPS) submitted an initiative to relax Switzerland's controversial banking secrecy regulations. It did not come to a vote until 1984, long after the issue had been displaced by others in the public eye. The proposition miscarried badly, winning only 27.0 percent of the vote.

This sort of delay has infuriated many initiative sponsors. Bernhard Böhi, the Basle businessman in the driver's seat of Switzerland's Auto party (devoted to representing Swiss motorists), has financed and orchestrated many initiatives. In 1988, he called off signature collection on two initiatives for a new Gotthard Tunnel out of frustration with the fate of two earlier initiatives that he financed. He angrily explained, "Today, initiatives are dispatched by the Federal Council through delaying consideration of the measure."[7] In 1989, he and his allies launched an initiative demanding the limitation of parliamentary and governmental consideration to two years. But the initiative failed to attract enough signatures before its November 1990 deadline. In any event, the proposal was strongly opposed by the conservative Radical party (FDP) in the National Council, which called for the lengthening of the parliamentary consideration period beyond four years, ostensibly to allow for a more equitable devotion of time to various initiatives and the grouping of proposals by subject matter.

A second problem, according to some critics, is the absence of the legislative initiative at the federal level. Although several cantons adopted the device in the mid-nineteenth century, it is still impossible for citizens to propose normal statutes. This has placed Switzerland in a curious position, in which the highest law of the land is more easily amendable by popular action than are routine statutes. Consequently,

---

7. Andreas Gross, "1988—ein Jahr erfolgloser Volksbegehren," *Tages-Anzeiger*, 5 January 1989, p. 9.

proponents of reform frame as constitutional amendments proposals that otherwise might have been enacted as normal laws, allowing the Swiss Constitution to become a hodgepodge of fundamental law mixed with routine legislation. An attempt was made to introduce the federal legislative initiative in 1961, but the move was rejected by 70.6 percent of the voters. Although the issue continues to receive sporadic government attention, no serious push for change has followed the 1961 vote.

A third problem has received considerable attention of late. Hotly contested battles on the field of direct democracy have involved greater and greater sums of money. This has been particularly evident in recent referendums on membership in international organizations. The amount spent on initiative campaigns has also increased markedly. In the early 1960s, the cost of a typical campaign in support of an initiative was likely to run more than 300,000 S.Fr. Today, the price varies from a general minimum of around 500,000 S.Fr. to well over 1 million S.Fr. spent on many initiatives. The sums spent to defeat initiatives have also risen accordingly. Groups opposing the initiative to abolish the army in November 1989, for example, spent approximately 4 million S.Fr.[8] Not surprisingly, a cottage industry has grown around the initiative device, providing services ranging from signature collection to direct mailing to professional campaign management (for similar developments in some American states, see chapter 7).

Volunteers working on initiative campaigns often complain of a significant disparity in resources, in that forces opposed to initiatives tend to have more money at their disposal. In 1988, for example, more than 20 million S.Fr. were spent by allied groups to defeat an initiative prohibiting real estate speculation. The sum dwarfed the resources available to the initiative's sponsors. Michael Kaufmann, secretary of the vanquished initiative committee, described the negative outcome as "purchased democracy."[9] Compounding this inequality is the fact that media exposure is generally of greater importance for proponents of an initiative than for opponents. Those launching an initiative need to explain their cause and convert uninformed voters to it. Those opposing an initiative have the easier task of defending the status quo before a fundamentally conservative electorate.

Although expenditures continue to spiral upward, there have always been notable cases in which the sponsoring organization spent very little and succeeded nevertheless. In 1971, a group of schoolmas-

---

8. Walter Biel (Independent MP in the National Council), interview by author, Zürich, Switzerland, 9 August 1989.

9. Gross, "1988—ein Jahr erfolgloser Volksbegehren."

ters and their supporters, for example, spent next to nothing on an initiative to reduce the criminal penalties applied against conscientious objectors. The proposal succeeded in prompting the Federal Council to make concessions, and the initiative was withdrawn. In 1982, sponsors of the successful price control initiative spent extraordinarily little, only 30,000 S.Fr., on the campaign. They did not even purchase posters to advertise their position.[10] Nonetheless, they won 56.1 percent of the national vote.

While it is questionable whether campaign expenditures can actually beget victory from defeat, money unquestionably affects the outcome to some degree. In a 1990 survey of both chambers of the National Assembly, fully 94 percent of members of Parliament (MPs) agreed that expenditure levels influence referendum and initiative outcomes. MPs also rated mass media exposure as the most effective means of influencing voter decisions in initiatives, over the exhortations of parties, politicians, and interest groups.[11] In the information age, media time can be essential to victory. Some issues, though, benefit from an expensive media blitz more than others. The more complicated the matter, the more likely it is that advertising will actually affect voter decisions. With more straightforward questions, voters typically hold a firm opinion on the matter already. Regardless, the extent of any unfairness due to unequal resources has always been difficult to assess. Protected by the Swiss tradition of financial confidentiality, referendum campaigns are not required to disclose the amounts or the sources of their expenditures.

There has been some effort to mitigate this potential bias in favor of wealthy organizations. The government provides equal amounts of free television time to both sides in a campaign and allows each to state its case to the electorate in government mailings. A campaign can always advertise over and above this free media time, however. It is still the case that the only real limit is the size of an organization's purse.

Referendum Outcomes

To an extent, the Swiss record speaks for itself. The voters have addressed virtually every conceivable area of national policy, often with

---

10. Monika Weber (MP in the Council of States and president of the Women's Consumer Forum, which launched the initiative), interview by author, Zürich, Switzerland, 16 August 1989.

11. This survey was carried out April through June 1990 by the author. The findings are based on eighty-six responses to a questionnaire sent to all 246 members of the Federal Assembly.

surprising results. Table 4–1 lists all the federal referendums held in Switzerland from 1848 through 1993, and table 4–2 shows the success rate for each type of ballot issue.

The Swiss have repeatedly demonstrated their willingness to reject the laws, proposals, and positions of their elected representatives. As illustrated in table 4–2, of the 275 constitutional amendments, challenged laws, and treaties that have come to a referendum since 1848, only 174 (or 63.3 percent) have survived. Routine laws and decrees have fared considerably worse in referendums than have constitutional amendments; only 48.7 percent of the routine laws have won popular approval, while the constitutional amendments have enjoyed a 72.7 percent success rate. This difference can largely be explained by the fact that a normal law must be challenged by petition before it can be subjected to a popular vote. Thus, only those laws that generate active opposition are eventually tested in a referendum. Constitutional amendments, in contrast, must always face a referendum, even if there is little public opposition to the measure.

Although these figures indicate a high propensity for the rejection of challenged laws and decrees, it must be remembered that many acts of the Federal Assembly never come before the people. Since 1874, approximately 7 percent of laws, decrees, and treaties susceptible to referendum have actually been challenged. A century ago, this figure was slightly higher. Between 1874 and 1908, the Federal Assembly passed 261 challengeable bills, of which 30 (or 11.5 percent) were forced to survive a referendum. In the postwar era, the percentage has been considerably lower, with 6–7 percent of legislation challenged in most years. This difference is mainly due to the advent of consociational democracy in the 1950s and to the increased legislative activity in recent decades. Much of this additional legislation is technical or uncontroversial; it therefore faces little or no opposition. There are also limits to the human and financial resources readily available for defeating laws by referendum.

The proportion of parliamentary measures rejected in referendums has changed with time. Table 4–3 illustrates a growing willingness among the electorate to accept legislative proposals. The high rate of rejection in the nineteenth century reflected the very different nature of Swiss direct democracy before the evolution of consociational government. Before the inclusion of the first Catholic Conservative on the Federal Council in 1891, the Radical party enjoyed virtually complete hegemony in federal political institutions. Catholic and conservative opposition groups used direct democracy as a vehicle for obstructionist politics and as a lever to pry open the door to power. Establishing common cause with federalist interests, they used the referendum to

TABLE 4–1
SWISS REFERENDUMS, 1848–1993

Type	Date	Subject	Success or Failure	Yes Votes Voters (%)	Yes Votes Cantons	Turnout (%)
1A	14 Jan. 1866	Weights and measures	F	50.4	9.5	—
2A	14 Jan. 1866	Equality for Jews	S	53.2	12.5	—
3A	14 Jan. 1866	Suffrage in communal matters	F	43.0	12.5	—
4A	14 Jan. 1866	Taxation of established citizens	F	39.9	8	—
5A	14 Jan. 1866	Suffrage in cantonal matters	F	48.0	10	—
6A	14 Jan. 1866	Religious liberty	F	49.1	11	—
7A	14 Jan. 1866	Exclusion of certain punishments	F	34.2	6.5	—
8A	14 Jan. 1866	Copyrights	F	43.6	9.5	—
9A	14 Jan. 1866	Prohibition of lotteries	F	44.0		—
10A	12 May 1866	Total revision of the Constitution	F	49.5	9	—
11A	19 Apr. 1874	Total revision of the Constitution	S	63.2	14.5	—
12D	23 May 1875	Civil status and marriage	S	51.0	—	—
13D	23 May 1875	Voting rights act	F	49.4	—	—
14D	23 Apr. 1876	Issue of banknotes	F	38.3	—	—
15D	9 July 1876	Tax on exemption from military duty	F	45.8	—	—
16D	21 Oct. 1877	Labor in factories	S	51.5	—	—
17D	21 Oct. 1877	Tax on exemption from military duty	F	48.4	—	—
18D	21 Oct. 1877	Voting rights act	F	38.1	—	—
19D	19 Jan. 1879	Subsidy to a private alpine railway	S	72.9	—	61.9
20A	18 May 1879	Permit capital punishment	S	52.5	14	60.4
21E	31 Oct. 1880	Create monopoly of banknotes	F	31.8	4.5	60.3

22A	30 July 1882	Protection of inventions	F	47.5	7.5	51.6
23D	30 July 1882	Prevention of epidemics	F	21.2	—	51.6
24D	26 Nov. 1882	Creation of a Federal Secretary of Education	F	35.1	—	76.3
25D	11 May 1884	Organization of the Department of Justice	F	41.1	—	60.1
26D	11 May 1884	Repeal tax on commercial travelers' license	F	47.9	—	60.1
27D	11 May 1884	Criminal code	F	44.0	—	60.1
28D	11 May 1884	Appropriation for secretary of legation at Swiss embassy in U.S.	F	38.5	—	60.1
29A	25 Oct. 1885	Inns and alcohol	S	59.4	—	60.4
30D	15 May 1887	Federal monopoly on liquor	S	65.8	—	62.5
31A	10 July 1887	Protection of inventions	S	77.9	20.5	42.4
32D	17 Nov. 1889	Bankruptcy act	S	52.9	—	70.9
33A	26 Oct. 1890	Compulsory health and accident insurance for workmen	S	75.4	20.5	59.8
34D	15 Mar. 1891	Law on pensions for officials	F	20.8	—	68.7
35A	5 July 1891	Popular initiative	S	60.3	18	49.3
36A	18 Oct. 1891	Monopoly on banknotes	S	59.3	14	61.9
37D	18 Oct. 1891	Customs tariff	S	58.0	—	61.9
38D	6 Dec. 1891	Nationalization of a railway	F	31.1	—	64.3
39B	20 Aug. 1893	Forbid slaughter of cattle by bleeding	S	60.1	11.5	49.1
40A	4 Mar. 1894	Extend power of federal government to allow uniform legislation on professions	F	46.1	7.5	46.7
41B	3 June 1894	Impose duty on the state to provide work for laborers	F	19.8	0	57.6

(Table continues)

TABLE 4–1 (continued)

Type	Date	Subject	Success or Failure	Yes Votes Voters (%)	Yes Votes Cantons	Turnout (%)
42B	4 Nov. 1894	Sharing of customs revenue among the cantons	F	29.3	8.5	72.9
43D	3 Feb. 1895	Diplomatic service	F	41.2	—	46.3
44A	29 Sept. 1895	Create government monopoly of matches	F	43.2	7.5	48.6
45A	3 Nov. 1895	Total centralization of the army	F	42.0	4.5	66.5
46D	4 Oct. 1896	Warranties in cattle trading	F	45.5	—	57.6
47D	4 Oct. 1896	Regulate accounts of railways for future purchase by government	S	55.8	—	57.6
48D	4 Oct. 1896	Disciplinary punishments in the army	F	19.9	—	57.6
49D	28 Feb. 1897	Create federal bank	F	43.3	—	64.7
50A	11 July 1897	Federal supervision of water powers and forests	S	63.5	16	38.5
51A	11 July 1897	Federal control of food products	S	65.1	18.5	38.5
52D	20 Feb. 1898	Nationalize railways	S	67.9	—	78.0
53A	13 Nov. 1898	Allow federal government to unify civil law	S	72.2	16.5	53.5
54A	13 Nov. 1898	Allow federal government to unify criminal law	S	72.3	16.5	53.5
55D	20 May 1900	Compulsory health, accident, and military insurance for workers	F	30.2	—	66.7

ID	Date	Description	Type			
56B	4 Nov. 1900	Proportional election of the National Council	F	40.8	10.5	59.0
57B	4 Nov. 1900	Popular election of the Federal Council	F	35.0	8	59.0
58A	23 Nov. 1902	Subsidies for public primary schools	S	76.3	21.5	46.6
59D	15 Mar. 1903	Customs tariff	S	59.6	—	73.2
60D	25 Oct. 1903	Military criminal law to punish instigation of evasion of duty	F	30.8	—	53.2
61B	25 Oct. 1903	Seats on the National Council	F	24.4	4	53.3
62A	25 Oct. 1903	Allow federal regulation of sale of liquor	F	40.7	4	53.1
63A	19 Mar. 1905	Protection of inventions	S	70.4	21.5	40.0
64D	10 June 1906	Food sales act	S	62.6	—	51.4
65D	3 Nov. 1907	Organization of the army	S	55.2	—	74.6
66A	5 July 1908	Extend power of federal government to allow uniform legislation on professions	S	71.5	21.5	48.7
67B	5 July 1908	Ban on absinthe	S	63.5	20	49.3
68C	25 Oct. 1908	Extend federal authority over water powers	S	84.4	21.5	48.2
69B	23 Oct. 1910	Proportional election of the National Council	F	47.5	12	62.3
70D	4 Feb. 1912	Compulsory health and accident insurance for workers	S	54.4	—	64.3
71A	4 May 1913	Human and animal diseases	S	60.3	16.5	36.0
72A	25 Oct. 1914	Administrative court	S	62.3	18	44.0
73A	6 June 1915	War tax	S	94.3	22	56.0
74A	13 May 1917	Stamp tax	S	53.2	14.5	42.1

(Table continues)

113

TABLE 4–1 (continued)

Type	Date	Subject	Success or Failure	Yes Votes Voters (%)	Yes Votes Cantons	Turnout (%)
75B	2 June 1918	Federal income tax	F	45.9	7.5	65.4
76B	13 Oct. 1918	Proportional election of the National Council	S	68.8	19.5	49.6
77A	4 May 1919	Navigation	S	83.6	22	53.9
78A	4 May 1919	New war tax	S	65.1	20	53.7
79A	10 Aug. 1919	Dissolution of the National Council	S	71.6	21.5	32.8
80D	21 Mar. 1920	Labor conditions	F	49.8	—	60.3
81B	21 Mar. 1920	Gambling houses	S	51.0	14	60.5
82C	21 Mar. 1920	Gambling houses	F	20.3	0.5	60.5
83A	16 May 1920	Entry into the League of Nations	S	56.3	11.5	77.5
84D	31 Oct. 1920	Working time in public transports	S	57.1	—	68.1
85B	30 Jan. 1921	Referendum on treaties	S	71.4	20	63.1
86B	30 Jan. 1921	Abolition of military justice	F	33.6	3	63.1
87A	22 May 1921	Legislation on cars and cycles	S	59.8	15.5	38.5
88A	22 May 1921	Aviation	S	62.2	20.5	38.4
89B	11 June 1922	Naturalization	F	15.9	0	45.6
90B	11 June 1922	Expulsion of foreigners	F	38.1	0	45.6
91B	11 June 1922	Civil servants in the National Council	F	38.4	5	45.6
92D	24 Sept. 1922	Federal criminal law	F	44.6	—	70.3
93B	3 Dec. 1922	Capital tax	F	13.0	0	86.3
94B	18 Feb. 1923	Internal security act	F	11.0	0	53.2
95F	18 Feb. 1923	Free trade convention	F	18.5	—	53.4

96B	15 Apr. 1923	Customs system	F	26.8	.5	65.8
97A	3 June 1923	Legislation on liquor	F	42.2	10	64.6
98D	17 Feb. 1924	Labor legislation (amendment)	F	42.4	—	77.0
99B	24 May 1925	Old-age and sickness insurance	F	42.0	6	68.3
100A	25 Oct. 1925	Status of foreigners	S	62.2	18.5	68.0
101A	6 Dec. 1925	Old-age and sickness insurance	S	65.4	16.5	63.1
102A	5 Dec. 1926	Supply of cereals	F	49.6	8	72.7
103A	15 May 1927	Subventions for alpine roads	S	62.6	21	55.3
104D	15 May 1927	Traffic law	F	40.1	—	57.8
105A	20 May 1928	Naturalization	S	70.6	19.5	45.2
106B	2 Dec. 1928	Gambling houses	S	51.9	14.5	55.5
107B	3 Mar. 1929	Supply of cereals	F	2.7	0	67.3
108C	3 Mar. 1929	Supply of cereals	S	66.3	21	67.3
109D	3 Mar. 1929	Customs tariff	S	66.4	—	67.3
110B	12 May 1929	Federal traffic law	F	37.2	3	65.0
111B	12 May 1929	Prohibition (liquor)	F	32.7	.5	66.4
112A	6 Apr. 1930	Legislation on liquor	S	60.6	17	75.7
113C	8 Feb. 1931	Prohibition of decorations	S	70.2	17	41.8
114A	15 Mar. 1931	Seats on the National Council	S	53.9	13.5	53.4
115A	15 Mar. 1931	Term of federal mandates	S	53.7	16	53.4
116D	6 Dec. 1931	Old-age pensions act	F	39.7	—	78.1
117D	6 Dec. 1931	Taxation of tobacco	F	49.9	—	78.1
118D	28 May 1933	Reduce salary of federal employees	F	44.9	—	80.5
119D	11 Mar. 1934	Protection of law and order	F	46.2	—	78.9
120D	24 Feb. 1935	Military instruction	S	54.2	—	79.9
121D	5 May 1935	Diversion of traffic	F	32.3	—	63.2
122B	2 June 1935	Measures against economic crisis	F	42.8	4	84.4
123B	8 Sept. 1935	Total revision of the Constitution	F	27.7	—	60.9

(Table continues)

TABLE 4–1 (continued)

Type	Date	Subject	Success or Failure	Yes Votes Voters (%)	Yes Votes Cantons	Turnout (%)
124B	28 Nov. 1937	Prohibition of Freemasonry	F	31.1	1	64.6
125A	20 Feb. 1938	Romansh as fourth national language	S	91.6	22	54.3
126B	20 Feb. 1938	Modification of the optional referendum	F	15.2	0	54.3
127B	20 Feb. 1938	Private armaments industry	F	11.5	0	54.3
128C	20 Feb. 1938	Private armaments industry	S	68.8	22	54.3
129D	3 July 1938	Swiss criminal code	S	53.5	—	57.0
130A	27 Nov. 1938	Federal finances	S	72.3	21	60.3
131B	22 Jan. 1939	Extension of constitutional jurisdiction	F	28.9	0	46.6
132C	22 Jan. 1939	Abuse of the emergency clause	S	69.1	21	46.6
133A	4 June 1939	National defense and prevention of unemployment	S	69.1	19	54.7
134D	3 Dec. 1939	Status of civil servants	F	37.6	—	63.4
135D	1 Dec. 1940	Premilitary instruction	F	44.3	—	62.2
136B	9 Mar. 1941	Legislation on liquor	F	40.2	—	60.1
137B	25 Jan. 1942	Election of the Federal Council	F	32.4	0	61.9
138B	3 May 1942	Reorganization of the National Council	F	34.9	.5	51.4
139D	29 Oct. 1944	Unfair competition	S	52.9	—	50.9
140D	21 Jan. 1945	National railways act	S	56.7	—	52.8
141C	25 Nov. 1945	Protection of the family	S	76.3	21.5	55.5

142C	10 Feb. 1946	Coordination of public transport	F	33.6	1	65.2
143B	8 Dec. 1946	Right to work	F	19.2	0	51.3
144B	18 May 1947	Economic reforms and labor legislation	F	31.2	0	59.4
145A	6 July 1947	Economic articles	S	53.0	13	79.7
146D	6 July 1947	Old-age pension act	S	80.0	—	79.7
147D	14 Mar. 1948	Monopoly of sugar	F	36.2	—	56.5
148A	22 May 1949	Emission of banknotes	F	38.5	1.5	61.0
149D	22 May 1949	Prevention of tuberculosis	F	24.8	—	61.0
150B	11 Sept. 1949	Direct democracy (emergency clause)	S	50.7	12.5	42.5
151D	11 Dec. 1949	Status of federal officials	S	55.3	—	72.0
152D	29 Jan. 1950	State aid for housing construction	F	46.3	—	52.8
153A	4 June 1950	Federal finances	F	35.5	6	55.3
154B	1 Oct. 1950	Speculation on real estate and labor	F	27.0	0	43.7
155A	3 Dec. 1950	Seats on the National Council	S	67.3	20	55.7
156A	3 Dec. 1950	Federal taxes from 1951 to 1954	S	69.5	20	55.7
157D	25 Feb. 1951	Transport by automobile	F	44.3	—	52.4
158B	15 Apr. 1951	Emission of banknotes	F	12.3	0	53.1
159C	15 Apr. 1951	Emission of banknotes	S	68.1	22	53.1
160B	8 July 1951	Taxation of public enterprises	F	32.6	—	37.6
161D	2 Mar. 1952	Construction of new hotels	F	46.1	—	40.1
162D	30 Mar. 1952	Agriculture act	S	54.0	—	64.1
163B	20 Apr. 1952	Federal sales tax	F	19.0	0	49.1
164B	18 May 1952	Financing of armaments	F	43.7	4	53.9
165A	6 July 1952	Financing of armaments	F	42.0	3	44.2
166D	5 Oct. 1952	Tax on tobacco products	S	68.0	—	52.6
167D	5 Oct. 1952	Antiaircraft shelters	F	15.5	—	52.6
168A	23 Nov. 1952	Control of prices	S	62.8	16	56.4
169A	23 Nov. 1952	Supply of cereals	S	75.6	21.5	56.4

(Table continues)

TABLE 4-1 (continued)

Type	Date	Subject	Success or Failure	Yes Votes Voters (%)	Yes Votes Cantons	Turnout (%)
170D	19 Apr. 1953	Postal tariff	F	36.5	—	52.7
171A	6 Dec. 1953	Federal finances	F	42.0	3	60.3
172A	6 Dec. 1953	Prevention of water pollution	S	81.3	22	59.1
173D	20 June 1954	Federal certificates of professional capacity	F	33.0	—	40.9
174D	20 June 1954	Aid for Swiss war victims	F	44.0	—	40.7
175A	24 Oct. 1954	Federal taxes from 1955 to 1958	S	70.0	21	46.8
176B	5 Dec. 1954	Protection of sites	F	31.2	1	51.9
177B	13 Mar. 1955	Consumers' and lessees' protection	F	50.2	7	55.5
178C	13 Mar. 1955	Consumers' and lessees' protection	F	40.6	8.5	55.5
179A	4 Mar. 1956	Control of prices	S	77.5	22	48.7
180B	13 May 1956	Utilization of hydraulic forces	F	36.9	2.5	52.1
181D	13 May 1956	State aid for a private timber enterprise in Graubunden	F	42.5	—	52.6
182A	30 Sept. 1956	Supply of cereals (amendment)	F	38.7	5.5	44.0
183C	30 Sept. 1956	Referendum on expenses	F	45.5	9	43.8
184A	3 Mar. 1957	Civil defense	F	48.1	14	53.1
185A	3 Mar. 1957	Radio and TV legislation	F	42.8	10.5	53.0
186A	24 Nov. 1957	Nuclear energy	S	77.3	22	45.5
187A	24 Nov. 1957	Supply of cereals	S	66.7	21.5	45.5
188B	26 Jan. 1958	Misuse of economic power	F	25.9	0	51.8
189A	11 May 1958	Federal finances	S	54.6	17.5	53.2

190A	6 July 1958	Cinema	S	61.3	20.5	42.3
191C	6 July 1958	Highway system	S	85.0	21	42.4
192B	26 Oct. 1958	Forty-four-hour workweek	F	35.0	.5	61.4
193A	7 Dec. 1958	Gambling in spas and casinos	S	59.9	20.5	46.2
194F	7 Dec. 1958	Utilization of the Spöl River	S	75.2	—	46.4
195A	1 Feb. 1959	Women's suffrage	F	33.1	3	66.7
196A	24 May 1959	Civil defense	S	66.3	22	42.9
197A	29 May 1960	Control of prices	S	77.5	22	39.0
198D	4 Dec. 1960	Legislation on milk production	S	56.3	—	49.8
199A	5 Mar. 1961	Legislation on pipelines	S	71.4	22	62.8
200D	5 Mar. 1961	Taxes on motor fuel	F	46.5	—	63.3
201B	22 Oct. 1961	Legislative initiative	F	29.4	0	40.1
202D	3 Dec. 1961	Watchmaking industry	S	66.7	—	45.8
203B	1 Apr. 1962	Nuclear arms prohibition	F	34.8	4	55.6
204A	27 May 1962	Nature and landscape protection	S	79.1	22	38.7
205D	27 May 1962	Salary of Parliament members	F	31.7	—	38.7
206A	4 Nov. 1962	Seats on the National Council	S	63.7	16	36.3
207B	26 May 1963	Nuclear arms	F	37.8	4.5	48.8
208A	8 Dec. 1963	Federal finances	S	77.6	22	41.8
209A	8 Dec. 1963	Scholarships	S	78.5	22	41.7
210A	2 Feb. 1964	Fiscal amnesty	F	42.0	3.5	44.3
211D	24 May 1964	Professional education	S	68.6	—	37.0
212A	6 Dec. 1964	Control of prices	S	79.5	22	39.2
213G	28 Feb. 1965	Limitation of credits	S	57.7	18.5	59.7
214G	28 Feb. 1965	Limitation of construction	S	55.5	17	59.7
215D	16 May 1965	Milk and milk products	S	62.0	—	37.4
216A	16 Oct. 1966	Swiss abroad	S	68.1	22	47.9
217B	16 Oct. 1966	Fight against alcoholism	F	23.4	—	48.0

(Table continues)

TABLE 4–1 (continued)

Type	Date	Subject	Success or Failure	Yes Votes Voters (%)	Yes Votes Cantons	Turnout (%)
218B	2 July 1967	Speculation on real estate	F	32.7	1	37.9
219A	18 Feb. 1968	Fiscal amnesty	S	61.9	22	41.8
220D	19 May 1968	Fixed prices on tobacco products	F	48.2	—	36.9
221D	1 June 1969	Federal technical high school	F	34.5	—	33.9
222A	14 Sept. 1969	Town and country planning	S	55.9	19.5	32.9
223D	1 Feb. 1970	Control of sugar	S	54.2	—	43.8
224B	7 June 1970	Foreigners, reduction of number	F	46.0	7	74.1
225A	27 Sept. 1970	Sports education	S	74.5	22	43.8
226B	27 Sept. 1970	Housing and family	F	48.9	8	43.8
227A	15 Nov. 1970	Federal finances	F	55.4	9	40.9
228A	7 Feb. 1971	Women's suffrage	S	65.7	15.5	57.7
229A	6 June 1971	Protection of the environment	S	92.7	22	37.9
230A	6 June 1971	Federal finances	S	72.7	22	37.8
231B	5 Mar. 1972	Construction of lodgings	F	28.9	0	35.7
232C	5 Mar. 1972	Construction of lodgings	S	58.5	21	35.7
233A	5 Mar. 1972	Protection of lessees	S	85.4	22	35.7
234G	4 June 1972	Control of the construction market	S	83.3	22	26.7
235G	4 June 1972	Defense of Swiss money	S	87.7	22	26.7
236B	24 Sept. 1972	Exportation of arms	F	49.6	7	33.1
237B	3 Dec. 1972	Old-age and sickness pension (amendment)	F	15.6	0	52.9
238C	3 Dec. 1972	Old-age and sickness pension (amendment)	S	74.0	22	52.9

239A	3 Dec. 1972	Free trade agreement with the EC	S	72.5	22	52.9
240A	4 Mar. 1973	Education	F	52.8	10.5	27.5
241A	4 Mar. 1973	Scientific research	S	64.5	19	27.5
242A	20 May 1973	Repeal of the confessional articles	S	54.9	16.5	40.3
243G	2 Dec. 1973	Prices and salary control	S	59.8	20	35.0
244G	2 Dec. 1973	Credit control	S	65.1	18.5	35.0
245G	2 Dec. 1973	Control of the construction market	S	70.4	20	35.0
246G	2 Dec. 1973	Limitation to amortization allowance	S	68.0	19.5	35.0
247A	2 Dec. 1973	Protection of animals	S	84.0	22	35.0
248B	20 Oct. 1974	Foreigners, reduction of number	F	34.2	0	70.3
249A	8 Dec. 1974	Federal finances	F	44.4	4	39.6
250A	8 Dec. 1974	Brake on federal expenses	S[a]	67.0	22	39.5
251B	8 Dec. 1974	Health insurance	F	26.7	0	39.7
252C	8 Dec. 1974	Health insurance	F	32.1	0	39.7
253A	2 Mar. 1975	Economic policy	F	52.7	11	28.4
254A	8 June 1975	Federal finances	S	56.0	17	36.8
255G	8 June 1975	Defense of Swiss money	S	85.5	22	36.8
256A	8 June 1975	Brake on federal expenses	S	75.9	22	36.8
275D	8 June 1975	Customs tariff, fuel	F	48.2	—	36.8
258D	8 June 1975	Financing of the highway system	S	53.5	—	36.8
259A	7 Dec. 1975	Freedom of domicile and social assistance	S	75.6	22	30.9
260A	7 Dec. 1975	Legislation on water resources	S	77.5	21	30.9
261D	7 Dec. 1975	Import and export of agricultural products	S	52.0	—	31.1
262B	21 Mar. 1976	Workers' participation	F	32.4	0	39.4
263C	21 Mar. 1976	Workers' participation	F	29.6	0	39.4
264B	21 Mar. 1976	More equal taxes	F	42.4	—	39.3

(Table continues)

TABLE 4–1 (continued)

Type	Date	Subject	Success or Failure	Yes Votes Voters (%)	Yes Votes Cantons	Turnout (%)
265A	13 June 1976	Compulsory unemployment insurance	S	68.3	21	34.5
266D	13 June 1976	Town and country planning	F	48.9	—	34.6
267F	13 June 1976	Loan to International Development Association	F	43.6	—	34.5
268A	26 Sept. 1976	Radio and TV legislation	F	43.3	3.5	33.5
269B	26 Sept. 1976	Federal liability insurance for cars	F	24.3	0	33.5
270G	5 Dec. 1976	Money and credit policy	S	70.3	22	44.8
271G	5 Dec. 1976	Control of prices	S	82.0	22	45.1
272B	5 Dec. 1976	Forty-hour workweek	F	22.0	0	45.2
273B	13 Mar. 1977	Foreigners, reduction of number	F	29.5	0	45.2
274B	13 Mar. 1977	Naturalization of foreigners	F	33.8	0	45.2
275B	13 Mar. 1977	Referendum on international treaties	F	21.9	0	45.0
276C	13 Mar. 1977	Referendum on international treaties	S	61.0	20.5	45.0
277A	12 June 1977	Introduction of value-added tax	F	40.5	1	50.0
278A	12 June 1977	Harmonization of cantonal taxes	S	61.3	17.5	49.9
279B	25 Sept. 1977	Protection of lessees	F	42.2	3.5	51.6
280C	25 Sept. 1977	Protection of lessees	F	41.2	1.5	51.6
281B	25 Sept. 1977	Air pollution from cars	F	39.0	1.5	51.7
282A	25 Sept. 1977	No. of signatures for a referendum	S	57.8	18	51.6
283A	25 Sept. 1977	No. of signatures for an initiative	S	56.7	19	51.6
284B	25 Sept. 1977	Free abortion in first 12 weeks	F	48.3	7	51.9

285B	4 Dec. 1977	Higher taxes on big incomes	F	44.4	2.5	38.3
286A	4 Dec. 1977	Civil service	F	37.6	0	38.1
287D	4 Dec. 1977	Exercise of political rights	S	93.7	—	38.1
288D	4 Dec. 1977	Balanced federal finances	S	62.4	—	38.2
289B	26 Feb. 1978	Democracy in highway construction	F	38.7	0	48.2
290B	26 Feb. 1978	Age of retirement	F	20.6	0	48.3
291A	26 FEb. 1978	Economic policy	S	68.4	22	48.0
292D	26 Feb. 1978	Old-age pension act (ninth revision)	S	65.6	—	48.3
293D	28 May 1978	Summer time	F	47.9	—	48.8
294D	28 May 1978	Customs tariff	S	54.8	—	48.8
295D	28 May 1978	Abortion act	F	31.2	—	48.8
296D	28 May 1978	University and research act	F	43.4	—	48.8
297B	28 May 1978	Twelve Sundays a year without motor traffic	F	36.3	0	48.8
298A	24 Sept. 1978	Creation of Canton of Jura	S	82.3	22	42.0
299D	3 Dec. 1978	Milk supplies	S	68.5	22	43.2
300D	3 Dec. 1978	Protection of animals	S	81.7	22	43.3
301D	3 Dec. 1978	Federal security police	F	44.0	6	43.3
302D	3 Dec. 1978	Professional education	S	56.0	17	43.3
303A	18 Feb. 1979	Vote at 18	F	49.2	9	49.6
304C	18 Feb. 1979	Pedestrian trails	S	77.6	22	49.6
305B	18 Feb. 1979	Ban liquor and tobacco advertising	F	41.0	.5	49.6
306B	18 Feb. 1979	Nuclear plants	F	48.8	9	49.6
307A	20 May 1979	Introduction of value-added tax	F	34.6	0	37.7
308D	20 May 1979	Revision of atomic energy	S	68.9	22	37.6
309B	2 Mar. 1980	Separation of church and state	F	21.1	0	34.7
310A	2 Mar. 1980	Supply of commodities	S	86.1	23	34.5
311D	30 Nov. 1980	Safety belts and crash helmets	S	51.6	13	42.1

(Table continues)

TABLE 4-1 (continued)

Type	Date	Subject	Success or Failure	Yes Votes Voters (%)	Yes Votes Cantons	Turnout (%)
312A	30 Nov. 1980	Suspend cantonal share of revenues from banking "stamp" tax	S	67.3	20	41.9
313A	30 Nov. 1980	Redistribution of alcohol tax receipts	S	71.0	21	41.9
314A	30 Nov. 1980	Price of cereals	S	63.5	20	41.9
315B	5 Apr. 1981	Policy toward foreign residents	F	16.2	0	39.9
316C	14 June 1981	Equal rights for men and women	S	60.3	15.5	33.9
317C	14 June 1981	Protection of consumer rights	S	65.5	20	33.9
318A	29 Nov. 1981	Federal taxation	S	69.0	23	30.4
319D	6 June 1982	Penal code on violent crimes	S	63.7	22	35.2
320D	6 June 1982	Law about foreigners	F	49.6	9	35.2
321B	28 Nov. 1982	Control of prices	S	56.1	17	32.9
322C	28 Nov. 1982	Control of prices	F	21.6	0	32.9
323A	27 Feb. 1983	Petrol tax	S	52.7	15.5	32.4
324A	27 Feb. 1983	Establish basis for federal energy policy	F	50.9	11	32.4
325A	4 Dec. 1983	Revise nationality law	S	60.8	20.5	35.8
326A	4 Dec. 1983	Ease naturalization policy	F	44.8	5	35.9
327A	26 Feb. 1984	Tax on trucks	S	58.7	15.5	52.8
328A	26 Feb. 1984	Highway tax	S	53.0	16	52.8
329B	26 Feb. 1984	Civilian service	F	36.2	1.5	52.8
330B	20 May 1984	Banking	F	27.0	0	42.5
331B	20 May 1984	No selling of land to foreigners	F	48.9	8.5	42.5

332B	23 Sept. 1984	End atomic development	F	45.0	6	41.7
333B	23 Sept. 1984	A safe energy policy	F	45.8	6	41.6
334A	2 Dec. 1984	Legislation on broadcasting	S	68.7	23	37.5
335C	2 Dec. 1984	Help for victims of violence	S	82.1	23	37.6
336C	2 Dec. 1984	Protection of motherhood	F	15.8	0	37.6
337A	10 Mar. 1985	End federal primary school subsidies	S	58.5	18	34.4
338A	10 Mar. 1985	End federal public health subsidies	S	53.0	13	34.4
339A	10 Mar. 1985	End federal education subsidies	F	47.6	8.5	34.4
340B	10 Mar. 1985	Length of paid vacation	F	34.8	2	34.6
341B	9 June 1985	"Right to life"	F	31.0	5.5	35.7
342A	9 June 1985	Suspend cantonal share of revenues from banking "stamp" tax	S	66.5	22	35.2
343A	9 June 1985	Reduce cantonal share of liquor tax revenues	S	72.3	22	35.2
344A	9 June 1985	Legislation on cereals	S	57.0	18.5	35.3
345C	22 Sept. 1985	Standardized school terms	S	58.8	16	41.0
346D	22 Sept. 1985	Insurance against innovation-related risk	F	43.1	0	40.9
347D	22 Sept. 1985	New law on husband and wife	S	54.7	14	41.1
348B	1 Dec. 1985	Prohibition of vivisection	F	29.5	0	38.0
349A	16 Mar. 1986	UN membership	F	24.3	0	50.7
350D	28 Sept. 1986	Subsidized sugar production	F	38.4	5	34.0
351B	28 Sept. 1986	Subsidy for arts	F	17.1	0	34.0
352C	28 Sept. 1986	Subsidy for arts	F	45.0	0	34.0
353B	28 Sept. 1986	Guaranteed vocational training	F	18.4	0	34.0
354C	7 Dec. 1986	Tenants' protection	S	64.4	18.5	34.0
355B	7 Dec. 1986	Taxation of heavy trucks	F	33.9	0	34.0
356D	5 Apr. 1987	Revision of political asylum laws	S	67.3	23	42.4

(Table continues)

TABLE 4–1 (continued)

Type	Date	Subject	Success or Failure	Yes Votes		Turnout (%)
				Voters (%)	Cantons	
357D	5 Apr. 1987	Revision of law regarding foreigners	S	65.7	23	42.2
358A	5 Apr. 1987	Double Yes on initiatives with a government counterproposal	S	63.3	21	42.3
359B	5 Apr. 1987	Right to referendum on all military expenditures	F	40.6	2.5	42.4
360D	6 Dec. 1987	"Rail 2000" project	S	56.7	18.5	47.7
361B	6 Dec. 1987	Stop Rothenturm military base (to protect the moors)	S	57.8	20	47.7
362D	6 Dec. 1987	Sickness and motherhood insurance	F	28.7	1	47.7
363A	12 June 1988	Coordination of transportation policy	F	45.5	3.5	41.9
364B	12 June 1988	Reduction of the age for receiving OAP benefits	F	35.1	2	42.0
365B	4 Dec. 1988	City and county prohibition of real estate speculation	F	30.8	0	52.8
366B	4 Dec. 1988	Forty-hour workweek	F	34.3	2	52.9
367B	4 Dec. 1988	Restriction of immigration	F	32.7	0	52.8
368B	4 June 1989	Protection of small farms	F	48.9	8	36.0
369B	26 Nov. 1989	Abolition of the army	F	35.6	2	68.6
370B	26 Nov. 1989	Raise highway speed limit to 130 kph	F	38.0	5	68.6
371B	1 Apr. 1990	Stop all new road construction	F	28.5	0	40.5
372B	1 Apr. 1990	Prevent highway between Murten and Yverdon	F	32.7	0	40.5

126

373B	1 Apr. 1990	Prevent highway between Wettswil and Kronau	F	31.4	0	40.5
374B	1 Apr. 1990	Prevent highway between Biel and Solothurn	F	34.0	0	40.5
375D	1 Apr. 1990	Wine import standards	F	46.7	11	40.5
376D	1 Apr. 1990	Revision of the federal judiciary law	F	47.4	7	40.5
377A	23 Sept. 1990	Establish basis for federal energy policy	S	71.0	23	39.6
378B	23 Sept. 1990	10-year moratorium on nuclear plant construction	S	54.6	19.5	39.6
379B	23 Sept. 1990	End use of nuclear energy	F	47.1	7	39.6
380D	23 Sept. 1990	Increase allowed width of trucks	S	52.8	15	39.6
381A	3 Mar. 1991	Reduce voting age to 18	S	72.8	23	31.1
382B	3 Mar. 1991	Transfer funds from road construction to public transportation	F	37.1	1.5	31.1
383D	2 June 1991	Introduce federal VAT to replace corporate tax	F	45.7	2.5	32.6
384D	2 June 1991	Decriminalize conscientious objection to military service	S	55.7	19	32.6
385F	17 May 1992	IMF and World Bank membership	S	55.8	18.5	36.6
386D	17 May 1992	Regulations governing involvement in the IMF and World Bank	S	56.4	18.5	36.4
387B	17 May 1992	Reduce amount of water in reservoirs to protect the environment	F	37.1	0	38.4
388D	17 May 1992	Less drastic reduction of water in reservoirs than in previous issue	S	66.1	18.5	38.5

(Table continues)

TABLE 4–1 (continued)

Type	Date	Subject	Success or Failure	Yes Votes		Turnout (%)
				Voters (%)	Cantons	
389D	17 May 1992	Regulation of genetic technology	S	73.8	22	38.0
390A	17 May 1992	Civilian service option for conscientious objectors	S	82.5	23	38.6
391D	17 May 1992	Decriminalize sex between minors, homosexuality; define rape in marriage	S	73.1	22	37.9
392D	27 Sept. 1992	Construction of cross-Alpine railway for automobiles	S	63.6	21	45.9
393D	27 Sept. 1992	Revised procedures for consideration, publication, and introduction of laws	S	58.0	17	45.4
394D	27 Sept. 1992	Change of banking "stamp" tax	S	61.5	23	45.7
395D	27 Sept. 1992	Farmers' inheritance regulations	S	53.6	15	45.7
396D	27 Sept. 1992	Increase salaries of MPs and funding for political parties	F	27.6	0	45.6
397D	27 Sept. 1992	Improved facilities and administrative services for MPs	F	30.6	1	45.5
398A	6 Dec. 1992	European Economic Area membership	F	49.7	7	78.3
399D	7 Mar. 1993	Raise gasoline tax by 20 cents per liter	S	54.5	15	51.3
400A	7 Mar. 1993	Legalize casino gambling	S	72.5	23	51.3
401B	7 Mar. 1993	Ban all animal experiments	F	27.8	0	51.3
402B	6 June 1993	Halt F/A-18 purchase and ban any new fighter aircraft until year 2000	F	42.7	4	54.5

403B	6 June 1993	Limit total number of army bases to 40	F	44.5	7	54.6
404A	26 Sept. 1993	Measures against abuse of weapons	S	86.3	23	39.4
405A	26 Sept. 1993	Annexation of Bern districts into Canton of Basle-Land	S	75.2	23	39.5
406B	26 Sept. 1993	Federal work-free holiday on 1 August	S	83.8	23	39.9
407D	26 Sept. 1993	Measures restricting cost increases in health insurance	S	80.5	23	39.8
408D	26 Sept. 1993	Unemployment insurance revisions	S	70.4	23	39.7
409A	28 Nov. 1993	Revision of the financial system	S	66.7	22	44.3
410A	28 Nov. 1993	Adopt federal VAT on all goods and services	S	60.6	20	43.8
411A	28 Nov. 1993	Increased contribution to federal revenues (VAT rate to 6.5%)	S	57.7	18	44.2
412A	28 Nov. 1993	Measures for preservation of social insurance	S	62.6	22	44.0
413B	28 Nov. 1993	Ban alcohol advertising	F	25.3	0	44.7
414B	28 Nov. 1993	Ban tobacco products advertising	F	25.5	0	44.7

— = no data available.

NOTES: The obligatory constitutional referendum was first provided for in the constitution of 1848. The first referendum of this sort did not occur until 1866. Types of votes: A. Amendment of the Constitution (obligatory referendum). B. Popular initiative. C. Counterproposal of Parliament (to proposed initiative). D. Facultative (optional) referendum on a law. E. Popular initiative for the total revision of the Constitution. F. Treaty referendum (optional). G. Urgent decree deviating from the Constitution.

a. Although it succeeded in winning a double majority, it had no effect because it was linked to 249.

SOURCE: Data through 1978 presented by Jean Francois Aubert in David Butler and Austin Ranney, eds., *Referendums: A Comparative Study of Practice and Theory* (Washington, D.C.: American Enterprise Institute, 1978), pp. 50–64. Subsequent data taken by author from various sources, including the embassy of Switzerland in Washington, D.C.

TABLE 4–2
OUTCOMES OF SWISS REFERENDUMS BY TYPE, 1848–1993

Type of Referendum	Total Number	Successful (Yes vote)	Failing (No vote)	Percentage Successful
Constitutional amendment proposed by Federal Assembly				
Total revision (1872, 1874)	2	1	1	50.0
Partial revision[a]	143	104	39	72.7
Constitutional initiative				
Total revision (1880, 1935)	2	0	2	0.0
Partial revision	110	11	99	10.0
Parliamentary counterproposal	27	17	10	63.0
Facultative (optional) referendum on laws and decrees	115	56	59	48.7
Optional treaty referendum	4	2	2	50.0
Urgent decrees deviating from the Constitution	11	11	0	100.0
Referendums on all government-initiated measures[b] (total excluding constitutional initiatives and parliamentary counterproposals)	275	174	101	63.3

a. The votes concerning entry into the League of Nations (1920), the free trade agreement with the EC (1972), and membership in the United Nations (1986) are all counted as constitutional amendments.
b. This category includes constitutional amendment referendums, facultative referendums, optional treaty referendums, and referendums on urgent decrees. Parliamentary counterproposals were not included because they are usually reactions to ideas presented from outside, rather than projects originating in the government.
SOURCE: Same as for table 4–1.

bring the federal government almost to a standstill between 1875 and 1884. The Social Democratic party employed similar tactics from the close of World War I until the magic formula of 1959 ensured their permanent inclusion in the Federal Council. This informal arrangement brought government-versus-opposition politics to a close and entrenched continuous power sharing among the four largest parties.

TABLE 4-3
Parliamentary Measures Rejected by Voters in Swiss Referendums, 1848–1993

	1848–79	1880–99	1900–19	1920–39	1940–59	1960–79	1980–93	Total
Total considered	20	30	17	30	40	77	61	275
Number rejected	14	16	3	13	19	21	15	101
Percentage rejected	70.0	53.3	17.6	43.3	47.5	27.3	24.6	36.7

Note: Includes constitutional amendments, laws, decrees, treaties, and urgent decrees deviating from the Constitution.
Source: Same as for table 4-1.

It is no coincidence that the most dramatic fall in the rejection rate came after 1959. A more inclusive Swiss government encountered less opposition to its measures in society. In the decades since 1959, roughly one-fourth of government proposals have been defeated. Nonetheless, there have been numerous dramatic rejections of specific policies in this period. In some cases, the governing parties were virtually unanimous in support of the defeated measure. In March 1986, for example, 75.7 percent of the voting electorate renounced the government's intended membership in the United Nations, a policy endorsed by the three largest parties and nearly all the major Swiss interest groups. In December 1992, Swiss voters narrowly rejected membership in the European Economic Area, another proposal that had enjoyed widespread support in Bern.

Direct Democracy and Parties

Direct democracy has contributed greatly to the relative weakness of political parties in Switzerland. It has rendered redundant an otherwise important party function, the aggregation and articulation of policy preferences in the electorate, by allowing citizens to express their opinions directly. At the same time, the initiative has undermined the parties' control of the national agenda. Referendums and initiatives have also weakened Swiss parties directly by undermining their unity. Ballot issues divide party membership on question after question, providing voters with repeated opportunities to defect from their party's official position. With most referendums, ad hoc alliances of interest groups, parties, other organizations, and public figures spring up on both sides of the issue. Individual voters cannot be prevented from pursuing their own preferences. Parties can do little more than endorse a position and hope that the declaration sways enough voters. Quite often, voters ignore this advice. Survey data over the 1977–1980 period revealed that, on average, 51 percent of FDP supporters knowingly went against the recommendations of their party, as did 55 percent of Christian Democrats and 60 percent of Social Democrats. Fully 75 percent of the supporters of the agrarian Swiss People's party disregarded their party's recommendations.[12]

The discord within parties at the ground level is often mirrored by division at the elite level. Leaders of parliamentary factions are rarely able to hold their MPs to the party line. It is completely normal

---

12. *Analyse der eidgenössichen Abstimmung vom 16 März 1986*, VOX Survey no. 29 (Bern: Forschungzentrum für Schweizerische Politik and the Schweizerische Gesellschaft für Praktische Sozialforschung, 1986), p. 6.

for MPs from the same party to endorse opposite positions publicly in a referendum campaign. In the 1986 debate on UN membership, for example, the presidents of the opposing umbrella committees were both MPs of the FDP. This open dissension only further encourages voters to ignore the pleas of their party of choice.

When referendums occur, loyalties are temporarily suspended and public policy becomes atomized. Unlike elections, in which voters are expected to endorse a whole platform of positions on disparate issues, referendums allow voters to express preferences on particular questions. Party allegiances lose relevance when voters inspect a list of specific proposals, unadorned with party labels or names of politicians.

Nevertheless, Swiss parties have long commanded unusually steadfast voter loyalty in elections. Party distributions in the National Council do not swing significantly from election to election. This combination of weak parties with strong voter loyalty is no mere coincidence. The referendum affords voters the opportunity to dissent from their party's position without actually leaving the party. Because Swiss voters are accustomed to disagreeing with their party of choice on specific issues, party loyalty in elections tends to be based on factors more lasting than transient policy positions. Traditional family allegiances and general party images are more important. Thus, referendums have fostered looser, but more resilient party ties.

Referendums have also influenced allegiances within the Swiss Parliament. There has been no consistent line of partisan division. Rather, alliances within the Federal Assembly have tended to be highly unstable. MPs of the governing parties have rarely remained united on important issues, mainly because of the splintering effect of direct democracy. If a coalition of parties stands a minimal chance of sticking together from referendum to referendum, there is little point in maintaining a tight alliance in Parliament. In much the same way that referendums encourage individual voters to break from their preferred party, they also encourage parties to break from parliamentary alliances. When voters defect, the parties are inevitably weakened. When parties defect, coalitions are similarly undermined. In Switzerland, majorities in Parliament and in the public tend to be concurrent, rather than cohesive.

One pattern in parliamentary and plebiscitary voting has appeared, however: the smaller, nongoverning parties oppose the government position much more frequently than is typical for countries with grand coalition governments. Such countries usually see considerable cooperation between the governing parties and those outside the coalition. Attempts to oppose such a large coalition are futile, so smaller parties accomplish more by cooperating. In Switzerland, however, the referendum offers a powerful weapon to small opposition parties. The protest of one quarter of the Parliament is augmented considerably when accompanied by the threat of a referendum. Emboldened by this power, the nongovernment parties in Switzerland often assume an opposition role. In 1989, for instance, the majority of small party MPs voted against the Federal Council position in eleven of the thirteen roll-call votes, or 85 percent of the time.

In recent years, otherwise antagonistic small parties have often found themselves working in concert to oppose government policies in referendum campaigns. The 1992 campaign against membership in the International Monetary Fund and the World Bank, for example, was waged by an alliance of opposites. The large parties and all the major economic interest groups (the Verbände) were united in favor of membership. Arrayed against this powerful bloc was a disparate collection of small parties and interest groups. The Swiss Left was against joining because of its opposition to IMF policies in the third world, and the Greens argued that IMF pressure to repay loans encouraged South American countries to destroy the rain forests. In league with them were organizations and parties of the Swiss Right, which raised the specter of excessive costs and generally argued against entanglements in international organizations. On 17 May 1992, voters approved IMF and World Bank membership, but only narrowly, with 55.8 percent in favor. Able to tap the *Neinsager* (naysayer) tendency of many Swiss citizens, such opposition campaigns pose an ever-present threat to government policies.

Participation Levels

In 1964, Max Imboden warned that declining participation in Swiss referendums foreshadowed a coming "democratic malaise."[13] By the late 1970s and early 1980s, it seemed that voter turnout was on an inexorable decline, unlikely to return above 40 percent except in isolated instances. Observers pointed to a disturbing 37 percent average rate of participation from 1978 through 1986.[14] The trend was widely attributed to the frequency with which Swiss voters were being called to the polls. It seemed that the people had been saturated with direct democracy.

---

13. Max Imboden, *Helvetisches Malaise* (Zürich: 1964), p. 8; cited in Benjamin Barber, "Participation and Swiss Democracy," *Government and Opposition*, vol. 23, no. 1 (Winter 1988), p. 40.

14. John Austen, David Butler, and Austin Ranney, "Referendums, 1978–1986," *Electoral Studies*, vol. 6, no. 2 (August 1987), p. 139.

Yet, in the late 1980s the downswing reversed, with unusually high turnouts on a number of controversial ballot issues. The initiative to reduce rents by prohibiting land speculation brought 52.8 percent of the electorate to the polls; and the question of whether the army should be abolished drew 68.6 percent participation. During the 1987–1989 period, participation averaged 48.2 percent, a significant rebound. The decade average for the 1980s ended at 40.3 percent, only slightly lower than the average for the 1970s (42.2 percent). And although in the first two years of the 1990s participation was fairly unimpressive, in 1992 and 1993 voters flocked to the polls again. In total, the first four years of the 1990s registered an average turnout of 45.1 percent.

In particular, the December 1992 referendum on membership in the European Economic Area saw participation soar. For the previous seven months, the issue had been argued exhaustively in a public debate that prompted the government to spend 6 million S.Fr. extolling the benefits of membership. The larger question of possible membership in the European Community loomed conspicuously in the background. On the day, an astonishing 78.3 percent turned out at the polls, the highest participation in forty-five years. The treaty was defeated, narrowly missing a popular majority with 49.7 percent voting in favor. Even if it had managed to take 50 percent of the national vote, however, it probably would have failed to gain the required double majority, because it won in only seven cantons. Interestingly, all the German-speaking cantons except Basel rejected the treaty (as did Italian-speaking Ticino); and all the French cantons voted in favor, some by large margins. The linguistic cleavage that has played a sporadic role in Swiss politics since the end of the Sonderbund War returned in striking fashion. In this instance, suspicion of German dominance of the European Community and regional insularity pushed German-speaking Switzerland to reject the treaty, while French-speaking Switzerland showed characteristically fewer inhibitions regarding partnership with the rest of Europe.

The gradual decline in participation since the early 1960s has finally leveled out near 40 percent, and a significant upswing may be in the making. Nevertheless, voter turnout has certainly declined since the referendum was introduced in 1848. Table 4–4 summarizes voter turnout since the 1880s, when participation figures were first routinely calculated. In the turbulent 1930s, average participation reached a high-water mark of 64.6 percent for the decade. In such an environment, taking part was of paramount importance in order to preserve democratic institutions from decay. At the same time, political extremists were keen to take part and usher in the radical changes they de-

135

TABLE 4–4
Voter Turnout in Swiss Federal Referendums by Decade, by Percentage of Electorate, 1880–1993

	1880s	1890s	1900s	1910s	1920s	1930s	1940s	1950s	1960s	1970s	1980s	1990–93
Average turnout[a]	60.6	57.8	56.2	50.6	63.2	64.6	58.8	50.8	43.2	42.2	40.3	45.1

a. Ballots with multiple questions were counted as only one ballot, because they represent a single trip to the polls. Considering them separately would have severely biased the calculation toward omnibus ballots.
Source: Same as for table 4–1.

136

sired. The most dramatic declines in turnout occurred in the 1940s, 1950s, and 1960s. Decade averages slipped by 21.4 percent during this period. Since then, participation seems to have reached a plateau at just above 40 percent, with intermittent peaks for highly controversial issues and valleys for more mundane questions.

It is debatable whether Switzerland is in a state of democratic malaise. According to a 1985 survey, 31 percent of Swiss citizens can be classified as "regular" participants in referendums.[15] These voters take part in most, if not all, federal referendums. The remaining 69 percent of Swiss citizens vote less frequently, participating in some referendums and abstaining in others, depending on the issue at hand. Thus, the 40 percent or so that vote in a given referendum are not entirely the same group of people that voted in the previous one; and the number of voters who participate in at least one referendum a year is considerably larger than 40 percent of the electorate.

In any event, participation in Swiss referendums has undeniably fallen since the 1940s. What explanations can be given? While it has been suggested that Swiss voters simply got tired of direct democracy, there are reasons to doubt this burnout theory. One cause for skepticism is the timing of the drop in participation. Why did it occur when it did and not earlier? Alternatively, why did the marked increase in the number of ballot issues coming before the electorate in the 1970s not produce a further drop in participation?

Accounting for the dramatic decline in referendum participation from the 1940s to the 1960s is not easy. Clearly, the most important political development during this period was the completion of Swiss consociational government with the magic formula of 1959. To the extent that this arrangement has minimized the number of people in society who find fault with government legislation, it has reduced the number wishing to express grievances through direct democracy. Voter indifference in Switzerland may also reflect general satisfaction with the political system and with the country's impressive postwar economic performance. This economic prosperity has been complemented by marked social and political stability. With the exception of the isolated Jura crisis of the late 1960s and early 1970s, involving the secession of the Jura region from the canton of Bern, incidents of social unrest have been relatively minor. These factors undoubtedly contribute to the willingness of much of the electorate to stay at home and let other citizens make referendum decisions.

Statistics on women's voting suggest an explanation for the slight drop in average turnout in the 1970s and 1980s, compared with that in

---

15. *Analyse der eidgenössischen Abstimmung vom 16 März 1986*, p. 6.

the 1960s. Newly enfranchised groups in virtually all democracies tend to participate in low numbers initially. For example, this was the case with early twentieth-century immigrants to the United States. A history of disenfranchisement depoliticizes such groups. Likewise, women in Switzerland did not flock to the polls after winning suffrage rights. This was illustrated clearly in the 1971 Federal Assembly election, the first in which women took part. In total, 56.9 percent of the electorate voted—a marked downturn from 65.7 percent in the previous (1967) election. Barely one out of two women went to the polls, compared with seven out of ten men.[16]

This phenomenon was not restricted to the 1970s. It typically takes at least two generations for such newly enfranchised groups to match the participation of the rest of the electorate.[17] Accordingly, disparities have persisted. In the March 1977 referendum, for example, only 47 percent of women in the electorate took part, compared with 64 percent of men—a gender gap of 17 percent.[18] In the March 1985 referendum, the gender gap was 14 percent;[19] and in April 1990, it was 16 percent.[20] Not surprisingly, 34 percent of men are regular referendum voters, compared with 28 percent of women.[21] If one assumes (conservatively) that the gender gap in participation has averaged 10 percent or more since 1971, this accounts for a drop in total turnout of at least 5 percentage points. In fact, participation figures in the 1980s were only three percentage points lower, on average, than they were in the 1960s. This is due to the fact that average participation levels for the male electorate have actually increased since 1971. This upward trend is further evidence that electoral burnout is not at work. It also bodes well for the future, as Swiss women gradually overcome their historical de-

---

16. Henry H. Kerr, "Swiss Electoral Politics," in Howard R. Penniman, ed., *Switzerland at the Polls: The National Elections of 1979* (Washington, D.C.: American Enterprise Institute, 1983), p. 74.

17. See Philip E. Converse, "Of Time and Partisan Stability," *Comparative Political Studies*, vol. 2 (1969), pp. 139–71.

18. *Analyse der eidgenössischen Abstimmung von 12/13 März 1977*, VOX Survey No. 1 (Bern: Forschungzentrum für Schweizerische Politik and the Schweizerische Gesellschaft für Praktische Socialforschung, 1977), p. 4.

19. *Analyse der eidgenössischen Abstimmung vom 10 Marz 1985*, VOX Survey No. 25 (Bern: Forschungzentrum für Schweizerische Politik and the Schweizerische Gesellschaft für Praktische Socialforschung, 1985), p. 5.

20. Florence Passy, Pascal Sciarini, Simon Hug, and Hanspeter Kriesi, *Analyse der eidgenössischen Abstimmung vom 1 April 1990*, VOX Survey No. 39 (Bern: Forschungzentrum für Schweizerische Politik and the Schweizerische Gesellschafte für Praktische Sozialforschung, 1990), p. 9.

21. *Analyse der eidgenössischen Abstimmung vom 16 März 1986*, p. 7.

politicization and add their numbers to the total active electorate.

The Exploitation of Apathy

Frequently during the 1970s and 1980s, turnout for specific referendums plummeted below 35 percent. It was at such moments that direct democracy was most vulnerable. The legitimacy of a referendum stems from the assumption that its result expresses the will of the majority. Extremely low participation, though, magnifies the possibility of distortion, in which the percentage voting Yes varies considerably from the percentage that would have resulted if all citizens had voted. In such instances of high voter apathy, a mobilized special interest may be well poised to take advantage of the situation. Trooping to the polls in great numbers while most of the electorate stays home, an activated minority can defeat a position held by the majority of citizens. The result can be described as a false majority (in which the final verdict on the proposal, had all citizens voted, would have been different). The exploitation of apathy is not necessarily deliberate. Affected interests have every incentive to urge their members to vote, and they cannot predict what the turnout will be. If the rest of the electorate participated as enthusiastically, such unrepresentative outcomes would never result.

Without a doubt, significant distortion occurs when voter turnouts are extremely low. It is difficult, however, to demonstrate with any certainty that false majorities have occurred. Since 1977, the Research Center for Swiss Politics at the University of Bern has conducted regular surveys immediately after every referendum.[22] These surveys draw from a pool of all citizens eligible to vote and therefore include both voters and nonvoters. In many referendums with a low turnout, the difference between the result of the vote and the support level of all citizens, as reflected in the survey, varied by a significant margin. Such instances point to the exploitation of voter apathy. Between 1977 and 1990, the variation between the survey result and the actual vote was nine percentage points or greater in nineteen cases, plainly illustrating

---

22. The results are presented in the VOX survey analyses, published jointly by the *Forschungszentrum für Schweizerische Politik* and the *Schweizerische Gesellschaft für Praktische Sozialforschung*. Since 1977, the surveys have polled a minimum of 700 subjects. From 1986 onward, 1,000 subjects have been used. The pre-1986 results are corrected slightly to account for a 4 percent bias in the Yes direction, since the surveys are conducted after the referendum results are known. See Claude Longchamp, "Die politische Sozialforschung am Beispiel der VOX-Analysen," in *Marktforschung Schweiz: Handbuch 1987–89* (Einseideln: Verband Schweizerischer Marktforscher, 1987).

TABLE 4–5
INITIATIVES AND COUNTERPROPOSALS AS A PERCENTAGE OF ALL SWISS
FEDERAL BALLOT ISSUES, 1950–1993

	1950–1959	1960–1969	1970–1979	1980–1993
Number of initiatives and counterproposals	14	5	30	41
Percentage of total	31.1	19.2	34.9	38.7

SOURCE: Same as for table 4–1.

the risk of warped referendum outcomes when voter turnout is low.[23] It is more difficult to determine with any confidence whether false majorities have actually occurred. The uncertainty associated with survey data prevents any definite conclusions. Nonetheless, it is a realistic possibility.

In one case in particular the exploitation of apathy may have yielded a false majority—the February 1983 vote on energy policy. This proposed constitutional amendment would have transferred authority from the cantons to the central government. In this instance, participation was at a particularly low 32.4 percent. The referendum yielded a narrow (50.9 percent) majority in favor. Survey data, however, indicated that only 41 percent of the entire population favored the amendment. In any event, the false majority had no real bearing on the final outcome, because the measure failed to gain the necessary majority of cantons. When the federal referendum was first instituted in Switzerland in 1848, anxious opponents warned that the excited and irresponsible masses would rise up to cast aside the carefully considered policies of their government. This prophecy was well off the mark. Most referendum outcomes express the basic conservative leanings of the Swiss electorate; and, as the above example illustrates, the greatest danger stems not from an excited citizenry but from an apathetic one.

The Rise of the Initiative

Without question, one of the most visible transformations in Swiss direct democracy has been the recent prominence of the initiative. Since the mid-1970s, a growing percentage of ballot issues presented to the electorate has been initiatives and parliamentary counterproposals made in response. That is to say, initiatives and counterproposals have taken up a larger share of the questions on each ballot. Table 4–5 illus-

---

23. For more detailed information on the nineteen cases, see Kris W. Kobach, *The Referendum: Direct Democracy in Switzerland* (Aldershot: Dartmouth, 1993).

TABLE 4–6
AVERAGE NUMBER OF INITIATIVES SUBMITTED PER YEAR IN SWITZERLAND,
1891–1993

	1891–1959	1960–69	1970–79	1980–93
Number of initiatives submitted	78	13	39	65
Average per year	1.1	1.3	3.9	4.6

SOURCE: Data compiled by author from records of the Swiss Federal Chancellory.

trates this trend. The figures in table 4–5 represent only the tip of the iceberg. A great number of initiatives are launched with little intention of carrying the venture all the way to a popular vote. They are withdrawn at some point after signature collection and formal submission, when sufficient policy concessions are won from the government.

A more accurate picture of the surge in initiatives can therefore be drawn by looking at the number of initiatives submitted in Bern with the requisite signatures each year. As table 4–6 indicates, recent decades have brought a marked upswing in initiative submissions.

This dramatic rise commenced in 1969. Following a sparse five-year period over which the average was only 0.8 initiatives per year, three initiatives were submitted in 1969. Four were launched in each of the next three years; and as table 4–6 indicates, the annual average has continued to climb virtually unchecked. There have been only two "dry" years since 1969, in which fewer than two initiatives were submitted: 1978 and 1988. In contrast, fifty-six of the seventy-eight years before 1969 were dry in this sense.

This so-called flood of initiatives has sometimes been attributed to the doubling of the electorate in 1971, with the introduction of women's suffrage. The timing of the two events is fairly close, and an electorate of twice the size makes the collection of signatures much easier. Undoubtedly, there is some connection. The number of initiatives per voter, however, still increased slightly between the 1960s and the 1970s;[24] and in the 1980s, the average number of submissions per voter continued to increase. Thus, the deluge of initiatives is not solely due to the swelling of the electorate. Moreover, the doubling of the number of required signatures and the imposition of an eighteen-month time limit for their collection (effective from the beginning of 1979) did little to stem the rate of submissions. The change was touted before its adop-

24. See Bruno Hofer, "Die Volksinitiative als Verhandlungspfand," *Schweizerisches Jarbuch für Politische Wissenschaft*, 27 (1987), p. 213.

tion in the September 1977 referendum as a means of "containing the initiative flood" unleashed by women's suffrage.[25] The mathematical assumption was obvious: double the size of the electorate and twice as many initiatives will materialize; double the required number of signatures and initiative submissions will drop off accordingly. Yet, in the decade that followed, more initiatives were submitted with the required number of signatures than in any other ten-year period before the change.[26] The failure rate (of initiatives falling short of the necessary number of signatures) barely changed, increasing from 30 percent in the decade before the change to 36 percent in the decade after.

Beyond the expansion of the electorate, other, more important forces have been behind the post-1969 surge. One is the rise of initiative entrepreneurs, high-profile individuals willing to dedicate time, effort, and money to the waging of initiative wars. This development is, in turn, a manifestation of deeper changes in the political culture. From the late 1960s onward, Switzerland has witnessed the growth of an activist approach to politics for which the initiative is ideally suited. The so-called *Aktivierungsprozesse* (activation process) involved unprecedented levels of participation in protests, rallies, and civil disobedience. Similar, contemporary movements in other democracies lent inspiration to Swiss activists. The transformation in Switzerland, however, was not confined to college campuses. Rather, a broadly based, grass-roots *Politik von unten* took hold in the 1970s. These changes coincided almost exactly with the rapid rise in initiative submissions. Although the number of protests and rallies dropped off in the 1980s, the use of initiatives continued to accelerate.

Another factor fueling the surge of initiative submissions was the economic crisis of 1974. Following on the heels of two decades of robust economic growth, the mid-1970s shock aroused great concern both in Bern and among the general public. Numerous initiatives dealing with the health of the economy were launched, particularly from the left side of the political spectrum and from the trade unions. In 1974, the Social Democrats and the Independent party (LdU), for example, started an initiative to minimize taxing discrepancies between cantons. It was rejected in a popular vote two years later, with 42.2 percent support for the measure. In 1975, the Social Democrats launched another initiative, which would have raised taxes on high-income groups and lessened the tax burden on lower incomes. This attempt at more progressive taxation was rejected by voters in December 1977 (44.4 percent voted Yes). Among other initiatives in the wake

---

25. Gross, "1988—ein Jahr erfolgloser Volksbegehren."
26. Forty-eight initiatives were submitted over the 1979–1988 period.

of the economic crisis were the protection of lessees (which failed, with 42.2 percent), worker participation (which also failed, with 32.4 percent), and the price control initiative, which, on its acceptance in 1982 (by 56.1 percent of voters), was Switzerland's first initiative to win popular endorsement in more than three decades. Successful or not, these proposals set the stage for subsequent initiatives in the area of managing the economy.

A fourth contributor to the flood of initiatives was a shift in the issue focus of the country. This shift came from below, rather than from above, and consequently found expression primarily in the initiative. The rise of postmaterialism in Europe in the 1970s and 1980s brought new concerns to the political agenda. Postmaterialist organizations sought to replace social goals based on economic prosperity and various distributions of wealth with the alternative objectives of protecting the environment and maintaining "quality of life." In most countries, the old distributional concerns demonstrated their staying power; and the postmaterialist aspirations remained subsidiary goals behind economic growth. Stealing the wind from Green sails, larger parties in most European countries incorporated Green planks into their platforms (or at least presented the appearance of doing so). In Switzerland, though, environmental organizations have had a more tangible effect on policy. Their limited parliamentary power has not hampered the environmental interests in the realm of direct democracy.

Initiatives on environmental protection, nuclear energy limitation, and road traffic restriction have figured prominently in the post-1969 initiative boom, particularly since 1974 (see table 4–7). Roughly a third of the initiatives submitted fell into this category. Yet amazingly, before 1973 not a single environmental initiative had been submitted. Although the recent profusion of initiatives is not entirely a product of postmaterialism, submissions in this topic area have dominated the field. Without them, the post-1969 surge would have been much less impressive.

The environmental movement gained momentum in the mid-1970s as various regional groups established national organizations and began launching initiatives. The environmental banner was carried by "outsider" interest groups and small parties, most notably the Green parties and the Independent party. Brushed aside by the Bern political establishment at first, environmental matters finally gained a prominent position on the formal agenda of the Swiss government in the early 1980s. In addition, the efforts of environmental organizations using direct democracy bore fruit in Parliament. A coalition of Green parties won 2.8 percent of the vote and five seats in the National Coun-

TABLE 4–7
DISTRIBUTION BY SUBJECT MATTER OF ALL INITIATIVES SUBMITTED IN
SWITZERLAND, 1974–1993

Subject	Number	Percentage of Total
Environmental and energy; traffic restrictions; animal rights	29	32.2
Consumer or renter protection; price controls	10	11.1
Defense; military policy	7	7.8
Antiforeigners	7	7.8
Taxes; economic policy	7	7.8
Workplace; employment	6	6.7
Social insurance	5	5.6
Women's issues; abortion	4	4.4
Agriculture	4	4.4
Alcohol, tobacco, and drug abuse	3	3.3
Education	2	2.2
Others	6	6.7

SOURCE: Data compiled by author from records of the Swiss Federal Chancellory.

cil in 1983. Four years later, they raised their take to 5.0 percent of the vote and nine seats. In 1991, they gained again, collecting fourteen seats with 6.1 percent of the vote. Like the Catholic Conservative party in the nineteenth century and the Social Democrats in the early twentieth century, the Greens used initiatives to introduce themselves and their cause to the electorate.

The fifth and final factor behind the rise in submissions of initiatives has been the proliferation of issue-oriented citizens' movements and interest groups. Fully two-fifths of all the initiatives submitted in the 1980s came from committees representing organizations new to the political stage. The possibilities for many of these groups to gain influence in representative institutions have remained limited. It is an irony of Swiss consociational democracy that, although it maximizes the participation of certain parties and groups in decision making, the formalization of this arrangement imposes informal barriers to entry. Interests that lack the resources, membership, and connections of the powerful *Verbände* are often unable to use the process of legislative "consultation" to full advantage. The initiative has served as the outsiders' primary recourse in attempting to exert political leverage. If their requests are ignored in Bern, they can take their case to the people. Once the signatures are collected, the sponsors of an initiative usually find that their demands obtain a more favorable reception. Between 1974 and 1992, more than four-fifths of the initiatives submitted came from outsider interest groups or nongovernment parties. The only insider organizations to submit initiatives in significant numbers were the Social Democratic party and the Swiss Federation of Trade Unions.

The most obvious manifestation of success for an initiative campaign is victory on the ballot. Under this definition of success, a truly dramatic reversal of fortune for initiatives has taken place during the 1980s and 1990s. After the adoption of an initiative in 1949 concerning referendums on "urgent" legislation, a thirty-three-year spell followed during which no initiative won at the polls. This string of defeats ended in November 1982 when the price control initiative launched by the Women's Consumer Forum three years earlier took 56.1 percent of the vote and carried seventeen cantons. The triumph was doubly impressive in that the initiative had to compete for votes with a government counterproposal. A victory in the presence of a counterproposal had been accomplished only once before, in 1920, with an initiative regarding gambling houses. Since the April 1987 reform allowing double-Yes voting, the counterproposal has posed less of a threat to initiatives. In December 1987, a second initiative met with success at the polls. This proposal to halt the construction of the Rothenturm military base on scenic moorland combined environmental worries with antimilitary sentiment to produce a popular majority of 57.8 percent.

In September 1990, the third initiative of recent years won a popular vote. Garnering 54.6 percent of the vote, the measure imposed a ten-year moratorium on nuclear plant construction. This victory was particularly startling because of the subject matter involved. Until the 1990 vote, nuclear energy policy had always been an area in which initiatives had made remarkably little impact. In 1979 and twice in 1984, Swiss citizens rejected initiatives to limit or end the use of nuclear power. In each case, the Federal Council had been unwilling to offer concessions; and the outcomes of the votes seemed to justify this intransigence. Finally, antinuclear organizations achieved a breakthrough in 1990 with the adoption of the ten-year moratorium. Successive initiatives had kept the issue on the national agenda until a proposal was framed in a way that attracted sufficient public support. Like the Rothenturm initiative, the moratorium initiative succeeded because it was able to find votes deep within the *bürgerliche* camp. Where single-issue parties like the Greens have been unable to attract many voters from the major parties in elections, they have often made real gains through direct democracy. Initiatives in the hands of allied inter-

145

est groups allied to single-issue parties have yielded far more substantial results than has representation in the National Council. For this reason, most initiatives will probably continue to flow from such sources in the future.

In September 1993, yet another initiative won at the polls. A proposal to establish a national work force holiday on the first of August, the date on which the creation of the Swiss confederation is traditionally celebrated, passed with 83.8 percent approval. In total, four initiatives had gained ballot victories in an eleven-year period. These successes appear particularly remarkable in the wake of the thirty-three-year string of defeats. They are less impressive, however, when the increase in initiative submissions is taken into account. In the twenty-five-year period of 1969–1993, exactly 107 initiatives were submitted, of which 4 were adopted by the voters. In the seventy-eight-year period of 1891–1968, 90 initiatives were submitted, of which 7 eventually won in the final vote. Thus, the ratio of adopted initiatives to submissions has actually been relatively low since the surge began.

Yet, it is a mistake to focus exclusively on victory at the polls. For sponsors of many Swiss initiatives, winning a popular vote is not necessary; and it may not even be an objective. Rather, initiatives are submitted with the intent of offering their withdrawal in bargaining for desired policy changes. This tactic arose only as recently as the postwar era. Before the late 1950s, the goal of most groups sponsoring initiatives was to circumvent the government entirely by taking a proposal all the way to a popular vote and winning. The vast majority of initiatives in the nineteenth century and the first half of the twentieth century were of this type. Ironically, none of this sort succeeded at the polls.

The establishment of a grand coalition government in 1959 encouraged a different type of initiative, one that sets forth a proposal in the hope that a consensus can be forged. Withdrawal of this type of initiative is not seen as defeat, and the sponsors of the initiative expect to bargain with the government for policy concessions. These concessions sometimes come in the form of a direct counterproposal to amend the Constitution. More often, however, the offers take the form of "indirect counterproposal"—normal legislation meeting some of the initiators' demands. In 1971, for example, an initiative was submitted to regulate sonic booms produced by supersonic aircraft. The sponsoring organization did not really expect to amend the Swiss Constitution as such; it simply wanted to force the government to act on the problem with legislation. Satisfactory regulations were agreed on, and the initiative was withdrawn fifteen months after submission. Treating an initiative as an expendable bargaining chip has the advantage of avoid-

TABLE 4–8
PROPORTION OF INITIATIVES WITHDRAWN IN SWITZERLAND, BY DECADE,
1891–1993

Decade	Number Submitted	Number Withdrawn	Percentage Withdrawn
1890s	3	0	0
1900s	5	1	20
1910s	6	0	0
1920s	11	1	9
1930s	20	5	25
1940s	10	8	80
1950s	23	12	52
1960s	13	8	62
1970s	39	13	33
1980–1993	65	14	22
Total	195	62	32

SOURCE: Same as for table 4–6.

ing the uncertainties and considerable expense involved in carrying a proposal to a popular vote. During the 1974–1986 period, forty-four initiatives were submitted. Of these, eight were met with a direct counterproposal; and fourteen were met with an indirect counterproposal. In all, a compromise was hammered out in exactly 50 percent of the cases.[27]

But the attractions of the withdrawable initiative have faded in recent years. As table 4–8 indicates, the proportion of initiatives withdrawn has actually declined since the 1960s. The proportion was highest in the 1940s, mainly because the war delayed the consideration of several initiatives. Proposals submitted before the war were no longer appropriate afterward and were consequently withdrawn. In all, six prewar submissions were withdrawn after the cessation of hostilities. In the 1950s and 1960s, more than 50 percent of initiatives were withdrawn. During this period, the use of the device as a bargaining chip was most prevalent. In the 1970s, however, withdrawals dropped to 33 percent. After 1980, the rate fell even lower, to 24 percent. It is the combination of increased submissions with reduced withdrawals that has produced the recent profusion of initiatives on Swiss ballots.

The infrequency of withdrawals reflects the hardening of the political climate in Switzerland. The consociational approach that guided

27. See Rolf App, "Initiative und ihre Wirkungen auf Bundesebene seit 1974," *Schweizerisches Jahrbuch für Politische Wissenschaft*, 27 (1987), p. 204.

147

the treatment of virtually all political questions in the 1950s and 1960s gave way to more majoritarian and confrontational attitudes in the late 1970s and early 1980s. Since then, as more subjects have tended to polarize parties and interest groups, the willingness to find compromises has dissipated considerably. Much of the change in attitude lies with those who launch the initiatives. Many proposals offer little room for compromise, or their sponsors are unwilling to concede any demands. Accordingly, groups launching initiatives are more likely to take measures to hinder future withdrawals. One tactic is to form initiative committees with as many members as possible, making it difficult to contact and convince half the members to endorse a withdrawal. The committee for the 1989 initiative to abolish the army, for example, had a committee of 100 members; and the 1988 initiative against real estate speculation had 76. For ad hoc groups sponsoring initiatives, this ploy holds another advantage. Because they lack the express backing of a major party or interest group, they need to demonstrate broad support to convince people to sign petitions. A large committee with well-known figures on board helps. It also demonstrates the group's resolve not to compromise and withdraw the initiative at a later stage.

Two other factors account for the relative unpopularity of withdrawals in the 1980s and early 1990s. First, as mentioned above, the signature hurdle for initiatives was raised to 100,000 in December 1977; and an eighteen-month deadline for collection was imposed at the same time. In the eight years before the change, ten of the thirty-one submitted initiatives were withdrawn (approximately 30 percent); in the seven years following the change, nine of the forty-three submitted initiatives were withdrawn (approximately 20 percent).[28] To collect twice as many signatures in a limited amount of time, groups had to magnify the importance of their cause and the problems of the status quo. In doing so, they committed themselves more firmly to their positions.

Second, the publication of collection deadlines in the government *Bundesblatt* and the national newspapers has combined with heightened attention from the broadcast media to alter the atmosphere considerably. Failure cannot go unobserved under this spotlight. The successful collection of the required signatures is treated as a preliminary victory, and public expectations mount accordingly. In this pressured climate of widespread publicity, withdrawal smacks of defeat. Consequently, the use of the initiative as a bargaining chip has become more difficult under public scrutiny.

---

28. See Hofer, "Die Volksinitiative als Verhandlungspfand," pp. 220–23.

Conclusion

Thus, the pendulum has swung back; the initiative is again being used primarily as a device of outright opposition. The sponsoring organizations—typically uninfluential interest groups or small parties without seats on the Federal Council—repeatedly challenge the government to defend the status quo. Even though organizations outside the corridors of power are the predominant sponsors of initiatives, however, MPs routinely participate individually in the launching and waging of such campaigns. A 1981 study of the National Council revealed that 84 of the 200 members were on the sponsoring committee of one of the various initiatives considered that year. Of these MPs, 51 were representatives of a governing party.[29] This is yet another manifestation of the fluidity and instability that direct democracy injects into parliamentary allegiances.

With virtually all initiatives, the proposed policy is something that the Federal Council and the Federal Assembly have been unwilling to endorse. When there is no avenue through the government, the initiative offers a path around the government. Proponents of change challenge the parliamentary majority by seeking the endorsement of a popular majority. Although the government usually wins such battles, the forces of opposition almost always make significant gains for their cause. The issue is catapulted into the national spotlight, volunteers are drawn to the campaign, the government sometimes concedes limited reforms to win over unsure voters, and occasionally enough momentum is created to produce reform even after defeat at the polls.

A particularly vivid example occurred after the defeat of the initiative to abolish the army in November 1989. The outcome of 35.6 percent in favor of the initiative vastly exceeded expectations, prompting the government to pursue significant reforms in its once-unshakable tradition of universal male conscription. In late 1990, the first few changes were enacted. Cuts were made in the size of the Swiss military, and regulations governing the basic-training period were relaxed. The government also yielded to widespread demands for a civilian service option for men unwilling to enter the military. An initiative proposing such a reform had been rejected by 63.8 percent of the voters in February 1984. But circumstances had changed dramatically in the wake of the November 1989 vote. The Federal Assembly decriminalized conscientious objection to military service, and 55.7 percent of voters approved the policy in a June 1991 referendum. A civilian service

29. See Hanspeter Kriese, *AKW-Gegner in der Schweiz* (Diessenhofen, 1982), p. 267.

amendment to the Constitution went before the electorate in May 1992, winning 82.5 percent of the vote—more than twice the approval shown for the 1984 initiative. Each of these subsequent reforms owed its success to the initiative of 1989. Yet, superficially the antiarmy initiative appeared to have failed. This illustrates one of the most important aspects of the postwar initiative in Switzerland: it has played a major role in shaping policy, but rarely through victory at the polls.

Much the same can be said about the facultative referendum device. It has also achieved its primary effect away from the ballot box. While the initiative has mainly been the weapon of the political outsider, whether employed in a conciliatory manner or in outright opposition, the facultative referendum has commonly been used by interests and parties at the center of power in Bern. That is to say, the *threat* of a referendum has commonly been used. Threatening to launch a referendum campaign has long been a favored tactic of MPs in legislative deliberations. When negotiations on a bill take a turn that disfavors a particular interest, the no-so-subtle threat of a referendum usually finds its way into the room. In a 1990 survey, fully 63 percent of Federal Assembly members said they would threaten to launch a referendum if they thought a bill that they strongly opposed was likely to pass; and 40 percent indicated that they had done so in the past. Of these, 77 percent reported that their threat had been successful.[30] If the MP speaks for an organization that can credibly make such a threat, the bill will almost always be changed. Legislating in Switzerland is the art of avoiding the referendum.

As noted previously, the grand coalition that has governed Switzerland since 1959 owes its existence, in large part, to the referendum. However, this seemingly permanent seat distribution on the Federal Council may not represent the final stage of Swiss political development. If changes are to come, there is no doubt that they will again be propelled by direct democracy. In fact, the seeds of transformation may already be taking root. In 1959, the four governing parties represented 85 percent of the voters in the National Council election. Although their share ebbed slightly in the ensuing quarter century, they still represented 78 percent of voters until 1987. Then in the 1987 and 1991 elections, combined support for the Federal Council parties dropped to 72.3 percent and 69.5 percent, respectively. The primary beneficiaries of these losses were two young parties that had risen to prominence on the back of the initiative—the Greens and the Auto party. Together accounting for 11.2 percent of the votes in 1991, neither of these archrivals had even existed as national parties a decade earlier.

---

30. Survey conducted by the author. See note 11.

These two new parties are very different from the governing four. Both began as spinoff organizations from interest groups dedicated to launching initiatives. Their appeal has been their commitment to a fairly narrow band of issues; and their primary activities remain geared toward direct democracy rather than representative democracy. Their greatest effect on policy has unquestionably been in this sphere. At the same time, their situation is much like that of the early Catholic Conservatives and Social Democrats, in that they have no real hope of outvoting the governing parties in the National Council. The four major parties took 145 of the 200 National Council seats in 1991; neither the Greens nor the Auto party can hope to form the core of an effective parliamentary opposition. As was the case in the late nineteenth century and the early twentieth century, parties with little real parliamentary power rely on the referendum to summon Switzerland's only potent opposition—the people. If these newcomers are to become more than a temporary blip on the radar screen, it will be because they continued to pose a threat to government policies by invoking direct democracy.

While these initiative-wielding parties may conceivably force a change in the distribution of Federal Council seats one day, Switzerland is unlikely to ever leave consociationalism behind. The presence of the referendum reinforces consociational behavior in too many ways. The fear of the popular veto of a law forces MPs to seek parliamentary consensus by negotiating the endorsement of every possible party and interest group. Moderate policies are the standard fare, because they are palatable to the greatest number of referendum voters. And, perhaps most important, direct democracy compensates for the inherent flaws of consociational arrangements. Consociational bargaining by political elites can easily lead to agreements that most voters would not endorse. The facultative referendum rectifies the problem when negotiations go astray. At the same time, the referendum and the initiative offer an escape from stalemate on issues that are too divisive to settle by consensus. Typically, this is the case with morally charged issues such as abortion, capital punishment, and gambling. Another general problem with consociational democracy is that it is rarely possible to allow every interested faction or group a seat at the bargaining table. The referendum offers such groups recourse by allowing them to take their case directly to the people.

In sum, the referendum and Swiss consociationalism have developed hand in hand. Consequently, Switzerland's *Konkordanz-Demokratie* is more firmly entrenched and more widely accepted than it might have been otherwise. Ironically, the blunt majoritarianism of the referendum has done much to foster the politics of consensus.

Bibliography

App, Rolf. "Initiative and ihre Wirkungen auf Bundesebene seit 1974." *Schweizerisches Jahrbuch für Politische Wissenschaft* 7 (1987): 190–206.

Austin, John, David Butler, and Austin Ranney. "Referendums, 1978–1986." *Electoral Studies* 6, no. 2 (August 1987): 139–47.

Barber, Benjamin. "Participation and Swiss Democracy." *Government and Opposition* 23, no. 1 (Winter 1988): 31–50.

Bucheli, Markus. *Die direkte Demokratie im Rahmen eines Kondordanz-oder Koalitionssytems.* Bern: Paul Haupt, 1979.

Butler, David, and Austin Ranney, eds. *Referendums: A Comparative Study of Practice and Theory.* Washington, D.C.: American Enterprise Institute, 1978.

Converse, Philip E. "Of Time and Partisan Stability." *Comparative Political Studies* 2 (1969): 139–71.

Gross, Andreas. "1988—ein Jahr erfolgloser Volksbegehren." *Tages-Anzeiger,* 5 January 1989, p. 9.

Hofer, Bruno. "Die Volksinitiative als Verhandlungspfand." *Schweizerisches Jahrbuch für Politische Wissenschaft* 27 (1987): 207–36.

Hughes, Christopher. *The Federal Constitution of Switzerland.* Oxford: Clarendon Press, 1954; Westport, Conn.: Greenwood Press, 1970.

———. *Switzerland.* New York: Praeger, 1975.

Kobach, Kris. *The Referendum: Direct Democracy in Switzerland.* Aldershot: Dartmouth, 1993.

Kriesi, Hanspeter. *Entscheidungsstrukturn und Entscheidungsprozesse in der schweizer Politik.* Frankfurt: Campus, 1980.

———. *AKW-Gegner in der Schweiz.* Diessenhofen, 1982.

Libbey, Kenneth. "Initiatives, Referenda and Socialism in Switzerland." *Government and Opposition* 5 (1969–1970): 307–26.

Linder, Wolf. *Politische Entscheidung und Gesetzesvollzug in der Schweiz.* Bern: Paul Haupt, 1987.

Longchamp, Claude. "Die politische Sozialforschung am Beispiel der VOX-Analysen." *Marktforschung Schweiz: Handbuch 1987–89.* Einsiedeln: Verband Schweizerischer Marktforscher, 1987.

Lowell, A. Lawrence. *Public Opinion and Popular Government,* 2d ed. New York: Longmans, Green and Co., 1914.

Neidhart, Leonard. *Plebiszit und pluralitäre Demokratie: Eine Analyse der Funktion des schweizerischen Gesetzesreferendums.* Bern: Franke, 1970.

Passy, Florence, Pascal Sciarini, Simon Hug, and Hanspeter Kriesi. *Analyse der eidgenössischen Abstimmung vom 1 April 1990.* VOX Survey no. 39. Bern: Forschungzentrum für Schweizerische Politik and the Schweizerische Gesellschaft für Praktische Sozialforschung, 1990.

Penniman, Howard R., ed. *Switzerland at the Polls: The National Elections of 1979.* Washington, D.C.: American Enterprise Institute, 1983.

Riklin, Alois, and Roland Key. *Stimmabstinez und direkte Demokratie.* Bern: Paul Haupt, 1981.

Sigg, Oswald. *Die Eidgenössischen Volksinitiativen 1892–1939.* Bern: Francke Verlag, 1978.

Steiner, Jürg. *Amicable Agreement versus Majority Rule: Conflict Resolution in Switzerland.* Chapel Hill: University of North Carolina Press, 1974.

Thürer, Georg. *Free and Swiss.* London: Oswald Wolff, 1970.

VOX Surveys, nos. 1–37. Bern: Forschungszentrum für Schweizerische Politik and the Schweizerische Gesellschaft für praktische Sozialforschung.

Zehnder, Ernst. *Die Gesetzesüberprüfung durch die schweizerische Bundesversammlung: Undersuchung der parlamentarischen Veränderungen von Vorlagen des Bundesrates in der Legislaturperiode 1971 bis 1975.* Entlebuch: Hober Druck AG, 1988.

Zimmerman, Kurt W. "Die Industrialisierung der Direkten Demokratie." *Politik und Wirtschaft,* 20 September–17 October, 1987, pp. 22–26.

5
Australia and New Zealand

Colin A. Hughes

Australia and New Zealand inevitably form a pair for comparative studies: histories, geographical locations, political and social institutions, and economies, all have combined to keep them on parallel tracks for the past one hundred and fifty years. In each country, the political culture during that period and even today reflects the industrial and political tensions of the British Isles early in the nineteenth century. Yet, in the use of the referendum, their experiences have diverged.

The Commonwealth of Australia was formed as a federation of the half-dozen British colonies occupying the continent. A federal form of government requires some degree of constitutional rigidity to prevent too easy and frequent amendment of the constitutional compact from undermining the original political bargain. Onto what was already a somewhat adventurous hybrid of British parliamentary and American federal arrangements was grafted a Swiss device, the constitutional referendum, to be the only means by which the text of the federal constitution might be amended. Its use on eighteen separate occasions in the ninety-odd years since federation may have led Australian electors to believe that this is what referendums are about, even though the six states have managed to hold almost as many referendums on a variety of questions, mostly social and only rarely constitutional (for a list of all nationwide referendums held in Australia up to 1992, see table 5–1).

New Zealanders, in contrast, abandoned an early flirtation with quasi-federalism and instituted a constitutional regime that resembled Britain's in its lack of rigidity. Thus, it is not surprising that New Zealand's referendums have been infrequent—three this century to Australia's eighteen—although the New Zealand figure disregards the routine, statute-programmed, national licensing polls at which electors voted triennially from 1911 to 1987, for a total of twenty-four times (for

TABLE 5–1
NATIONWIDE REFERENDUMS IN AUSTRALIA, 1906–1988
(percent of valid votes cast)

Date	Subject	States in Favor	Yes Votes	Turnout of Electorate
12 Dec. 1906	Senate elections	6	82.7	50.2
13 Apr. 1910	Finance	3	49.0	62.2
13 Apr. 1910	State debts	5	55.0	62.2
26 Apr. 1911	Legislative powers	1	39.4	53.3
26 Apr. 1911	Monopolies	1	39.9	53.3
31 May 1913	Trade and commerce	3	49.4	73.7
31 May 1913	Corporations	3	49.3	73.7
31 May 1913	Industrial matters	3	49.3	73.7
31 May 1913	Railway disputes	3	49.1	73.7
31 May 1913	Trusts	3	49.8	73.7
31 May 1913	Nationalization of monopolies	3	49.3	73.7
28 Oct. 1916	Conscription for overseas services[a]	3	48.4	82.7
20 Dec. 1917	Conscription for overseas service[a]	2	46.2	81.3
13 Dec. 1919	Legislative powers	3	49.7	71.3
13 Dec. 1919	Nationalization of monopolies	3	48.6	71.3
4 Sept. 1926	Industry and commerce	2	43.5	91.1
4 Sept. 1926	Essential services	2	42.8	91.1
17 Nov. 1928	State debts	6	74.3	93.6
6 Mar. 1937	Aviation	2	53.6	94.1
6 Mar. 1937	Marketing	0	36.3	94.1
19 Aug. 1944	Postwar reconstruction and democratic rights	2	47.0	96.5
28 Sept. 1946	Social services	6	54.4	94.0
28 Sept. 1946	Marketing	3	50.6	94.0
28 Sept. 1946	Industrial relations	3	50.3	94.0
29 May 1948	Rents and prices	0	40.7	93.6
22 Sept. 1951	Communism	3	49.4	95.6
27 May 1967	Parliamentary nexus	1	40.3	93.8

(Table continues)

155

TABLE 5–1 (continued)

Date	Subject	States in Favor	Yes Votes	Turnout of Electorate
27 May 1967	Aborigines	6	90.8	93.8
8 Dec. 1973	Prices	0	43.8	93.8
8 Dec. 1973	Incomes	0	34.4	93.4
18 May 1974	Simultaneous elections	1	48.3	95.5
18 May 1974	Procedure for constitutional amendment	1	48.0	95.5
18 May 1974	Democratic elections	1	47.2	95.5
18 May 1974	Local government	1	46.9	95.5
21 May 1977	Simultaneous elections	3	62.2	92.3
21 May 1977	Senate vacancies	6	73.3	92.3
21 May 1977	Territory franchise for referendums	6	77.7	92.3
21 May 1977	Judges' retirement	6	80.1	92.3
1 Dec. 1984	Senators' terms	2	50.6	94.0
1 Dec. 1984	Interchange of powers	0	47.1	94.0
3 Sept. 1988	Parliamentary terms	0	32.9	92.1
3 Sept. 1988	Fair elections	0	37.6	92.1
3 Sept. 1988	Local government	0	33.6	92.1
3 Sept. 1988	Rights and freedoms	0	30.8	92.1

a. Not proposing constitutional amendment
SOURCES: 1906–1977; Don Aitkin, "Australia," in David Butler and Austin Ranney, eds., *Referendums: A Comparative Study of Practice and Theory* (Washington, D.C.: American Enterprise Institute, 1978), pp. 126–27; 1984–1990: Australian Electoral Commission, *Referendum Statistics* (Canberra: Australian Government Publishing Service, 1987, 1990).

a list of New Zealand's nationwide referendums through 1993, see table 5–2).[1]

After New Zealand's upper house, the Legislative Council, had been abolished in 1950, concerns about the resultant loss of checks and

1. In selecting what electoral events qualified for inclusion in table 5–2 (New Zealand) and table 5–3 (the Australian states), local option polls in which electors decide how many licensed premises if any should be allowed to open, or to remain open, in their own area have been excluded. Table 5–3, however, does include two polls in which only part of an Australian state's area and electorate were involved: one because the possible creation of a new state is such a significant matter on which to vote, the other because although

TABLE 5–2
NATIONWIDE REFERENDUMS IN NEW ZEALAND, 1949–1993
(percent of valid votes cast)

Date	Subject	Yes Votes	Turnout of Electorate
9 March 1949	Off-course betting	68.0	56.3
9 March 1949	Bar closing at 6 p.m.	75.5	56.3
3 Aug. 1949	Compulsory military training	77.9	61.5
23 Sept. 1967	Extension of parliamentary term of House of Representatives	31.9	71.2
23 Sept. 1967	Variable closing hours for bars	64.4	71.2
27 Oct. 1990	Extension of parliamentary term of House of Representatives	30.7	85.2
19 Sept. 1992	Electoral system	84.7	55.2
19 Sept. 1992	Mixed member proportional electoral system	70.5	55.2
6 Nov. 1993	Mixed member proportional electoral system	53.8	82.6

SOURCES: 1949–1967: J. O. Wilson, *New Zealand Parliamentary Record 1840–1984* (Wallington: Government Printer, 1985), p. 301; 1990: Stephen Levine and Nigel S. Roberts, "The New Zealand General Election of 1990," *Political Science*, vol. 43 (1991), pp. 1, 16; 1992: Stephen Levine and Nigel S. Roberts, "The Referendum Results," in A. McRobie, ed., *Taking It to the People? The New Zealand Electoral Debate* (Christchurch: Hazard Press, 1993), p. 57; 1993: New Zealand Department of Justice.

balances led to modification of the Electoral Act of 1956, including entrenched provisions dealing with basic constitutional matters: maximum terms and number of members of the House of Representatives, secret ballot, minimum voting age, and redistricting procedures. S. 189 of the act required that none of these might be amended or repealed except by a majority of 75 percent of the house's total membership or by a majority of electors at a referendum. S. 189 itself, however, was not entrenched; instead, reliance was placed on the unanimous vote for its passage to protect the substantive clauses.[2]

shopping hours may not be so vital an issue, any poll covering Adelaide involves 65–70 percent of South Australia's population.

2. See L. Cleveland and A. D. Robinson, eds., *Readings in Australian Government* (Wellington: Reed Educational, 1972), p. 272.

The referendum as a piece of constitutional machinery for involving the people in decision making at a high level can carry considerable ideological baggage. The initial drive for its adoption in the English-speaking Southwest Pacific early in the twentieth century reflected the contemporary North American enthusiasms of the Populist and Progressive movements mixed with evangelical Protestant initiatives through international organizations such as the Women's Christian Temperance Union and local bodies such as the New Zealand Alliance. Consequently, the referendum was often bracketed with the initiative and the recall, the other components of direct democracy endorsed by Populists and Progressives, although neither took root in Australia and New Zealand as firmly as the referendum did. Moreover, outside the sphere of constitutional amendments, the referendum was used mainly to settle those same WASP (White, Anglo-Saxon, Protestant) and rural-flavored moral issues: curbing the drink trade and promoting religious instruction in state schools (which was possible in the absence of an American-style First Amendment). Distrust of professional politicians and of the middle-class middlemen, who in economic and political matters were seen as misleading and exploiting the real producers of wealth, was a shared attitude on both sides of the Pacific.

In Australia and New Zealand, however, the institutions of parliamentary government were sufficiently well regarded for the more radical initiative and recall to attract little support outside the emerging Labor party and there only briefly. James Bryce's assessment at the time was that "Australian radicalism has not found them necessary" when Labor politicians relied more on their own disciplined caucus than on the electorate.[3] In 1913, a Labor party government in Western Australia did introduce an initiative and referendum bill that would have allowed legislation (other than appropriation measures) to be introduced on petition of 15 percent of the electorate: if passed, bills would become law; if not passed, they would be put to a referendum. The bill threatened the conservative Legislative Council, which defeated it. In 1919, the New Zealand Labour party included the initiative, referendum, and recall in its election policy but ran a poor third at the polls; when that party eventually came to office in 1935, direct democracy had been forgotten.

More recently, referendums on daylight saving time display similar anxieties about urban ignorance of, or hostility to, the rural way of life. In Australia, the second and strong wave of enthusiasm for the referendum and the initiative (but still with little attention to the recall)

---

3. James Bryce, *Modern Democracies*, vol. 2 (London: Macmillan, 1923), pp. 264–65.

has been actively stimulated by a strand of the Populist inheritance from America, Christian Patriot and Radical Right groups, and their local allies. During the first wave, the referendum was one device among many taken up by a reforming multigoaled Labor party; now the cause is championed most vigorously by small political parties, usually labeled by some single-issue derivation of direct democracy—Citizens Electoral Councils, Citizens Initiated Referendum Alliance, and the like—even though they may promote a wider range of far Right causes. In New Zealand, the right-wing Social Credit movement has endorsed the initiative, and the Left-Libertarian Values party increased use of the referendum.

Five uses for the referendum, as either employed or proposed, can be identified in Australia and New Zealand:

1. initial provision as the sole means of constitutional amendment
2. subsequent introduction to entrench a particular institution, like an upper house, or its powers or an electoral formula
3. legitimation of an especially important choice, such as a new state or an electoral system
4. removal of a controversial lifestyle question from the party-political arena
5. overturning of a major decision made by one part of the constitutional regime

The categories are not mutually exclusive. The first and fifth combined in Australia, for example, when the High Court declared unconstitutional the Menzies government's legislation aimed at banning the Australian Communist party, and a constitutional amendment was sought to secure for the federal legislature the power that the High Court had said it did not have. The electorate rejected the proposal in 1951. The first and second categories combined in Australia when opponents of malapportionment sought to add to the federal Constitution a one-vote–one-value formula binding on both the commonwealth and the states. The electorate rejected that proposal in 1988. In New Zealand, where constitutional flexibility largely avoids the other three, the third and fourth categories have predominated. There could, however, be a combination of the second and third whereby a major innovation, such as an enforceable bill of rights, is both legitimated and entrenched by a referendum.

Constitutional Amendment

Only the federal government has the power to initiate the process for altering the Australian federal Constitution, which ends with a referendum. While S. 128 of the Constitution allows for the possibility that either chamber might act by itself for this purpose, in practice the governor-general must issue a writ for the referendum to be held and acts only on the advice of the prime minister. Thus, the Senate's formal power is nugatory, and it would be impossible to carry a proposal if the House of Representatives acted alone against a hostile Senate.[4] Suggestions for alternative methods included allowing one or some proportion of the state legislatures to initiate; allowing special conventions or commissions to propose or to initiate; and introducing a citizens' initiative.[5]

There had also been some support for replacing the constitutional requirement of a double majority, a majority of the states and a majority of the electors, with only half (thus three rather than four) of the states and a majority of electors. Two amendments failed in 1946 because of the double majority provision; another two (1937, 1984) achieved narrow national majorities but were carried in only two states. The case for easing the rule had seemed especially pressing when more than 60 percent of electors nationally failed to carry a simultaneous House and Senate elections proposal in the necessary fourth state in 1977. But when support for a similar proposal was only half that figure a decade later in the 1988 referendums, enthusiasm for amending the amending procedure virtually disappeared.

In his earlier account of the strikingly poor success rate of constitutional referendums in Australia (even worse now than when he wrote, with only eight of forty-two proposals passed), Don Aitkin speculated that three factors worked against them: the high level of partisanship, the electorate's lack of information, and procedural hurdles such as the double majority.[6] There can be no doubt about the first factor and its adverse effect, although there may also be something of a skew visible on the record. The Australian Labor party, ostensibly the party of change, has been more ready to support amending proposals emanating from a coalition government formed by the Liberal and National parties than the coalition has been to throw its weight behind a

---

4. An extensive account of experience and recent proposals for change is provided by *Final Report of the Constitutional Commission*, vol. 2 (Canberra: Australian Government Publishing Service, 1988), chap. 13.

5. The most elaborate case for more extensive use of the referendum and initiative in Australia is Geoffrey deQ. Walker, *Initiative and Referendum: The People's Law* (Sydney: Centre for Independent Studies, 1987).

6. Don Aitkin, "Australia," in David Butler and Austin Ranney, eds., *Referendums: A Comparative Study of Practice and Theory* (Washington, D.C.: American Enterprise Institute, 1978), p. 124.

Labor party move. Indeed, the coalition in 1974 and 1978 campaigned against a proposal for simultaneous elections for the House and Senate that it had put forward itself in 1977, when in office. As the coalition parties proclaim their commitment to federalism and condemn the Labor party's half-hearted advocacy of centralism, and as proposals for altering the federal Constitution are unlikely to prune or abandon federal government powers, this is not surprising. But consequently, only when the coalition is in office will an amendment likely secure bipartisan support. Even then, there is no guarantee of success. In 1967, for example, the Democratic Labor party (a minor party commanding about 10 percent of the national vote) and a handful of rebel Liberal senators resoundingly defeated a bipartisan proposal to end the nexus of membership numbers of the two chambers of the federal legislature, the House of Representatives being required to have "as nearly as practicable" twice as many members as the Senate.

One related question is whether a referendum held by itself may be less at risk from partisan influences. The first problem is that a separate referendum costs a lot of money. The 1988 referendums cost A\$34.4 million (U.S.\$23.4 million at A\$1 = U.S.\$0.68); the additional cost (more paper and postage for the pamphlet, slightly longer hours for counting votes) for four questions rather than one would have been minor. Tacked onto a parliamentary election, the bill might have been an extra A\$10 million, spent almost entirely on printing, postage, and advertising. Apart from the, say, A\$25 million difference, a separate referendum might be less contaminated by partisanship, but hostility to the extra public expenditure and the likelihood of scare campaigns being heard in the quieter environment could cancel that advantage.

Another consideration is whether to combine a number of issues in one "question" or to keep them separate, to be voted on separately. In the 1944 "Fourteen Powers" referendum, one more affirmative vote would have given the commonwealth Parliament power for a transitional, postwar period of five years to legislate on a list of social and economic matters as well as to protect freedom of religion and speech and power against delegated legislation. In 1988, several rights and freedoms were combined in the one question. Both failed to pass, and comparison with other referendum votes at the same time or reasonably close in time suggests that an accumulation of negatives can be marginally harmful.

The point becomes important when a substantial and controversial change is contemplated—as replacing the monarchy with a republic is currently. The federal Labor government's starting position has been minimalist: pick out the provisions relating to the monarchy and replace them with equivalents for an elected president with identical powers. But many supporters of constitutional reform do not wish to pass up an opportunity to advance other favorite causes, such as reducing the Senate's powers, introducing fixed terms, and adding a bill of rights. On the other side, defenders of the monarchy argue that unless the conventions that supposedly fetter the sovereign's nominee in discharging widely drafted powers are made enforceable by inclusion in the Constitution, an elected president would be a potential dictator of at least Cromwellian proportions. If the government were to compromise with either in an attempt to broaden support, it would risk making the matter more complex and making an affirmative vote even more of a leap in the dark that partisans can make terrifying to the voters.

Moreover, seeking to change so fundamental an element in the federal Constitution opens up questions of what impact the changes might have on the constitutional arrangements of the six states. Would it be possible to introduce a republican form of federal government and still retain monarchical governments in some or all of the states? Should each state hold a simultaneous referendum to determine its own form of government? Do states need to do so? S. 106 of the present federal Constitution provides, somewhat obscurely, that after federation, each state constitution is "subject to" the federal Constitution "until altered in accordance with" the state constitution. Fearing a republican coup by an earlier Labor federal government, Queensland sought to entrench the office of state governor and through it the monarchy by prescribing a referendum for any state-level change. Other states now under coalition governments might rush to introduce the same defensive strategy if a federal referendum comes closer. There is also some uncertainty, however, as to whether the states' ability to entrench institutions using the referendum device extends past the legislature to the executive. Whatever the final ruling on the constitutional law, which could take years of experimental legislation and litigation to resolve, it would be difficult to deny voters wearing their state hats the same right to choose between queen and president that they have when wearing their federal hats.

Political partisanship might also help to explain why Australian referendum results—exceptionally so by the experience in New Zealand and other countries—so often fall between the parameters of 60 and 40 percent that traditionally have marked the extremes of the electoral pendulum's swing. Electoral behavior in New Zealand, however, so closely resembles Australian patterns that their divergence on this point would require a more convincing explanation than the present referendum voting studies in either country allow.

Solid evidence as to whether an uninformed electorate handicaps constitutional referendum proposals is lacking. Market research associated with recent attempts to review and revise the federal Constitution found that a high proportion of electors were unaware that there *was* a federal Constitution, much less having any command of its detail. There also appears to be much uncertainty about the existence in each state jurisdiction of two separate constitutions, one federal, the other state. When asked to alter something about which they know nothing, the argument goes, electors behave rationally and refuse to do so. Conversely, there is an apparent tendency for support for passing an amendment to be higher at the start of each campaign than at the end: as electors become better informed, they are more likely to vote No to any change. Quite possibly "better informed" really means "more alarmed." Barely a month before the Australian 1988 referendum, polls showed each question with a clear majority, but each question then dropped between twenty-five (local government) and forty (rights and freedoms) percentage points over that month and were soundly defeated.[7]

The information made available to electors comes from three sources. Media coverage includes the better daily newspapers, which do a reasonable job; the rest of print, which say little; and the electronic media, which are not naturally suited to referendum-type questions unless they can be turned into human interest stories in the way a daylight saving vote can. That coverage is supplemented by advertising in the media by interested groups and to a modest extent by the political parties. When a parliamentary election is held on the same day the volume of referendum-oriented advertising may be augmented by party or candidate-oriented material, but when the referendum is held by itself, party purse strings are unlikely to be loosened much.

That throws the burden for educating and informing the electorate onto the third source, the official pamphlet posted to every elector on the national roll by the federal electoral agency, the Australian Electoral Commission (AEC). The text is supplied by those who voted for and against the particular referendum's enabling legislation as it passed through the federal Parliament.[8] A national telephone poll (*n* = 996) conducted three days before the 1988 referendums reported 87

---

7. Morgan Gallup Poll, *Bulletin*, 23 August 1988, p. 20.

8. The Commonwealth's Referendum (Machinery Provisions) Act of 1984 parallels the Commonwealth Electoral Act of 1918 provisions in most voting arrangements. It regulates the pamphlet's number of words (2,000 for and 2,000 against for each proposal), and, since 1984, prohibits the federal government from spending any money to present arguments for or against, except on the pamphlet (including translations and sight-impaired versions).

percent of respondents saying that they had received their pamphlet and 62 percent saying that they had read it, with the older electors more likely to have read it than the younger. Because of the sensitivity of such information, only after the poll had been conducted did the AEC obtain from the polling organization the responses it had secured at the time as to how electors intended voting on the four questions. Consistently over all questions, those who claimed to have read the pamphlet were less likely to vote affirmatively than those who had received it but not read it or had not received it; they were also less likely to be undecided.[9]

The less-routinized referendums of New Zealand and the Australian states often have comparable arrangements. For the 1992 electoral system referendum, the minister of justice set up a panel presided over by an ombudsman to conduct a public education campaign, which included a brochure sent to every household, a more detailed guide, three television programs, and a videotape. Partisan cases were advanced by the Electoral Reform Coalition, which had been in existence for some years, and the Campaign for Better Government formed to oppose change.

To Aitkin's three factors might be added a fourth, antipathy to the federal government per se. To the extent that Canberra is perceived as a remote, hostile, and selfish force in Australian politics, any proposal to tamper with the federal constitution is perceived as a potential Trojan horse for the aggrandizement of alien influences. The role of the Senate as guardian of states' rights has been enhanced, after the introduction of the single transferable vote form of proportional representation in 1949, by the likelihood that the government of the day will lack a majority in it. Thus, any proposal to diminish the Senate, for example, by requiring it to be elected on the same day as the House of Representatives, will be portrayed as a dangerous attack on the federal principle that protects the states, especially the smaller states.

Initially, there were considerable variations in the readiness of individual states to amend the Constitution. Before 1949, when the coalition returned to federal office for a protracted stay, the two larger states in twenty-three opportunities voted for change six times (New South Wales) and nine times (Victoria). Two of the smaller states were much more ready to support change: Western Australia voted Yes eighteen times, and Queensland, sixteen. One, South Australia, was slightly more ready, voting Yes eleven times; the smallest state, Tasmania, was

---

9. Australian Electoral Commission, *Sources of Electoral Information: Research Report No. 1 of 1989* (Canberra: Australian Government Publishing Service, 1989), chap. 5.

TABLE 5–3
VOTING BY STATE AND TERRITORY IN AUSTRALIA, 1988
(percent of valid votes cast)

State	Parliamentary Terms	Fair Elections	Local Government	Rights and Freedoms	Total Vote (millions)
New South Wales	31.7	35.6	31.7	29.6	3.298
Victoria	36.2	40.1	36.1	33.4	2.491
Queensland	35.2	44.8	38.3	32.9	1.552
Western Australia	30.7	32.0	29.8	28.1	0.845
South Australia	26.8	30.6	29.8	26.0	0.874
Tasmania	25.3	28.9	27.5	25.5	0.283
Australian Capital Territory	43.6	52.0	39.8	40.7	0.149
NT	38.1	43.0	38.8	37.1	0.056
AUS	32.9	37.6	33.6	30.8	9.548

SOURCE: Australian Electoral Commission, *1988 Referendums Statistics* (Canberra: Australian Government Publishing Service, 1990).

the least ready, at only five times. But since 1949, only the largest state, New South Wales, stands out, voting for change on eleven of the nineteen possible occasions, when each of the other states did so only five times. The latest referendums, the four voted on in 1988, recorded remarkably uniform results among the states (table 5–3).

Although the average would suggest that an attempt to amend the federal Constitution occurs about once every five years, the record is more irregular (see table 5–1). In particular, the long gap between 1951 and 1967—three times the average spacing—is attributed to Sir Robert Menzies's frustration with the communism referendum of 1951,[10] close run though it was, and his reluctance to risk another such rejection by the electorate. The exceptionally low affirmative votes in 1988, it might be thought, counsel another long period of abstention. The people do not want constitutional change and have said so loudly when rejecting a mixed lot of proposals. The symbolic attraction of the coincidence of the start of the next millennium with the centenary of the federal Constitution in 2001, however, has encouraged yet another period of amending ferment in which a proposal to replace the hereditary monarch with an elected president is the most prominent feature.

---

10. See Leicester Webb, *Communism and Democracy in Australia: A Survey of the 1951 Referendum* (Melbourne: F. W. Cheshire, 1954).

Entrenching

Unlike the Australian federal Constitution, the New Zealand and the several Australian state constitutions are capable of self-modification to vary the "manner and form" of the legislative process by requiring a special majority when the legislature itself is voting or by requiring the consent of the electorate at a referendum (for a list of state referendums held in Australia through 1992, see table 5–4).[11] In 1908 in Queensland, for example, following a state election in which the proposal had been canvassed, a moderate coalition government including some ex-Labor members repealed the previous requirement of two-thirds majorities for amendments to the state's constitutional legislation and introduced the Parliamentary Bills Referendum Bill, which would have put to a referendum bills that the upper house had rejected or refused to pass. As Queensland was one of the two states that had retained a nominated upper chamber, dissolution as a means of resolving intercameral disagreements was not available. The bill's passage had the desired effect of moderating the upper house's obstruction until the acid test came in 1917. Then, legislation to abolish the Legislative Council was itself defeated in the upper house and subsequently rejected by the electorate in the ensuing referendum. Instead, the Labor government had to pack the council with new members, who voted for its abolition, and a subsequent Labor government then entrenched unicameralism by requiring that a referendum be held before legislation to restore an upper house could be valid.

In 1933 in New South Wales, the other state to retain a nominated upper house, attempts to pack the council failed when some members of the suicide squad reneged. In a series of steps, coalition governments then secured an indirectly elected upper chamber modeled on the recommendations of the United Kingdom's Bryce Conference of 1917 and protected from abolition by requirement that a referendum be inaugurated.[12] When in the 1970s a Labor government wished to replace indirect election with direct election, a further referendum was required. It was carried, with almost 85 percent of the electorate agreeing to the change.

Important Choices

An elected government faced with a difficult and potentially unpopular decision may legitimately believe that it lacks a mandate and, rather

---

11. See R. D. Lumb, *The Constitutions of the Australian States* (St. Lucia: University of Queensland Press, 1963 and later editions).

12. See Ken Turner, *House of Review: The New South Wales Legislative Council, 1934–68* (Sydney: Sydney University Press, 1969), chap. 1.

TABLE 5–4
AUSTRALIAN REFERENDUMS AT THE STATE AND TERRITORY LEVEL, 1903–1993
(percent of valid votes cast)

State	Date	Subject	Yes Votes
New South Wales	16 Dec. 1903	Reduced size of legislative assembly	72.9
	10 June 1916	Bar closing at 6 p.m.	62.4
	1 Sept. 1928	Prohibition of liquor sales	28.5
	23 May 1933	Reform & Legislative Council	51.5
	15 Feb. 1947	Bar closing at 6 p.m.	62.4
	13 Nov. 1954	Bar closing at 10 p.m.	50.3
	29 Apr. 1961	Abolition of Legislative Council	44.7
	29 Apr. 1967	New state in Northeast New South Wales (voting in proposed new state area)	45.8
	29 Nov. 1969	Open bars on Sundays	42.0
	1 May 1976	Daylight saving time	63.0
	17 June 1978	Direct election of Legislative Council	84.8
Victoria	1 June 1904	Keep public education secular	58.6
	1 June 1904	Scripture lessons in schools	53.0
	1 June 1904	Use of certain prayers and hymns	51.2
	21 Oct. 1920	Local-option sale of liquor	52.9
	29 Mar. 1930	Abolition of liquor licensing	42.9
	8 Oct. 1938	Abolition of liquor licensing	33.6
	24 Mar. 1956	Bar closing at 10 p.m.	39.7
Queensland	13 April 1910	Religious instruction	56.7
	5 May 1917	Abolition of Legislative Council	39.3
	30 Oct. 1920	Prohibition of liquor sales	41.6
	6 Oct. 1923	Prohibition of liquor sales	36.2
	23 Mar. 1991	Extension of Parliament term of Legislative Assembly	48.7
	22 Feb. 1992	Daylight saving time	45.5
Western Australia	4 Apr. 1925	Prohibition of liquor sales	34.9
	8 Apr. 1933	Secession from the Commonwealth	66.2
	8 Apr. 1933	Constitutional convention	42.5

(Table continues)

167

TABLE 5–4 (continued)

State	Date	Subject	Yes Votes
	9 Dec. 1950	Prohibition of liquor sales	26.5
	8 Mar. 1975	Daylight saving time	46.3
	7 Apr. 1984	Daylight saving time	45.6
	4 Apr. 1992	Daylight saving time	46.9
South	26 Apr. 1911	Raise parliamentary salaries	32.5
Australia	27 Mar. 1915	Bar closing at 6 p.m.	56.3
	20 Nov. 1965	Establishment of state lottery	65.7
	19 Sept. 1970	Shopping hours (voting in metropolitan area only)	48.0
	6 Nov. 1982	Daylight saving time	71.6
	9 Feb. 1991	Electoral redistricting	76.7
Tasmania	25 Mar. 1916	Bar closing at 6 p.m.	58.7
	14 Dec. 1968	Establishment of Wrest Point casino	53.0
	12 Dec. 1981	Gordon River hydroelectric power development	54.7
Australian Capital Territory	15 Feb. 1992	Single transferable vote electoral system	65.3

Sources: 1903–1978: Don Aitkin, "Australia," in David Butler and Austin Ranney, eds., *Referendums: A Comparative Study in Practice and Theory* (Washington, D.C.: American Enterprise Institute, 1978), p. 125; 1981–1992: official returns published by the respective state and territory electoral commissions and offices.

than try to focus the electorate's attention on the matter in a general election called for the purpose, may put it to the people directly by referendum. But there are also times when a political hot potato is tossed to the people for less worthy motives, such as to avoid splitting the government or to overwhelm an opposition's resistance to the measure. Governments constantly face important choices but rarely turn them into popular referendums; the process that directs a government's thoughts in that direction is not easily identified.

Federal Australia's two votes on conscription for overseas service in 1916 and 1917, both narrowly defeated, are good examples although they came at a time when interest in the referendum was still strong. New Zealand's equivalent vote on peacetime conscription took place much later, early in the cold war, but again reflected British Commonwealth solidarity. It was carried easily with the endorsement of both major parties, though with a low (for New Zealand) turnout of only 63 percent. Recourse to the referendum was probably intended more to circumvent opposition within the governing Labour party than to let the people decide.[13]

The other federal Australian vote was for the selection of a national song (rather than a national anthem), concurrently with the constitutional referendums of 1977; "Advance, Australia Fair" came close to a majority (43.4 percent) over three alternatives. The subsequent general acceptance of the song makes it likely that should a replacement for the present national flag be proposed, that choice too would be put to a referendum.

Another incident of manipulation was the new state referendum of 1967 in New South Wales. The Liberal majority in a coalition government subverted the long-standing aspirations of their Country party partner for the secession of the northeastern corner of the state to form a solid Country party fiefdom. Such an outcome would have made it more difficult for the Liberals ever to win a majority in the part of the state that remained. The voting territory was arbitrarily extended southward to include the Hunter Valley region, where hostility to the idea overturned the majority in the area that should have been making the decision. More virtuously, the Askin government commissioned a local political science department to produce cases both for and against the proposal.

A more complicated affair was the 1981 vote in Tasmania, which followed cabinet dissent leading to the deposition of the premier and bitter conflict between the House of Assembly and the Legislative Council. Electors were told that both houses favored a new hydroelectric scheme on the Gordon River and they could choose whether it would be placed below the junction with the Franklin River or above the junction with the Olga River. A third of the ballot papers were marked "no dams"; 45 percent of those were declared invalid because their marking departed from a strict interpretation of the special stat-

---

13. Arend Lijphart's suggestion that the occasional use of referendums in New Zealand mitigates that country's otherwise overwhelming majoritarianism has been rejected on the ground that political manipulation is often the explanation. In 1949, the National party, which wanted conscription, was prepared to help the Labour party out of its internal difficulties, while in 1967 inclusion of a choice between a three-year term and a four-year term was a makeweight to the real question, which was the 10 o'clock closing of bars, thrown to the electors to give them something to vote against while easing licensing hours. See Keith Jackson, *The Dilemma of Parliament* (Wellington: Allen and Unwin, 1987), p. 29.

ute under which the referendum had been conducted.[14] The lesson learned was that a combination of compulsory voting with a formulation of a referendum question that ignores the wishes of a large part of the electorate will produce a messy result.

More interesting for political scientists have been the relatively recent New Zealand and Australian Capital Territory (ACT) referendums to select electoral systems. ACT residents were aggrieved about a strange hybrid of party list and single transferable vote procedures cobbled together in the federal Parliament and imposed on the ACT with somewhat bizarre results.[15] Unable to agree on what might replace it, the federal government and opposition could at least agree to let the local electorate decide. New Zealanders felt growing dissatisfaction with the vote-counting procedure of first past the post, which grossly exaggerated swings and frequently gave a majority of seats to the party that did not have a majority of votes.

The erratic voting patterns of the 1984 Australian election brought a reforming Labor government into office. Subsequently, a royal commission was appointed to look at the national electoral system. Its impressive report included a recommendation for a referendum to select a new electoral system and a proposal to extend the term for the House of Representatives (which already required a referendum).

During the 1987 election campaign, the prime minister unexpectedly promised to hold referendums for a longer term and for the introduction of proportional representation. A referendum on the first was held with the 1990 general election; the Labor government was soundly defeated, and extension of the House's term to four years just as soundly rejected. The new National government then chose to implement its predecessor's second referendum commitment in 1992 as a double-barreled question. First, did the electors wish to retain the first-past-the-post method; second, which of four alternatives did they prefer? If there were a vote for change, the government promised, there would then be a second—this time binding—vote to choose between the existing system and whichever of the four alternatives had been most popular at the first referendum. In both cases, observers were surprised at the size of the majorities for substantial change—in the case of the ACT, contrary to the wishes and interests of the dominant

14. Terry Newman, *Referenda in Tasmania* (Hobart: Tasmanian Parliamentary Library, 1984).

15. Commonwealth of Australia, Parliament, Joint Standing Committee on Electoral Matters, *Inquiry into the ACT Election and Electoral System* (Canberra: Australian Government Publishing Service, 1989).

party, the Labor party, and in the case of New Zealand, contrary to the interests of both major parties.[16]

The final referendum in New Zealand was held with the November 1993 general election. As two substantial minor parties shared the vote with the two unpopular major parties, this promised, and delivered, a vivid demonstration of the failings of the existing first-past-the-post system. The National government with 35 percent of the vote secured an absolute majority by one seat, while the balance of power nearly went to the two minor parties: their 27 percent of the vote gave them merely 4 percent of the seats. In the referendum itself, business interests campaigned expensively for the status quo and strong government. Survey support for the proposed proportional system declined sharply during the campaign, one poll even showing it slightly behind retention of first past the post. A vote of 54 percent in favor of change, however, appears to have settled the matter, coupled as it was with a high turnout of 82.5 percent (because of the simultaneous general election) and the blatant disparity between votes and seats recorded.

The decline in support for a proportional system might be attributed in part to the failure of the two new alternatives to the two old parties to make convincing cases as to why they ought to be in Parliament, in part to improving economic conditions having rehabilitated the parties that had appeared responsible for so much hardship. Had the outgoing government come closer to an absolute majority of votes, there might have been a temptation to advocate caution in changing an electoral system that might be rectifying past problems, but the disparity between votes and seats remained too wide for that.

Lifestyle Questions

Two early questions—drinking alcoholic beverages and reading the Scriptures in schools—have predominated, though gambling by off-course betting, state lottery, or casino has accounted for a few referendums. At the first licensing poll in 1911 in New Zealand, a majority (55.8 percent) actually voted for prohibition; it was not implemented, but many bars were closed and the minimum drinking age set at

---

16. Stephen Levine and Nigel S. Roberts, "The New Zealand Electoral Referendum of 1992," *Electoral Studies*, 12(2) (1993): pp. 158–67; Alan Simpson, ed., *Referendums: Constitutional and Political Perspectives* (Wellington: Department of Politics, Victoria University of Wellington, 1992); Alan McRobie, *Taking it to the People? The New Zealand Electoral Referendum Debate* (Christchurch: Hazard Press, 1993).

twenty-one. During World War I, support for prohibition remained high, and further majorities were narrowly missed at the two polls held in 1919: only the votes from troops still overseas tipped the balance.[17] Neither drinking, religious instruction, nor gambling is likely to produce major political conflict today, but new issues can. In the 1978 election, the New Zealand Labour party promised such a referendum on abortion.

Since the mid-1970s, conflict over daylight saving time in the three Australian states with the largest areas has been passed to the electorate to resolve because, as the electoral commissioner of Queensland wrote in his report on the 1992 referendum in that state, "the issue divided Queenslanders as no other single issue has done [and] was one which recommended itself to a direct appeal to the people of Queensland for resolution."[18] The general empathy for those experiencing the hardships of rural life undercuts the vote for commercial interests and relaxation in the largest cities. The outcome is likely to be a conservative vote for "God's time," which is what some rural people call standard time.

Overturning Decisions

The poor rate of success of constitutional referendums has given the referendum device a reputation for conservatism in Australia: when asked, people are likely to vote for the status quo and reject change. Entrenchments that require a referendum may provide more secure protection for elements of constitutional machinery, an upper house or the lack thereof, than would special majorities, which might be overwhelmed by wide swings of the electoral pendulum under the majoritarian alternative vote. In the late 1970s, the federal High Court began to appear more adventurous, in particular when it allowed the treaty-making power to extend the federal government's competence into previously state spheres such as race relations and environmental questions. At that time, proposals were made that the referendum might be employed to rein in a runaway court, for example, by putting new treaties to a referendum or by amending the Constitution to subject the nomination of High Court justices to wider scrutiny, possibly by state governments.

Following their latest and most controversial decision, which over-

---

17. For statistics, see J. O. Wilson, *New Zealand Parliamentary Record, 1840–1984* (Wellington: Government Printer, 1985), pp. 298–300.

18. Electoral Commission Queensland, *Statistical Returns 1992: Daylight Saving Referendum* (Brisbane: Goprint, 1992), p. 1.

turned the common law's doctrine of *terra nullius* and thereby allowed the possibility of a limited number of land claims by some Aboriginal and Torres Strait Islander groups, one hostile state premier has proposed that a referendum be held to establish whether the people want the High Court judgment reversed and the previous common-law position restored. Similarly, local government authorities threatened with boundary alterations or amalgamations as a consequence of state government reforms demand that a referendum be held before any change is made or conduct their own to display the evidence that the people do not want change. For some years to come, interest in the referendum—in Australia at least; the position in New Zealand is less certain—will be as much about putting the device to new or relatively little-known uses as about its traditional role with written constitutions.

6
Eastern Europe and the Former Soviet Union

Henry E. Brady and Cynthia S. Kaplan

Cataclysmic political change destroys old authority structures and triggers a search for new forms of legitimacy. The referendum is one device among many others such as military force, terror, strikes and protests, elections, and elite bargaining that can be used to bolster or undermine authority. Referendums have the great virtue that, in this age of democratic aspirations, they produce legitimate authority using the gold standard of political support: individual ballots cast in an election.

The resort to referendums in Eastern Europe and the former Soviet Union has ebbed and flowed during the past seventy-five years with the region's passage through three sweeping transformations: (1) the post–World War I breakup of the Russian, Austro-Hungarian, and German empires and the formation of the Soviet Union and weak democratic states in Eastern Europe; (2) the post–World War II creation of Communist states in Eastern Europe; and (3) the breakup of the Soviet bloc and the Soviet Union itself between 1989 and 1991. After each upheaval, the authority to rule and the legitimacy to support that rule had to be created anew—providing ample reason for leaders to turn to the referendum.

Yet referendums have grave limitations. To put a question to the populace, one must have enough authority to carry out a referendum,

Our thanks to Sabine Hüebner Monien for meticulous and dedicated research assistance. In addition, our thanks go to the National Science Foundation for grant number SES-9122389, to the U.S. Institute of Peace for grant number USIP-049-92F, to the John D. and Catherine T. MacArthur Foundation, the Committee on Science and Technology, Supreme Soviet, USSR, and the Academy of Sciences, USSR. For help in collecting the data on citizen participation in Russia and Estonia, we thank William Smirnov, Vladimir Andreenkov, and Andrus Star.

and authorities inevitably shape, or even squash, referendum questions to protect their own interests. To enforce the results of a referendum, especially if it contradicts the position of established authorities, there must be a devotion to democracy and democratic principles that may be lacking. Referendums, as a truly democratic device, work best with leaders in a knife-edge situation where they have enough authority to carry out and respond to the results of the referendum but not so much authority that they can disdain inconvenient outcomes or, in extreme cases, determine the outcome. Yet when such conditions prevail, when leaders have just enough authority to carry out a referendum but no more than that, referendums put leaders at the mercy of a fickle public who can confer legitimacy but little authority and at the whim of other elites who may choose to protect their authority by ignoring the public. For these reasons, referendums have been less important than elite bargaining, military force, and police repression in shaping Eastern European and Soviet history, but at the moments when these techniques have faltered or when elites have sought other methods, referendums have been important.

After World War I, the Wilsonian ideals of self-determination and democratic settlement of disputed sovereignties led to the third European episode of widespread experimentation with referendums.[1] The League of Nations used plebiscites to decide postwar territorial disputes. The frail new governments of Eastern Europe employed referendums to obtain the legitimacy needed for governance. This sometimes led to Bonapartism—plebiscitary democracy as the servant of authoritarian regimes. But it was nevertheless the first widespread use of referendums for governing. After World War II, political leaders, the large military occupation forces, and the rapid onset of the cold war provided little room for democratic solutions to questions of sovereignty or governance, and referendums were little used.

From 1987 to the present, referendums have arguably been as important as strikes, protests, and elections as tools for refashioning authority. They have, in Poland, Hungary, and the Soviet Union, shown Communist party elites that they could not bulwark their faltering power with popular support. They have been vital in determining sovereignty and independence throughout the Soviet Union, and they have, so far, played a largely constructive role in creating democratic

---

1. In France, between 1791 and 1804 there were at least twelve national and regional referendums. Between the democratic uprisings of 1848 and the Franco-Prussian War of 1870, there were over twenty referendums in nations or subparts of Europe (see appendix A of this book). Referendums, not surprisingly, proliferate when democracy is in fashion.

175

systems. It still remains to be seen whether they will also become the tools of emperors, führers, or "conducators."[2]

Seventy-five Years of Referendums

The Number of Referendums. The first free referendum in Eastern Europe since World War II occurred in Poland in 1987. Before this date, from 1900 to 1986, there were seventeen countrywide referendum questions (on fifteen separate dates) in Eastern Europe[3] (see table 6–1) and five plebiscites in disputed areas involving Eastern European countries. Ten of the seventeen countrywide referendums occurred in

---

2. The reference is to Napoleon I and Napoleon III, both of whom used the title *emperor*, Adolf Hitler who used *führer*, and General Ion Antonescu of Romania who called himself *conducator* (a term meaning "exalted leader"). All four used referendums in their rise to power. Nicolae Ceausescu, in addition to Antonescu, also called himself conducator and abused the referendum device.

3. The area covered in this chapter includes the fifteen union republics of the Soviet Union and what became known as Eastern Europe after World War II—namely, the German Democratic Republic, Poland, Czechoslovakia, Hungary, Romania, Bulgaria, Albania, and Yugoslavia. For the sake of simplicity, we will refer, sometimes anachronistically, to the fifteen republics that were part of the USSR in the late 1980s, as the Soviet Union or the former Soviet Union. The Central Asian republics are Kazakhstan, Kirghizia, Tadjikistan, Turkmenistan, and Uzbekistan. The Caucasian republics are Armenia, Azerbaijan, and Georgia. The Baltics are, of course, Estonia, Latvia, and Lithuania. We include the Baltics as part of Eastern Europe for the interwar years but place them among the Soviet Republics from 1945 onward. By the Balkans, we mean the four countries on the Balkan peninsula that had Communist governments until 1989—namely, Romania, Bulgaria, Albania, and Yugoslavia. This excludes the Balkan countries of Greece and the European part of Turkey. We will use the locution *East Central Europe* to refer to the remaining states of Poland, Czechoslovakia, Hungary, and sometimes also the German Democratic Republic.

Including Austria, Germany, and Greece (all arguably part of the area we are studying) would have added fifteen nationwide referendums to our list. All but four held in Greece between 1946 and 1974 took place during the interwar period. In the text, we allude to the series of five right-wing and fascist referendums in Germany from 1929 to 1938. (There was also one in 1926 in Germany on the confiscation of royal property.) The eight referendums in Greece all dealt with the form of government, whether monarchy or republic, in one way or another. The one referendum in Austria involved the approval of the Anschluss in 1938. There were also five referendums in subordinate territories in Austria and Germany in the years after World War I (Vorarlberg, Tyrol, Salzburg, Schleswig, and the Saar) and one in the Saar in 1955. These events provide additional evidence for the points made in the text.

TABLE 6–1
REFERENDUMS IN EASTERN EUROPE, 1900–1986

Country/Question	Date	Percent Yes	Percent Turnout
The Baltics			
Estonia			
Restore religious instruction	17–19 Feb. 1923	71.7	66.2
Constitutional reform	19 Aug. 1932	49.2	90.5
Presidential government	10–12 June 1933	32.6	66.5
Presidentialism and ministerial responsibility	14–16 Oct. 1933	72.6	77.9
Convene Constituent Assembly	23–25 Feb. 1936	76.1	80
Latvia			
Minority religious rights	Summer 1931	No	
Lithuania None			
The Balkans			
Albania None			
Bulgaria			
Trials for "war crimes"	19 Nov. 1922	73.1	
End monarchy	8 Sept. 1946	95.1	89.2
Approve constitution	16 May 1971	99.7	99.7
Romania			
Approve constitution	24 Feb. 1938	99.9	92
Approve Antonescu government	2 Mar. 1941	99.9	
Approve Antonescu government	9 Nov. 1941	99.9	
Reduce spending by 5 percent	23 Nov. 1986	100.0	
Yugoslavia None			
Countrywide Referendums in East Central Europe			
Czechoslovakia None			
German Democratic Republic			
Approve constitution	16 Apr. 1968	94.5	98.1
Hungary None			
Poland			
Abolish Senate	30 June 1946	68.0	87.6
Economic system permanent	30 June 1946	77.1	87.6
Approve Baltic and eastern frontiers	30 June 1946	91.4	87.6

(Table continues)

TABLE 6–1 (continued)

Country/Question	Year	Percent Yes	Percent Turnout
Plebiscites in Disputed Areas in East Central Europe			
Allenstein			
Germany, not Poland	11 July 1920	97.8	87
Marienwerder			
Germany, not Poland	11 July 1920	92.1	87
Klagenfurt			
Austria, not Yugoslavia	10 Oct. 1920	59.0	95.8
Sopron			
Hungary, not Austria	17 Dec. 1921	65.1	89.5
Upper Silesia			
Germany, not Poland	20 Mar. 1921	59.7	97.5

SOURCE: David Butler and Austin Ranney, *Referendums: A Comparative Study of Practice and Theory* (Washington, D.C.: American Enterprise Institute, 1978), appendixes A and B.

the interwar years, and all five plebiscites occurred in 1920 and 1921. During Communist rule in Eastern Europe from 1946 to 1986, only seven referendum questions were posed in Eastern Europe—and except for the three Polish questions of 1946, the outcome of these referendums was a foregone conclusion as they elicited participation of over 98 percent and agreement of over 95 percent. No referendums occurred in the Soviet Union during this entire period.

The absence of referendums in the Soviet Union and their circumscribed use in Eastern Europe under Communist rule is especially striking given the early Bolshevik enthusiasm for self-determination and referendums. The Petrograd Soviet, in one of its first decrees on 8 November 1917, mentioned plebiscites as a method of ensuring self-determination. At the Brest-Litovsk Peace Conference, Leon Trotsky, the Soviet commissar of foreign affairs, demanded that free referendums be used to decide the fate of occupied areas and national groups; and in its initial relations with the Ukraine and Georgia, the Soviet government promised referendums. The Soviet Constitution of 6 July 1923 even provides for the right of each union republic to withdraw from the union, although the method is not specified. Bolshevik practice soon departed from these principles, and no referendums were ever held.[4] The Petrograd Soviet's endorsement of self-determination

---

4. Sarah Wambaugh, *Plebiscites since the World War* (Washington, D.C.: Carnegie Endowment for International Peace, 1933), pp. 7–10.

TABLE 6-2
REFERENDUMS IN EASTERN EUROPE, 1987–1993

Country/Question	Date	Percent Turnout	Percent Yes
The Balkans			
Albania None			
Bulgaria None			
Romania			
New constitution	8 Dec. 1991	77.3	69.1
Yugoslavia (See table 6–7)			
East Central Europe			
Czechoslovakia None			
Hungary			
Presidential elections after parliamentary elections	26 Nov. 1989	55	50.0
Party out of workplace	26 Nov. 1989	55	95.1
CP give account of assets	26 Nov. 1989	55	95.4
Workers' guards disbanded?	26 Nov. 1989	55	94.9
President elected	29 July 1990	13.9	85.9
Poland			
CP economic reform	29 Nov. 1987	67.3	64
CP political reform	29 Nov. 1987	67.3	69

SOURCES: Compiled by the authors from Foreign Broadcast Information Services, Daily Report, *East Europe*, 1987–1993; Andras Bozoki, Andras Korosenyi, and George Schopflin, eds., *Post-Communist Transition: Emerging Pluralism in Hungary* (New York: St. Martin's Press, 1993); George Sanford, ed., *Democratization in Poland, 1988–90: Polish Voices* (New York: St. Martin's Press, 1992).

and populist democracy yielded to the Leninist dictatorship of the proletariat, Stalinist nationalities' policy, which assumed a withering away of nationalities during the building of a Communist state, and the *Realpolitik* of European security, which had little patience with national aspirations.

Once the fermenting brew of nationalism, self-determination, democracy, and economic change was shaken by Gorbachev's policies of *perestroika* and *glasnost*, it could be stoppered no more, and from 1987 to the end of 1993, thirty-three referendum questions were posed: eight in Eastern Europe listed in table 6–2 (not including at least sixteen referendums in parts of Yugoslavia listed in table 6–7) and twenty-five[5]

5. The 17 March 1991 All-Union referendum detailed in table 6–3 counts as only one referendum. All referendums (at least seven) in autonomous republics within Russia and Georgia are also excluded.

on the territory of the former Soviet Union listed in tables 6–3 to 6–5. Indeed, all but two of these referendum questions (those posed in the 1987 Polish referendum) were asked between 1989 and 1993. This extraordinary explosion of activity has accompanied the transition crises faced by these countries.

Transition Crises. In a transition period, three major decisions must be faced: What nation-state is this? What form of government shall it have? What policies shall it follow? The thirty-three referendums in Eastern Europe and the former Soviet Union since 1987 can be readily placed into these three categories. Twelve of these referendums were concerned with sovereignty or independence, nine with constitutions or the form of governance, and twelve with policy issues including confidence in leaders, the economic system, and the disposition of armies and militia.[6]

Referendums in earlier periods can also be classified in this way. After World War I, many regions of the former German, Austro-Hungarian, and Russian empires had to redefine their nationhood. Although their problems differed, ranging from Czechoslovakia's and Yugoslavia's need to invent themselves to Poland's and Lithuania's need for reinvention, almost all faced substantial uncertainty about who and what they were. At the Paris Peace Conference (1919), many nationalities found themselves at odds with the peacemakers' plans. Initially, President Wilson's support for self-determination led many to believe that the Peace Conference would endorse a wholesale use of referendums to determine sovereignty, but Wilson himself apparently did not favor plebiscites, and they were proposed for only four areas

---

6. Independence and sovereignty referendums were easily classified because they contained those words. Referendums on the form of government all referred to constitutions or constitutional features of the political system (for example, presidency for the Russian Soviet Federated Socialist Republic, the Union Treaty for the USSR, the powers of the presidency in Lithuania, or the way the president would be chosen in Hungary). The 1987 Polish referendum was also included here even though it merely referred to the "Polish model of deep democratization of political life" because it amounted to an endorsement of Jaruzelski's approach to governmental reform. Referendums on policy issues ranged from those on economic reform in Poland and Russia, on confidence in the current leader in Azerbaijan and Russia, on broad (and vague) policy statements in Turkmenistan, the role of the Communist party and the militia in Hungary, the rights of noncitizens in Estonia, the withdrawal of the Red Army from Lithuania, or on the need for early elections in Russia. Some of these, such as those on voting rights or the role of the Communist party, might be considered votes on forms of government.

in Eastern Europe.[7] As Sarah Wambaugh noted,

> It is true that the Allies avoided a plebiscite in every region of first importance save that of Upper Silesia, and that when they resorted to a plebiscite it was as a method of compromise, to escape from a dilemma rather than as a deliberate choice. Nevertheless, the treaties made at Paris . . . provided for by far the most important plebiscites ever held concerning changes of sovereignty.[8]

Referendums were particularly important for some countries as they tried to define the type of government they would have. Outside Eastern Europe, referendums punctuated the movement toward authoritarian rule in Germany and Italy, and they served the same role in Estonia and Romania. In Germany, Hitler used a series of four referendums between 1933 and 1938 to consolidate his rule. Mussolini did the same in Italy through two referendums in 1929 and 1934, and General Ion Antonescu followed suit in Romania through two referendums in 1941. In all these cases, a succession of referendums with nearly 100 percent turnouts and 100 percent Yes votes marked the onset of authoritarian rule. The four referendums in Estonia between 1932 and 1936 showed less unanimity, and the authoritarian government of Konstantin Päts was correspondingly less draconian than its counterparts in Germany, Italy, or even Romania. Nevertheless, in all these countries, the referendum was primarily a device whereby right-wing parties consolidated their power, and not a method whereby democracy was served.

Although the referendum device was, by historical standards, much used during this period, there were also many more opportunities for its use. The map of Europe was completely redrawn after World War I; there were more democracies in Europe than ever before; and many areas, including parts of what was to become the Soviet Union— the Baltic states, the Caucasus, and the Central Asian republics—were in the process of defining themselves and their forms of government. Perhaps democratic impulses were weak; after all, almost all these nations had known only autocracy. Yet many of them had competitive elections during this period. Perhaps, then, referendums, despite their long use in Switzerland and in France, were thought to be too populist—a dangerous mechanism in the hands of neophyte democrats and citizens. Their use to consolidate authoritarian regimes suggests that this fear was justified. In any case, despite Wilsonian rhetoric about

---

7. The plebiscite in Sopron occurred as a result of mediation by Italy between Austria and Hungary.

8. Wambaugh, *Plebiscites since the World War*, p. 42.

self-determination, the referendum was less used than might have been expected.

After World War II, definitions of nation-states and decisions about forms of government had little to do with democratic forms and everything to do with the policies of the great powers. On the Soviet side, Marxist-Leninist ideology militated against bourgeois notions of electoral democracy, especially popular referendums. The dictatorship of the proletariat does not square easily with referendums.

Directly after the war, referendums were undertaken in only two places, Poland and Bulgaria, and the Polish experience revealed the dangers, to Communist parties at least, of unfettered democracy. In June 1946, under the watchful eyes of the world, the Communists chose the referendum as a way to show their strength in Poland. They proposed three questions they thought Poles, no matter what their politics, would answer affirmatively. Stanislaw Mikolajczyk, the former head of the non-Communist Polish government in London and by 1946 the deputy premier, decided to campaign for Yes votes on two of the three questions and one No vote on the abolition of the Senate. The question on the Senate became a vote of confidence in the government's domination by the Communists. The government announced the referendum results on the Senate question as 68 percent to 32 percent, but Jerzey Morawski, one of the Communist leaders, later admitted,

> I found out afterwards that the results had been faked. In reality the situation was probably just the reverse: two-thirds had voted for what Mikolajczyk was asking. . . . It was a warning which showed how strong the influence of Mikolajczyk's opposition was in Poland. It showed how much effort to pressurize, destroy, intimidate and discredit Mikolajczyk's opposition was still needed in order to win the elections.[9]

No doubt the experience in Poland sent a clear-cut message to both Moscow and the Communist parties of Eastern Europe to avoid referendums. A referendum was held in Bulgaria in September 1946 to abolish the monarchy, but only after the Communists had already consolidated power through a campaign of terror. Although the referendum was conducted "in a manner less than fair, . . . had it been held under free conditions, the end result—the declaration of a republic— might well have been the same, . . . since the monarchy had suffered severe losses of prestige as a result of Bulgaria's disastrous [wartime] alignments."[10]

---

9. Neal Ascherson, *The Struggle for Poland* (London: Michael Joseph, 1987), p. 144.

10. J. F. Brown, *Bulgaria under Communist Rule* (New York: Praeger, 1970), p. 11.

For the next forty years, from 1947 to 1986, only three referendums were held in Eastern Europe and the Soviet Union, and none of them involved turnout of less than 98 percent and Yes votes of less than 94.5 percent. Two involved approval of constitutions (Bulgaria in 1971 and the German Democratic Republic in 1968), and one was a proposal to reduce defense spending by 5 percent in Romania. The 1986 referendum in Romania, probably the most repressive of all Eastern European countries by then, included the nicety of signed ballots and produced the dark burlesque of no negative votes and only 228 nonvoters in an eligible electorate of over 17 million.

The Romanian referendum epitomized the mockery that could be made of the referendum device. In the next seven years, the referendum would be both redeemed as an instrument of democracy and abused in new ways that would suggest the limits of its usefulness. In Poland in 1987, in Hungary in 1989, and in the Soviet Union in 1991, referendums were the last-ditch attempts of putatively reformist but increasingly overwhelmed Communist elites to bulwark their failing defenses by calling in the plebiscitary armies. In all three cases, we shall show how Communist reformers failed to get enough support on the crucial issues.

In the Soviet republics, a series of independence and sovereignty referendums in early 1991 revealed the deep fissures within the Soviet Union. These referendums led first to the increasing desperation of the conservative cabinet installed by Mikhail Gorbachev in the fall and winter of 1990 and the failed coup attempt of August 1991; then to more independence referendums; and finally to the crucial independence referendum of Ukraine on 1 December 1991, that catalyzed the breakup of the Soviet Union and the resignation of Gorbachev on 25 December 1991. These referendums, it might be argued, constituted the redemption of the referendum device.

The referendum, however, has not been an altogether perfect device. Referendums on the form of government and policy since 1991 have had a mixed effect. The preeminent example is the failure of the April 1993 Russian referendum to resolve the continuing legitimacy crisis. In Yugoslavia, referendums have been manipulated as part of the war among ethnic groups, and the Yugoslavian experiences demonstrate that only a minimal amount of order and authority is necessary to carry out a referendum, although the result under these circumstances is often a Pyrrhic victory. In other countries, it has become obvious that authorities can delay or squash referendums even when most of the population or the elites want them. The most notable case may be Czechoslovakia: public opinion, even in Slovakia, favored unity and a referendum on keeping the federation together; President

Vaclav Havel and others wanted a referendum; but the stalemate of elites made a referendum impossible. We review these matters in our last four sections.

Failed Communist Reformism—
Poland 1987, Hungary 1989, and the USSR 1991

Poland 1987. Referendums in Poland marked the beginning and the end of Communist hegemony in Eastern Europe. After the Polish Communist party manipulated and misreported the 1946 referendum to suit its needs, there followed a forty-year period without free competitive elections or meaningful referendums throughout Eastern Europe. In 1987, the defeat of General Jaruzelski's referendum in Poland marked the beginning of a new period in which elections would become meaningful and fully competitive.

After the 1980 Solidarity uprisings and the December 1981 imposition of martial law, the military regime of General Jaruzelski had been slowly building support for a form of consultative democracy in which elections, while not offering competitive candidates, provided voters a chance to indicate their loyalty to, if not approval of, the regime. That regime had enjoyed reasonable turnout in the 1984 People's Council elections and the 1985 Senate elections, and it was increasingly popular as General Jaruzelski relaxed martial law. By 1987, Jaruzelski could take solace in the apparent weakness of Solidarity after the total amnesty of September 1986 and the pope's visit of June 1987. But he had to confront the dilemma created by pressure from the International Monetary Fund for price increases and a recalcitrant population that had balked at earlier economic reforms.

In these difficult economic circumstances, Jaruzelski decided that the successes of the 1984 and 1985 elections might be repeated in a referendum that would allow the regime to institute some painful reforms. Two questions were posed, one on the economy and one on democratization. The first asked voters to approve a "full implementation of the program [price increases] for radical stabilization of the economy . . . , a program that aims at significantly improving the quality of life, knowing that this will bring with it rapid change and a difficult period of two to three years." The second proposed the Polish model of "a profound democratization of political life, the goal of which is to strengthen industrial autonomy, increase the rights of citizens, and enlarge their role in governing the country."[11] Solidarity

---

11. The text of the referendum questions is taken from Lech Walesa, *The Struggle and the Triumph* (New York: Arcade Publishing, 1991), p. 122.

asked its supporters to boycott the referendum, and workers did boycott it. Many rural inhabitants showed their loyalty to the regime by voting, but many also voted No on both propositions. The referendum, for the first time, allowed citizens to make two statements: one about loyalty to the regime by turning out or not voting and another about approval or disapproval of policies by choosing Yes or No on the ballot. The results constituted a "spectacular defeat for the authorities."[12]

Although the regime won a majority of votes on each question, it fell about five percentage points short of the majority of the eligible electorate that it had said it needed. After the failure of the 1987 referendum, Jaruzelski, faced with the dire necessity to do something, increased prices. This precipitated the rout of the regime—strikes in mid-1988, Jaruzelski's offer for round-table talks with Solidarity in August, and finally the elections of June 1989, in which the Communists were trounced wherever they allowed competition. By August 1989, Solidarity had formed a government, and communism unraveled all over Eastern Europe.

Hungary 1989. Following Poland's example, round-table talks began in Hungary in June 1989. The Communists in the form of the Hungarian Socialist Workers' party (HSWP) wanted a strong president elected directly by the people because they believed that Imre Pozsgay, a Communist reformer and popular politician, would be elected. An agreement was reached on a weak presidency, but no consensus was attained on who should elect the president (Parliament or the people) and when this election should occur (before or after parliamentary elections). Initially, the Opposition Round Table, composed of those groups opposing the HSWP, was united in wanting the president elected by Parliament after new elections to ensure the primacy of Parliament and to minimize the power of the HSWP, but eventually the opposition split into moderate and radical groups. The final agreements of the Round Table were signed by the HSWP and the moderate groups, but the radical groups felt "that no democratic state could evolve if the Workers' Militia survived, if the election of the President preceded the parliamentary elections, if the HSWP did not give an account of its wealth, and if it did not leave the places of work."[13]

---

12. Krzysztof Jasiewicz and Tomasz Zukowski, "The Elections of 1984–89 as a Factor in the Transformation of the Social Order in Poland," in George Sanford, ed., *Democratization in Poland, 1988–90: Polish Voices* (New York: St. Martin's Press, 1992), p. 103.

13. Andras Bozoki, "Political Transition and Constitutional Change in Hungary," in Andras Bozoki, Andras Korosenyi, and George Schopflin, eds., *Post-Communist Transition: Emerging Pluralism in Hungary* (New York: St. Martin's Press, 1992), p. 68.

Using the very liberal initiative law formulated by the Round Table, the radicals devised a proposal for a referendum on the presidency and their three other concerns, and they easily obtained the 100,000 signatures required to get it on the ballot. Facing an initiative that might upset their last hope for retaining power through the election of Pozsgay to the presidency, the reform Communists quickly abolished the workers' guards, removed party cells from the workplace, and promised a full accounting of the party's assets before the referendum. Nevertheless, on the crucial issue of not having presidential before parliamentary elections, the radical opposition won by the narrowest of margins with only a 55 percent turnout (barely satisfying the necessary 50 percent) and with only 50.07 percent of those voting agreeing to have parliamentary elections first.

The referendum campaign served two purposes. It sullied the reform Communists by focusing on the limits of their reform efforts, and it ensured that the Parliament would be elected before the president. According to Andras Bozoki,

> It was the plebiscite of 26 November which ultimately removed all the obstacles in the way of free elections and made possible what the parties of the Opposition Roundtable were not strong enough for: the completion of the dismantling of the party state so that preparations for the elections could start.[14]

The Communists used the initiative themselves to force a 29 July 1990 vote on the direct election of the president (the new Parliament had decided to name the president itself), but this was the fourth election in eight months, and turnout was only about 14 percent—insufficient for the results to matter and a pitiful commentary on a party that could once report 99 percent turnout in elections throughout Eastern Europe.

USSR 1991. The 17 March 1991 All-Union referendum in the USSR easily set records for the largest number of votes ever cast (almost 150 million) and the widest geographical area ever encompassed by a referendum, but these statistics do not begin to suggest its importance. More tellingly, it was the first *and* the last referendum in the Soviet Union's history. As with the Polish and Hungarian referendums, the Communist party no longer had the wherewithal to produce such clearly contrived but nevertheless daunting outcomes as the 1986 Romanian referendum. Yet, Mikhail Gorbachev no doubt started down the road toward a referendum with great hopes that it would provide him with the legitimacy he needed to reshape the Soviet Union.

---

14. Ibid., p. 68.

As Gorbachev found himself increasingly squeezed between democrats, reformers, and independence-minded republics on the one side and a skeptical and recalcitrant party and *apparat* on the other side, he turned to the mass public to obtain the authority he needed to keep the Soviet Union intact. He had used this strategy with some success in the 1989 elections to the Congress of People's Deputies. In 1990, as he faced a cascade of sovereignty declarations from the fifteen union republics, the increasing power of Boris Yeltsin as head of the Russian Parliament, and the need to refashion relations between the center and the republics, he decided to use the referendum to gain support for a new Union Treaty to replace the one that had created the Soviet Union in 1922. In December 1990, Gorbachev proposed a referendum on the new Union Treaty to the Fourth Congress of People's Deputies. Within two weeks, a law on national referendums was approved by the Supreme Soviet based on provisions of the 1977 constitution, and the date of 17 March 1991 was set for a referendum on the question, "Do you consider necessary the preservation of the Union of Soviet Socialist Republics as a renewed federation of equal sovereign republics, in which the rights and freedoms of an individual of any nationality will be fully guaranteed?"

From the outset, both the idea of a referendum and the wording of the proposition were criticized from all sides. The nationalist leaders of the Baltics, who had already declared their independence from the Soviet Union, were in no mood to consider a Union Treaty that kept power in Moscow. The conservative leaders of other republics, such as those in Central Asia, were dismayed by the prospect of a vote that might bring the "radical democracy" of the Baltic republics to their doorstep. They complained that there was no need for a referendum because their citizenry was already in favor of a renewed union. In addition, everyone noted the internal contradictions and confusions in the question itself: how could one vote on the preservation of something that was being renewed? What was the point of the last clause about guaranteeing the rights and freedoms of individuals of any nationality? And why was the union described as one of "socialist" republics? The referendum question provided plenty of ambiguity, and it seems likely that Gorbachev wanted it that way.

The frailty of Gorbachev's authority quickly became evident as the Supreme Soviets of six republics—the three Baltic states (Estonia, Latvia, and Lithuania), Armenia, Georgia, and Moldavia—adopted resolutions against the referendum and refused to set up central referendum commissions. Lithuania, Estonia, Latvia, Georgia, and Armenia went even farther and proposed independence referendums. The Supreme Soviets of five of the nine other republics took the more modest but still disruptive step of either changing the question, as in Kazakhstan,[15] or adding questions of their own. Kirghizia, Uzbekistan, and the Ukraine added questions emphasizing their "sovereignty" within the new union, and Russia added a question on an elected president. Only Azerbaijan, Belorussia, Tadjikistan, and Turkmenistan presented the referendum to their citizens as Gorbachev had intended. (See columns 2, 3, and 4 of table 6–3 for a summary of what happened.)

Gorbachev still had enough authority to control the referendum in some important ways. He launched it. He defined the initial question. He remained vague about the method of counting votes across republics so that success could be claimed for a variety of different outcomes. He prevented opponents, especially Boris Yeltsin, from obtaining media time. He initiated a mobilization campaign complete with traditional Soviet slogans such as "Your Motherland is calling you. Say 'Yes' " and "Let there always be blue sky. Say 'Yes.' "[16] In his televised speech on 15 March 1991, he argued hyperbolically that "our 'Yes' will preserve the unity of the state, which is a thousand years old and which has been created through labor and intelligence as well as immense suffering of many generations. . . . Our 'Yes' guarantees that never again will the flame of war scorch our land, which has had enough trials as it is."[17] And he had some success even in getting local and regional soviets, factories, labor unions, and units of the Soviet army and navy to set up their own polling stations and election commissions in the republics that had decided to boycott the referendum. In Latvia, for example, about one-quarter of the population (probably about 40 percent of the eligible voters) voted despite the fact that the Latvian Supreme Soviet had decided to boycott the referendum.[18]

---

15. The question put in Kazakhstan was, "Do you consider it necessary to maintain the USSR as a Union of sovereign states of equal rights?" Although the question appears closer to those added by Kirghizia, the Ukraine, and Uzbekistan (except that it substituted "states" for "republics"), Gorbachev supporters argued that the Kazakhstan question was "reconcilable" with the question proposed by the Supreme Soviet of the USSR.

16. Commission on Security and Cooperation in Europe, *Presidential Elections and Independence Referendums in the Baltic States, the Soviet Union, and Successor States* (Washington, D.C.: Commission on Security and Cooperation in Europe, 1992), p. 26.

17. Serge Schmemann, "Soviet Vote Becomes Test of Loyalties," *New York Times*, 16 March 1991.

18. The turnout in these areas seems directly related to the size of the local Russian population and to the militancy with which the local republic tried to discourage voting. Estonia and Latvia have the largest Russian populations (30 to 50 percent) and were least confrontational. Georgia and Armenia have small

Yet, Gorbachev had sufficient authority to control the referendum only in those areas where there was nothing to prove. In those areas where the results mattered, he lacked the authority to get the referendum held the way he wished. In the end, Gorbachev won the vote—in the five Central Asian republics at least 93.7 percent of the voters approved the Union Treaty;[19] and in the remaining republics at least 70 percent of the voters voted Yes (see table 6–3).[20] But he had already lost in the implementation of the referendum: six republics boycotted it, and five others changed the question or added questions of their own. In the words of the report on presidential elections and independence referendums of the Commission on Security and Cooperation in Europe,

> Considering how much time, effort, money, hoopla, vitriol, and panic-mongering went into the first referendum in Soviet history, its actual significance appears small. As various analysts had predicted, it resolved no problems and produced no clear answers to any questions. . . . The first referendum in Soviet history produced plebiscitary paralysis, and the stand-off between the center and the republics continues.[21]

Soviet Republics in 1991

There were two rounds of referendums in the union republics in 1991. The nine referendums (in the three Baltic republics, Armenia, Georgia, Kirghizia, Uzbekistan, Russia, and the Ukraine) announced before 17 March were precipitated by Gorbachev's decision to hold the All-Union referendum. The decision by those nine to hold referendums and the questions they chose to ask reveal a great deal about the strate-

---

Russian populations (less than 10 percent) and were strongly opposed to the referendum. See Darrell Slider, "The First 'National' Referendum and Referenda in the Republics: Voting on Union, Sovereignty, and Independence," *Journal of Soviet Nationalities*, forthcoming.

19. The *Economist* commented that these figures "suspiciously approach the good old days of 99.9% communist voting" (23 March 1991, p. 54), and the report of the Commission on Security and Cooperation in Europe, *Presidential Elections and Independence Referendums*, notes reports of much lower turnout in a number of the republics.

20. But Gorbachev fared badly in many major cities. In Moscow, the vote was only 50.02 percent for the Union Treaty, in Leningrad, 53 percent, and in Sverdlovsk (where Yeltsin had once been the local Communist party boss), only 34 percent.

21. Commission on Security and Cooperation in Europe, *Presidential Election and Independence Referendums*, p. 58.

TABLE 6-3
ALL-UNION REFERENDUM IN THE FORMER SOVIET UNION, 17 MARCH 1991

Republic	Boycott[a]	Independence Referendum?[b]	Sovereignty Referendum?[c]	Registered Vote as Percentage of Population	Percent Turnout	Percent Yes
Soviet Union				56.60	80.00	76.40
Baltics						
Estonia	Yes	Yes	No	19.10	74.20	95.00
Latvia	Yes	Yes	No	25.00	65.10	95.10
Lithuania	Yes	Yes	No	15.80	86.10	98.90
Caucasus						
Armenia	Yes	Yes	No	.02	72.10	71.60
Azerbaijan	No	No	No	55.00	75.10	93.30
Georgia	Yes	Yes	No	6.70	57.80	98.90

	Was there an official boycott?[a]	Was there an independence referendum announced before March 17, 1991?[b]	Was there a sovereignty question added (add) to the March 17, 1991, ballot, or was the Gorbachev question changed (chg.)?[c]	Turnout[d]		
Central Asian republics						
Kazakhstan	No	No	Chg.	60.46	88.20	94.10
Kirghizia	No	No	Add	54.57	92.90	94.60
Tadjikistan	No	No	No	49.87	94.40	96.20
Turkmenistan	No	No	No	52.27	97.70	97.90
Uzbekistan	No	No	Add	51.68	95.40	93.70
Slavic republics and Moldavia						
Belorussia	No	No	No	72.11	83.30	82.70
Moldavia	No	Yes	No	19.39	83.30	98.30
Russia	No	No	Add	71.68	75.40	71.30
Ukraine	No	No	Add	72.98	83.50	70.20

a. Was there an official boycott?
b. Was there an independence referendum announced before March 17, 1991?
c. Was there a sovereignty question added (add) to the March 17, 1991, ballot, or was the Gorbachev question changed (chg.)?
d. The turnout as a percentage of population is calculated from population data given in table 2, appendix 2, of Graham Smith, *The Nationalities Question in the Soviet Union* (New York: Longman, 1990); and from the number of registered voters reported in Darrell Slider, "The First 'National' Referendum and Referenda in the Republics: Voting on Union, Sovereignty, and Independence," *Journal of Soviet Nationalities*. For Georgia, the reported registered voters used were just those for South Ossetia and Abkhazia.

SOURCE: Compiled by authors from sources listed in the selected references section of this chapter.

gic situation of each republic at a crucial moment in the history of the USSR. The five referendum questions posed from 26 October onward (two in Turkmenistan; one each in the Ukraine, Azerbaijan, and Uzbekistan) were the endgame for the Soviet Union after the August putsch had made independence for the republics essentially a matter of declaring it. What remained in doubt was whether the Soviet Union might persist in some reduced fashion—possibly as a union of Slavic states with some Central Asian republics as well. The referendum in Turkmenistan suggested that the Central Asian republics were unlikely to remain, but, more important, the Ukrainian referendum of 1 December made it clear that the Ukraine wanted its independence. This marked the end of the Soviet Union. (See table 6–4.)

Referendums Announced before 17 March 1991. By proposing a referendum, Gorbachev opened the floodgates for more referendums, and he presented the republics with dilemmas concerning their sovereignty and authority, the role of the center, and the Soviet Union itself. For the Baltic states, the goal was clear: complete independence from the center. The path to this goal was not so clear. With their large Russian populations, Estonia and Latvia faced the danger that holding the all-union referendum would provide these Russians with a chance to voice their misgivings about independence,[22] while boycotting would give Gorbachev a pretext to recommence the military crackdown that had begun in January. This dilemma was solved by simultaneously boycotting the All-Union referendum, while preempting it with independence referendums on 9 February in Lithuania and 3 March in Estonia and Latvia.[23] There was some danger to this approach—the Baltics did not want to be seen as following the arduous and, to their minds, inapplicable and corrupt Soviet secession law. For this reason, both Lithuania and Latvia labeled their referendums "public opinion polls."

The results revealed a widespread and fervent desire for independence. Turnout was over 83 percent in all the Baltic republics. The votes for independence were 90.5 percent in Lithuania, 77.7 percent in Esto-

---

22. The degree of possible embarrassment is indicated by the results of the Estonian Citizen Participation Study (conducted by Cynthia Kaplan and Henry Brady), which interviewed 6,884 residents of Estonia in January and February 1991. Whereas only 3 percent of the ethnic Estonians supported the Union Treaty, 79 percent of the Slavs (Russians, Ukrainians, and Belorussians) supported it.

23. Lithuania, with its much smaller Russian population, could afford to go first. After Lithuania's success, it was easier for Estonia and Latvia to take the same step.

TABLE 6–4
REFERENDUMS IN THE FORMER SOVIET UNION, 1991–1993

Republic or Country/Question	Date	Percent Turnout	Percent Yes
The Baltics			
Estonia			
Independent Estonia[a]	3 Mar. 1991	83.0	77.7
Approve constitution	24 June 1992	66.8	91.3
Voting for noncitizens	24 June 1992	66.8	46.1
Latvia			
Independent Latvia[a]	3 Mar. 1991	87.6	73.7
Lithuania			
Independent Lithuania[a]	9 Feb. 1991	84.4	90.5
Presidential powers	23 May 1992	57.0	69.2
Withdrawal of Russian Army	14 June 1992	75.8	90.8
Caucasus			
Armenia			
Independent Armenia[a]	21 Sept. 1991	95.1	99.3
Azerbaijan			
Independent Azerbaijan[a]	29 Dec. 1991	95.3	99.6
No confidence in president	30 Aug. 1993	92.0	97.5
Georgia			
Independent Georgia[a]	31 Mar. 1991	90.6	99.1
Central Asian Republics			
Kazakhstan None			
Kirghizia			
Equal sovereign republic[a]	17 Mar. 1991	81.6	62.0
Tadjikistan None			
Turkmenistan			
Independent Turkmenia[a]	26 Oct. 1991	97.4	94.1
Approve policies	26 Oct. 1991	97.4	93.5
Uzbekistan			
Equal sovereign republic[a]	17 Mar. 1991	93.0	93.9
Independent Uzbekistan[a]	29 Dec. 1991	94.0	98.2
Slavic Republics and Moldova			
Belarus None			
Moldova None			

(Table continues)

TABLE 6–4 (continued)

Republic or Country/Question	Date	Percent Turnout	Percent Yes
Russia			
Presidency for RSFSR	17 Mar. 1991	75.1	69.9
Confidence in Yeltsin	25 Apr. 1993	65.0	57.4
Approve Yeltsin's economics	25 Apr. 1993	65.0	53.7
Early elections for president	25 Apr. 1993	65.0	49.1
Early elections for deputies	25 Apr. 1993	65.0	70.6
Approve Yeltsin's constitution	12 Dec. 1993	58.4	54.8
Ukraine			
Equal sovereign state[a]	17 Mar. 1991	83.5	80.2
Independent Ukraine[a]	1 Dec. 1991	84.2	90.3

a. Independence or sovereignty referendums.
SOURCES: Same as for table 6–3.

nia, and 73.7 percent in Latvia. Even in many heavily Russian areas, 50 percent or more of the population voted for independence. The Baltic independence referendums undermined Gorbachev's claim that a union was still viable, and they handily legitimated the Baltic quest for independence.

The Central Asian republics faced a much different situation. Their conservative governments were dominated by Communist party officials who depended on the center for support and sustenance. They wanted the union to stay intact, and they did not want a referendum to disturb their peace. Not surprisingly, the leaders of Kazakhstan, Turkmenistan, and Uzbekistan all initially opposed the referendum, but once it became clear that it would occur, they sought a way to co-opt nationalist sentiment. Kirghizia and Uzbekistan added questions asking voters to approve the "preservation of the USSR as a renewed federation of equal sovereign republics." Kazakhstan modified the all-union question to ask whether voters considered it necessary "to maintain the USSR as a union of sovereign states of equal rights." Only Tadjikistan and Turkmenistan offered the unadorned and unmodified Gorbachev question.[24] The strong support for the two sovereignty

24. The data reported in table 6–4 for these referendums do not square with those in table 6–3 for the All-Union referendum. It is odd, to say the least, that the turnout for the sovereignty question in Uzbekistan was 93 percent but for the All-Union question turnout was 95.4 percent. Odder still is the discrepancy in Kirghizia, where turnout was 81.6 percent for sovereignty but 92.9 percent for the All-Union question. We are tempted to put greater faith in the results

questions and for Kazakhstan's modified question suggested that nationalist sentiment could be co-opted, and this became the central strategic ploy of these governments.

In the Caucasus, Georgia and Armenia had well-developed independence movements, and Azerbaijan had festering grievances with the center over the Nagorno Karabakh conflict. Following the Baltic lead, Georgia decided to boycott the All-Union referendum and to hold its own independence referendum to coincide with municipal elections on 31 March 1991. The reported 99.1 percent Yes vote is undoubtedly an exaggeration, given areas such as South Ossetia and Abkhazia where Georgian independence was unlikely to be popular. But the figure captures the essential result of the referendum—Georgians overwhelmingly favored independence. Armenia rejected participation in the All-Union referendum and decided to follow the April 1990 USSR law of secession, which required several referendums and a two-thirds Yes vote on the first one. On 1 March 1991, Armenia chose 21 September 1991 for its referendum. By doing so, it became the first, and ultimately only, Soviet republic that elected to follow Soviet law on secession. By the time the vote came around, the failed August putsch and the disintegration of the center had made an assertion of independence virtually superfluous so that "Armenia's vote on independence went forth in a festive, almost carefree atmosphere," according to one report.[25] Azerbaijan had the weakest democratic movement in the Caucasus and a strong, conservative Communist party leader, Ayaz Mutalibov. Like leaders in the Central Asian republics, Mutalibov saw no real reason for the All-Union referendum, and much less reason for sovereignty or independence declarations. The Azerbaijanis' major concern was the continuing dispute over Nagorno Karabakh, which colored all their dealings with the center. After a heated debate, Mutalibov convinced his parliament to hold the referendum as the best strategy for dealing with the center and advancing their interests in Nagorno Karabakh.

Finally, there were the dilemmas faced by the Slavic republics.[26]

for the sovereignty questions, but no source even notes this discrepancy so we can only speculate about its cause or meaning.

25. Commission on Security and Cooperation in Europe, *Presidential Elections and Independence Referendums*, p. 68.

26. The fifteenth republic, Moldavia (known as Moldova since independence), includes mostly Romanians, but its significant Russian and Ukrainian minorities (over 25 percent), coupled with its small size and precarious geopolitical location, have created a complicated situation characterized mostly by stalemate. Even though the Popular Front controlled the Supreme Soviet and nationalism could arguably be served by boycotting the All-Union referendum, the vote against it was very close. Sovereignty and independence were

Belorussia, economically weak, with the smallest population of the Slavic republics (one-fifth the size of Ukraine) and with close ties to Russia and the Ukraine, had no choice but to sit tight and wait for others to make their moves. Moreover, nationalism was a relatively weak force in Belorussia in 1991 (only 37 deputies of the 345-member Parliament were members of the Popular Front), and the Communists controlled the Parliament. Belorussia and Tadjikistan took the most conservative course of all the Soviet republics: they did not boycott, they posed an unaltered version of Gorbachev's referendum question, and they did not undertake any other referendums between 1991 and 1993.

Russia and the Ukraine faced much more complicated strategic problems. For Russia's Boris Yeltsin, the challenge was to maintain the coalition of reformers and westernizers who wanted to speed up reform on the one hand and on the other hand Russian nationalists and even hard-line Communists who wanted to return to the peace and tranquillity of the days before *perestroika* and *glasnost.* For the hard-liners, Yeltsin could not seem to be rejecting the idea of a Soviet Union. For the reformers, he had to show his commitment to change. The approach he chose, it can be argued, was the masterstroke that carried him through the next few years. He decided to allow the 17 March All-Union referendum to proceed without his endorsement or overt disapproval, but he added a referendum question on creating a popularly elected presidency. The call for *popular election* of the president pleased the reformers. The call for a *strong* president (embodied in the draft Russian constitution that the referendum would help to enact) pleased those who wished for a return of strong central authority and Russian, if not Soviet, greatness. In effect, Yeltsin ignored the Union Treaty and changed the subject to one on which he could win.

Yeltsin succeeded in getting a mandate for an elected presidency (with 70 percent support from voters) and was elected to the post in June 1991. The legitimacy he derived from being a popularly elected president was essential to his success during the August coup attempt in 1991 and during the violent confrontation with the Russian Congress of People's Deputies in October 1993.

The nature of Yeltsin's dilemma, and the success of his strategy, can be gleaned from table 6–5, based on data from the 1991 study of Russian Citizen Participation conducted by Cynthia Kaplan and Henry Brady. In this study, we asked respondents to choose "the best course

---

too explosive to put on the ballot, given the minority populations and the differences of opinion between those who wanted to rejoin with Romania and those who wanted independence.

TABLE 6–5
PARTICIPATION IN 17 MARCH 1991 REFERENDUM IN RUSSIA AND PUBLIC OPINION ON SELECTED ISSUES ACCORDING TO RESPONDENT'S PREFERRED PATH OF DEVELOPMENT
(percent)

Turnout	Monarchy (1.2%)	Stalinism (3.2%)	Brezhnevism (18.3%)	Democratic Socialism (16.1%)	Capitalism and Socialism (22.3%)	Western Society (21.7%)
For referendum	62.1	71.0	81.5	87.8	77.8	73.4
For union treaty	60.7	87.3	91.6	92.7	72.9	60.7
For elected president	83.1	72.2	72.7	66.5	78.7	84.1
For Gorbachev	12.1	14.9	15.3	34.2	16.2	9.9
For Yeltsin	52.8	42.5	36.7	24.7	34.5	48.1

NOTE: Percentages of respondents specifying a path of development do not add to 100 because some respondents did not state a preference.
SOURCE: Russian citizen participation study, conducted in April–June 1991 by the authors. This was a scientific survey of over 12,000 respondents in Russia.

of development" for their country from among six responses that attempted to mimic the rhetoric of the times. We label these responses Monarchy, Stalinism, Brezhnevism, Democratic Socialism, Capitalism and Socialism, and Western Society.[27] As shown at the bottom of table 6–5, roughly one-fifth of the population chose one of the last four categories, about 3 percent chose Stalinism, and about 1 percent chose Monarchy. About 17 percent chose no category at all, and we have omitted these people from our table. Because our survey was conducted immediately after the 17 March vote, we took the opportunity to ask respondents whether they had voted and how they had voted on each question. We also asked them whom they preferred, Gorbachev or Yeltsin or neither.

There are several remarkable features of table 6–5. First, turnout increases to a peak at the Democratic Socialist option. Second, support for Gorbachev also peaks at the Democratic Socialist option, suggesting that this course of development might be called "Gorbachevism." Third, Yeltsin's support, not surprisingly, is the inverse of Gorbachev's—peaking at each end of the table. Fourth, support for the Union Treaty (the second row) peaks at the Democratic Socialist option—as we would expect given the high degree of support for Gorbachev among those who chose that course of development. Fifth, support for an elected president in Russia is highest at the extremes and lowest in the middle, as we would expect given the pattern of support for Yeltsin. Yeltsin, by his strategy, had managed to win support from wildly disparate groups: monarchists, Stalinists, and Brehznevites, who saw in Yeltsin a chance for order and stability, and westernizers and capitalists who saw in him a chance for real economic and political reform.[28]

The strategic problem in the Ukraine was probably the most com-

---

27. The text of each response is: Monarchy—"revival of the before-1917 monarchy"; Stalinism—"return to the system of 1930–1950"; Brezhnevism—"return to the system of 1960 to the early 1980s before *perestroika* began"; Democratic Socialism—"build a society on the basis of a humane, democratic socialism"; Capitalism and socialism—"build a society based on a combination of capitalism and socialism at their best"; Western society—"build a western-type society."

28. Our data also show that 95 percent of Gorbachev supporters and 89 percent of current members of the Communist party of the Soviet Union (CPSU) were strong supporters of the Union Treaty, whereas only 31 percent of Yeltsin supporters and 28 percent of former CPSU members supported it. Conversely, 89 percent of Yeltsin supporters and 87 percent of former CPSU members supported an elected Russian president, while only 34 percent of Gorbachev supporters and 33 percent of current CPSU members supported an elected presidency.

plex of all. The large Russian population in the Ukraine (over 20 percent) could be expected to support the Union Treaty as a way of
maintaining contact with Russia. This population was heavily concentrated in the Crimea (about 67 percent Russian) and in the eastern
provinces. The Ukrainian population, concentrated in the west, was
more favorable toward independence, especially in the three western
Galician provinces added to the Ukraine from Poland after World War
II, in which there was a very strong independence movement. Against
this backdrop, the politically adroit Communist chairman of the Supreme Soviet, Leonid Kravchuk, proposed a sovereignty question similar to those proposed in Kirghizia and Uzbekistan. The Communist
party leadership supported both the All-Union question and the Ukrainian Republic's question on sovereignty for the Ukraine within the
USSR. The Ukrainian independence movement, Rukh (with the exception of its chapters in some west Ukrainian oblasts), supported the sovereignty question as well. In the three west Ukrainian oblasts, the
Galician Assembly proposed a third question on independence and
opposed both the All-Union and the sovereignty questions.

Table 6–6 summarizes data on ethnic composition and voting for
the Union Treaty and sovereignty on 17 March. The data are averages
across oblasts[29] placed into five geographical areas running from east
to west. In the first column, the percentage of the Ukrainian population
increases from the eastern Ukraine to the western Ukraine, and in the
second column the percentage of Russian population declines or stays
roughly the same. This summarizes the basic geopolitical fact about
the Ukraine—Russians in the east, Ukrainians in the west. The northwestern and western oblasts are separated because of the unusually
intense political activity, including the convening of the Galician Assembly, in the west. The southwest is treated separately because these
two oblasts have substantial minorities and a distinctive politics based
on their proximity to Romania, Czechoslovakia, and Hungary.

The most obvious fact about the average support for the All-Union
referendum on 17 March is the substantial drop-off from east to west,
especially in the western oblasts. Putting the western oblasts aside, the
drop-off in support is more than twenty percentage points from east
to west. For the sovereignty question, except for the three western

---

29. The eastern oblasts are Dnepropetrovsk, Donetsk, Zaporozhe, Crimea,
Lugansk, Nikolaev, Odessa, Khar'kov, and Kherson; the central oblasts are
Vinnitsa, Zhitomir, Kiev City, Kiev Rural, Kirovograd, Poltava, Sumy, Cherk-
essk, and Chernigovsk; the northwestern oblasts are Volyna, Rovno, and
Khmel'nitskii; the western oblasts are Ivano-Frankovsk, L'viv, and Ternopol';
the southwestern oblasts are Transcarpathia and Chernovitsa.

TABLE 6–6
ETHNIC COMPOSITION AND SUPPORT FOR REFERENDUMS, BY REGIONS IN UKRAINE, 1991

Region	Ethnic Composition[a]		Support for Referendums			Number of Oblasts
	% Ukrainian	% Russian	% for union treaty[b]	% for sovereignty[c]	% for independence[d]	
Eastern Ukraine	59.4	34.7	82.1	86.1	83.8	9
Central Ukraine	86.5	10.4	75.0	87.2	94.5	9
Northwestern Ukraine	92.8	4.9	61.9	81.8	96.2	3
Western Ukraine	94.1	5.4	18.0	39.1	98.2	3
Southwestern Ukraine	74.6	5.4	60.5	76.3	92.7	2

a. Percentages add to less than 100 because of ethnic groups other than Ukrainian and Russian.
b. 17 March 1991.
c. 17 March 1991.
d. 1 December 1991.
SOURCE: Same as for tables 6–4 and 6–5.

oblasts in which there was a third question on independence (which passed by over 83 percent in each oblast), there is less than a 10 percent drop-off with virtually no noticeable relationship between approval of the sovereignty question and the percentage of Ukrainian or Russian population. The sovereignty question, with the exception of the western oblasts, was fairly successful in gaining support from Ukrainians and Russians alike. Kravchuk's compromise had its intended effect.

In the Ukraine, we clearly see the ethnic cleavages that underlay the moves toward independence in many of the republics. We also see how cunningly devised compromise referendums such as the one on sovereignty could cut through this cleavage, although counter maneuvers by highly mobilized independence groups such as those in the Galician Assembly could get the independence issue back on the agenda and destroy the delicate balance created by the sovereignty question.

In short, the 17 March referendum taught many lessons—all worrisome for Gorbachev's program of keeping the union together. In the Baltics and Georgia, it was clear that independence would come soon. In the Central Asian republics, it might be possible to maintain the union, but it would require a careful appeal to national sentiments. In Russia, Yeltsin was keeping together an unlikely coalition that made him a formidable opponent, and he was developing widespread legitimacy by his willingness to use the referendum to create a popularly elected presidency. In the Ukraine, maneuvers of opposition groups easily unleashed the powerful divisive forces of ethnicity. Gorbachev's attempt to get authority back for the center had almost entirely backfired, because he vastly underestimated the disgust with the center and the desires of ethnic groups to be free of the Soviet Union. Moreover, referendums seem to be excellent devices for taking power away from the center but ineffective methods for getting power for the center.

Referendums after the August Coup Attempt. Six referendums were held after the August coup attempt. The first, on 21 September in Armenia, had been planned since March and ratified what was, by then, obvious—Armenia would become independent. The next two, on 26 October, were an attempt by Turkmenistan's leaders to demonstrate their popular support as they declared independence. The 97.4 percent turnout and over 93 percent support for both independence and a vaguely worded question about support for the domestic and foreign policy of the president and Supreme Soviet of Turkmenistan made this seem plebiscitary democracy at its worst. The 29 December referendums in Azerbaijan and Uzbekistan were anticlimactic, occurring after Gorbachev's resignation and the dissolution of the Soviet Union.

Only the Ukrainian referendum of 1 December was of any importance, and it was crucial in the final breakup of the USSR. Even after the failed coup attempt, a union of republics (probably not of Socialist or Soviet Republics, however) was conceivable, albeit without the Baltics or the Caucasian republics. The three Slavic republics of Belorussia, Ukraine, and Russia were a formidable bloc, and the Central Asian republics, especially Kazakhstan with its sizable Russian population, might well have stayed in some form of union with them. Without the Ukraine, however, a union seemed almost unthinkable. The Ukraine's decision on 1 December, then, would decide the fate of the union.

The vote was overwhelmingly clear. Even in the Crimea, with a population two-thirds Russian, a majority favored independence, although table 6–6 shows that the 1 December vote was strongly related to ethnicity in the expected fashion, with Ukrainians much more likely to favor independence. One analytical method commonly used with data like these (ecological regression)[30] suggests that almost 100 percent of the Ukrainians and 51 percent of the Russians voted for independence, whereas almost 100 percent of the Russians and only 69 percent of the Ukrainians voted for the Union Treaty. Russians and Ukrainians outside the western provinces voted for sovereignty in equal proportions so that ethnicity had no effect. Despite Kravchuk's attempt to find a compromise, national sentiments finally prevailed—determining the outcome of the 1 December election and dooming the Soviet Union.

Referendums on the Form of Government and Policy since 1991

Since 1991, there have been ten referendums in the fifteen republics of the former Soviet Union (see table 6–4).[31] After severing their relationship with the Soviet Union, the republics faced the difficult problem of reconstituting themselves and their authority. This often required going to the people to get approval for a constitution or to deal with a difficult issue that created deadlock within the creaky institutions left over from the Soviet regime. In Estonia, in June 1992 there was a vote on a constitution and on the vexing issue of allowing noncitizens to vote. Estonians approved the constitution but rejected voting for non-

---

30. To get the results for the Russians, we regressed the total fraction voting for a referendum in each oblast on the percentage of Russians in the oblast. We omitted the three western oblasts in these regressions. The results for Ukrainians were obtained in a similar way.

31. There was only one referendum in Eastern Europe from 1990 to 1993—a vote on the Romanian Constitution on 9 December 1991; see table 6–2.

citizens. In Azerbaijan, the failure of the democratically elected Elchibey government led to a referendum on 30 August 1993 on "no confidence" in President Elchibey to clear the way for the return of former Communist leader, Heydar Aliyev, who had assumed effective authority in June. In Lithuania in May 1992, President Landsbergis tried to break the deadlock between himself and an opposition bloc of leftists and independents by asking for the creation of a strong presidency. Although Landsbergis received a majority of the votes cast, he failed to get the majority of eligible voters necessary to pass the referendum. A month later, the overwhelming approval of a referendum on the withdrawal of the Russian army provided a club to use against the Russians. In each of these cases, the nations involved employed a referendum to break through a deadlock created by ethnic cleavages (voting in Estonia), the failure of institutions (Azerbaijan and Lithuania), or the residues of empire (troops in Lithuania).

The most important referendum of this period was the 25 April 1993 vote in Russia, which pitted the Russian Parliament against Boris Yeltsin. This vote, which dealt with a deadlock of titanic proportions, illustrates how referendums are used in the painful process of developing new institutions and new forms of authority.

The story can be told in five acts. In act I of December 1992, Boris Yeltsin's emergency powers, originally conferred after the abortive coup of August 1991, are curtailed by the Congress of People's Deputies. After Yeltsin strikes a deal with the Congress regarding reforms and his cabinet, the Congress reneges on the deal. Act II opens with Yeltsin deciding to challenge the Congress by calling for a referendum on 24 January 1993, which will ask people whom they want to lead the country out of economic and political crisis—the president or the Congress? The Congress, unenthusiastic about reform and wanting to displace Yeltsin, counters with a proposal for a referendum on early elections to the presidency and the Congress. On 12 December a compromise is reached that calls for a referendum on 11 April 1993 on the draft principles of the new Russian Constitution.

Act III begins with democratic parties supporting a referendum on a new constitution, with centrist and conservative parties opposed to a referendum or proposing a question on early presidential and parliamentary elections, and the head of the Constitutional Court also opposed and calling for a postponement. Yeltsin presents a draft of four referendum questions, all asking about significant institutional changes, to Parliament on 7 March. He proposes questions on whether the Russian federation should be a presidential republic, whether the supreme legislative body should be a bicameral parliament, whether the new constitution should be adopted by a constitutional assembly, and whether citizens have a right to private property. On 12 March, the Congress of People's Deputies curtails Yeltsin's powers by annulling the compromise of December 1992, by which he had retained his emergency powers, and they cancel the referendum. Yeltsin and his followers walk out of the Congress on the morning of 12 March.

The climax comes in act IV. On 20 March, Yeltsin, infuriated by what he views as the duplicity of the Congress, calls for a referendum to be held on 25 April. He proposes a vote of confidence, a vote on the draft of a new constitution, and a vote on a draft law on elections to a national parliament. On 27 March, after a week of tactical maneuvering, Yeltsin appears before the Congress to propose a compromise. The Congress replies with a motion to impeach the president, which fails. Then it sets out its own questions for the referendum: "(1) Do you trust the president of the Russian Federation? (2) Do you approve of the social-economic policy carried out by the president and the government of the Russian Federation since 1992? (3) Do you deem it necessary to hold early presidential elections? (4) Do you deem it necessary to hold early elections for people's deputies?" The second question is clearly intended to embarrass Yeltsin by focusing on the most unpopular aspect of his rule. The third and fourth questions are designed either to force Yeltsin to reject presidential elections for himself, while endorsing them for the Congress—thus making him look hypocritical—or to accept elections for himself as well. Moreover, the Congress proposes that approval of any question will require half the eligible electorate, thus making success for Yeltsin on the three questions he cares about (trust, approval of his economic policy, and early elections for the Congress of People's Deputies) unlikely. Yeltsin is placed in a difficult strategic situation, and for a while he thinks about a parallel plebiscite. In the end, though, he goes along with the questions proposed by the Congress, and he gets the Constitutional Court to require only a majority of those voting (instead of a majority of all eligible voters) for passage of the first two questions.

In the final act, the referendum is held, and Yeltsin wins a majority of the vote on all three questions that he cares about but fails to win the majority of eligible voters he needs on the crucial question of elections to the Congress. Despite the fact that 70.6 percent of the voters endorse new elections, a 65 percent turnout means that only 45.9 percent of the eligible voters have recorded this opinion. Sadly, nothing is resolved, and the struggle continues until the tragedy that begins in September 1993 with Yeltsin's dissolution of Parliament.

The machinations during the five months leading up to the referendum of 25 April reveal the unsettled character of Russian politics, and the methods used by Russian elites to gain advantage—question wording, counting rules, and timing—illustrate the ways that referendums can be manipulated. The outcome also suggests the limitations of referendums. Even though Yeltsin achieved a substantial victory, he could not turn it into a complete success as long as the Congress felt emboldened to ignore the results. These circumstances foster the growth of authoritarianism, as leaders become increasingly frustrated with democratic institutions and seek other methods to resolve stalemates. The referendum device, as in Germany, Italy, Romania, and Estonia during the interwar years, may still play a prominent role as this happens, but increasingly it may be a mask for antidemocratic methods.

The destructive confrontation between Yeltsin and the Congress of People's Deputies in September 1993 and the subsequent constitutional referendum of 12 December 1993 suggest that this may be happening in Russia. Yeltsin's constitution omitted many features of earlier drafts such as sovereignty guarantees for republics within Russia, and the constitution appeared to facilitate a centralization of power by strengthening the presidency and creating a weak parliament. During the campaign, Yeltsin's advisers tried to get two electoral blocs removed from the list of contenders simply because they advocated rejecting the new constitution. After the vote, some observers expressed concern over the length of time before the Central Electoral Commission reported the results, and the final tally announced eight days after the election suggested a narrow victory for Yeltsin with 54.8 percent of eligible voters participating and 58.4 percent of them voting Yes, implying approval by less than one-third of the eligible voters. Some claimed that this vote was insufficient for approval under the 1990 Russian referendum law (signed by Yeltsin at that time in his capacity as chairman of the RSFSR Supreme Soviet), which had required approval of at least 50 percent of the eligible voters. The announced results, of course, did satisfy the requirements set down for the April 1993 referendum. But even if the votes were sufficient, the referendum met with significant opposition in many ethnic republics. It was not held in all places (for example, the Chechen Republic); turnout was very low in many others (only 13.8 percent, for example, in Tatarstan, where nationalist parties had called for a boycott); and voters in the Tuvan Republic rejected the Russian Constitution and approved a Tuvan Constitution that conflicted with it. Despite these problems and auguries of future difficulties, the new Russian Constitution went into effect on 24 December 1993.

More referendums appear to be on their way in the former Soviet Union. In addition to the Tuvan constitutional referendum, at least three other Russian republics (Dagestan, Karelia, and Komi) held referendums on the introduction of a presidency concurrently with the 12

December 1993 Russian constitutional referendum. On 29 November, Kirghizia's president proposed a referendum on his presidency for 24 January 1994. On 28 December 1993, Turkmenistan's Parliament of Notables met to propose a referendum for 15 January 1994 on the extension of the president's term of office. On 30 December 1993, President Leonid Kravchuk of Ukraine proposed a 27 March 1994 referendum about the type of political system, but it was not held. These referendums demonstrate the continuing need for popular mandates to break impasses and provide legitimacy.

In Yugoslavia, an Anarchy of Referendums

In the USSR, referendums played an important role in mobilizing nationalities and advancing independence movements without bloodshed. In Yugoslavia, where referendums have taken second place to the threat and use of force, they have often seemed more like the battle cries of highly mobilized and desperate populations than instruments of deliberative democracy.

The Socialist Federal Republic of Yugoslavia, like the USSR, was an amalgam of numerous ethnic groups separated by language, history, and religion. Of the seven largest groups,[32] all but the Albanians had a national home based in one of the six Yugoslavian republics: Serbs in Serbia proper (where they constituted 96 percent of the population), Croats in Croatia (75 percent), Muslims in Bosnia and Herzegovina (44 percent), Slovenes in Slovenia (91 percent), Macedonians in Macedonia (64 percent), and Montenegrins in Montenegro (70 percent). In addition, two areas—Kosovo with 83 percent Albanians and Vojvodina with 70 percent Serbs and 22 percent Hungarians—were included as "autonomous provinces" in Serbia. Except for Serbia proper and Slovenia, however, all these republics had significant fractions of other groups, and this was the curse of Yugoslavia.

The history of Yugoslavia revolves around attempts to bring these very different groups, especially the large Serbian and Croatian populations, together in one nation. Serbs and Croats speak similar languages; but Serbs use the Cyrillic alphabet and belong to the Orthodox Church, while Croats use the Latin alphabet and belong to the Roman Catholic Church. Serbs also have two lengthy episodes of nationhood dating back to the nineteenth century and the Middle Ages, while

---

32. In order of size, the groups are: Serbs (about 40 percent of Yugoslavia's population); Croats (about 20 percent); Muslims (9 percent); Albanians (9 percent); Slovenes (8 percent); Macedonians (5 percent); and Montenegrins (about 2.5 percent).

Croats were part of the Austro-Hungarian empire until they joined with the Serbs after World War I to form Yugoslavia. For Croats, Serbian numerical predominance in Yugoslavia and Serbia's history of state building threaten Croatian identity. As for Serbs, they retain the memory of the systematic annihilation undertaken by the fascist Croatian state, which collaborated with Italy and Germany during World War II.

Other ethnic groups present still more bases for conflict. Most non-Albanian Muslims speak Serbo-Croatian and share a history with Serbs and Croats, but their religion and their minority status even in their own republic of Bosnia and Herzegovina have forced them to tack back and forth with the winds of ethnic strife in Yugoslavia. Slovenes, who speak a language closely related to Serbo-Croatian, are mostly Roman Catholics; but as the most concentrated nationality in the most homogeneous republic with relatively high industrial development, they have the least in common with the rest of Yugoslavia.[33]

Referendums have given these groups voice in Yugoslavia. The chorus, however, has been more babble than melody. Referendums provide an easy way, possibly too easy, for subparts of a country to declare their independence, and the Yugoslavian experience shows that referendums can be undertaken by groups that have little constituted authority. The parade of referendums (see table 6–7) began in Yugoslavia in 1990, when Serbs in Croatia, seeing a resurgence of Croatian nationalism, organized an unofficial parliament (the Serbian National Council) and called for a referendum on Serbian autonomy. In the results announced by this council, 99.96 percent of the Serbs who voted supported Serbian autonomy.

Fearing the consequences of Serbia's resurgent nationalism led by former Serbian Communist boss Slobodan Milosevic and other even more radical Serbs, the Slovenian Assembly held a referendum on Slovenian independence in December 1990. The overwhelming support for independence led Slovenia to announce its secession from Yugoslavia in June 1991. After a May 1991 Croatian referendum had demonstrated strong support for independence, the Croatians proclaimed their independence in June as well. The Yugoslav Constitutional Court nullified these declarations of secession, and the Yugoslav leadership, increasingly dominated by Serbia, sent troops to both Slov-

---

33. In addition, Macedonians speak a language close to Bulgarian—so close that there is recurrent debate about whether it is a separate language at all. Montenegrins speak Serbo-Croatian, attend Orthodox churches, and often consider themselves Serbs, but they have the distinction of having had, until their absorption into Yugoslavia, one of the oldest republics in the world.

TABLE 6–7
REFERENDUMS IN REPUBLICS AND PARTS OF YUGOSLAVIA, 1990–1993

Area	Date of Referendum	Issue	Percent Turnout	Percent Yes	Who Proposed
Serbia	1–2 July 1990	Constitution	76	97	Serbian Assembly
Serbs in Croatia[a]	19 Aug. and 2 Sept. 1990	Autonomy	—	99	Serbian National Council
Slovenia	23 Dec. 1990	Independence	94	89	Slovenian Assembly
Serbs in Krajina (Croatia)[a]	12 May 1991	Unite with Serbia	73	99	Krajina Serb Assembly
Serbs in Slavonia, Baranja, Srem (Croatia)[a]	15–18 May 1991	Unite with Serbia	—	High	Serbian National Council
Croatia	19 May 1991	Independence	84	93	President of Croatia
Croatia	19 May 1991	Stay in Yugoslavia	84	5	President of Croatia
Macedonia	8 Sept. 1991	Independence	72	95	Macedonian Assembly
Kosovo[a]	26–30 Sept. 1991	Independence	87	99	Kosovo Assembly
Muslims in Sandzak[a]	25–27 Oct. 1991	Autonomy	Low	Low	Muslim National Council
Serbs in Bosnia-Herzegovina[a]	9–10 Nov. 1991	Stay in Yugoslavia	—	90	Serbian Democratic Party in Bosnia-Herzegovina
Albanians in Macedonia[a]	11 Jan. 1992	Independence	Low	Low	Two Albanian parties
Bosnia-Herzegovina	1 Mar. 1992	Independence	64	99	Bosnian Assembly
Montenegro	1 Mar. 1992	Stay in Yugoslavia	52	75	Montenegrin Assembly
Serbia	11 Oct. 1992	Early elections	—	—	Serbian Assembly
Serbs in Bosnia-Herzegovina[a]	15–16 May 1993	Peace plan	92	96	Bosnian Serb Assembly
Serbs in Bosnia-Herzegovina	15–16 May 1993	Independent Serb state	92	96	Bosnian Serb Assembly
Serbs in Krajna (Croatia)[a]	19–20 June 1993	Unite with Serbs in Bosnia	—	—	Krajina Serb Assembly

— = no data available.
a. The referendum was proposed by nonstate authorities.
SOURCE: same as for table 6–3.

enia and Croatia. Fighting also broke out between Croatians and Serbians in Croatia, leading to a bloody civil war.

An independence referendum in Macedonia in September 1991 led to its secession from Yugoslavia in 1992. In September 1991, the Kosovo Assembly, which had been disbanded by Milosevic, sponsored another independence referendum, which suggested overwhelming support for independence. Serbia, however, was not about to let Kosovo, which has tremendous historical importance for Serbs, follow Slovenia, Croatia, and Macedonia.

By the fall of 1991, the maelstrom had broadened to include non-Albanian Muslims, ethnic groups within republics, and Bosnia and Herzegovina. In October 1991, the Muslim National Council of the Sandzak Muslims, a group living at the intersection of the Serbian, Montenegrin, and Kosovo republics, undertook a referendum on autonomy for which the turnout and support were apparently quite low. Just a few weeks later, in this war of referendums, the Serbs in Bosnia and Herzegovina held a referendum on Bosnia's remaining in Yugoslavia. According to the reports of the Serbian Democratic party, which organized the referendum, more than a million Serbs voted, and 90 percent supported remaining in Yugoslavia. In Macedonia, just two months later, the large population of Macedonian Albanians held a referendum on independence, but turnout was disappointing. The independence referendum organized by the Assembly of Bosnia-Herzegovina for 1 March 1992, led to relatively low turnout but overwhelming support for independence among those who voted. In the mostly Serbian republic of Montenegro, a referendum on the same date asked voters whether they wanted to stay in Serbian-dominated Yugoslavia. Among the bare majority of the voters who participated, three-quarters supported remaining. A 15–16 May 1993 referendum by Serbs in Bosnia and Herzegovina led to the rejection of the Vance-Owen peace plan and strong support for an independent Serbian state. And a 19–20 June referendum of Serbs in the Krajina region of Croatia called for union between this region and the Serbs in Bosnia.

In short, referendums marked each stage in the seemingly endless splintering of Yugoslavia. Referendums preceded independence proclamations for the Yugoslavian republics of Slovenia, Croatia, Macedonia, and Bosnia and Herzegovina. Referendums were also used by such minorities as Croatian Serbs, Sandzak Muslims, Serbs in Bosnia and Herzegovina (twice), and Macedonian Albanians to assert their autonomy or independence. Only among the mostly Serbian Montenegrins was there a referendum that led to fusion (with Serbia) instead of fission. Once again, referendums were used by provincial elites, and even by the leaders of compact minorities, to serve the divisive interests of nationalism instead of Yugoslavian state building. When territorially concentrated ethnic groups are asked whether their nationality should have its own homeland, the appeals of ethnic identity tied to a nation-state appear irresistible. Conversely, it is all too easy for elites to reject attempts to create states embracing different ethnic groups, and an attempt from September 1990 to mid-1991 to have a Yugoslavia-wide referendum on the future of the country failed because ethnic and republic elites could not agree on a formulation of the question.

Why Referendums Do Not Occur

Eastern Europe. Squashed referendums reveal as much, and maybe more, about a polity as those that are held. The inability even to get the question of Yugoslavian nationhood before the public suggests the profound disagreements among elites in Yugoslavia. Other stillborn referendums suggest similar maladies (see table 6–8). The failure of the Polish people to get a referendum on the country's punitive abortion law despite the collection of over 1.3 million signatures suggests how much the reform government needed the support of the Catholic Church and wanted to stay away from a divisive moral issue while it focused on economic reform.

Czechoslovakia presents an even more interesting story. The differences between Czechs and Slovaks go deep and involve language, religion, and identity. Immediately after independence in early 1990, these differences erupted in the debate over what to name the new republic, and after several false starts, it was christened the Czech and Slovak Federal Republic (CSFR). This recognition of Slovakia did not, however, assuage the Slovakian separatists who immediately began pushing for independence. Throughout the next two years, a referendum of some sort—either in Slovakia alone or throughout the Federal Republic—was a constant topic of debate. By 14 March 1991, President Vaclav Havel, in a televised address, pressed for a referendum throughout both the Czech and the Slovak Republics. Four months later, a referendum law was promulgated by the CSFR Federal Assembly, which stated that secession by either republic could be decided only by a referendum called by the Federal Assembly or by the National Council of the Czech or the Slovak Republic. An absolute majority of eligible voters in either republic would be enough to sanction secession.

In October 1991, Havel, addressing the federal Parliament, proposed a referendum for December. Despite Havel's support for a referendum, most parties remained opposed to it. At the 12 November session of the Parliament, none of six different wordings for a referen-

TABLE 6–8
Some Proposed Referendums in Eastern Europe, 1990–1992

Country	Topic	Date Proposed	Who Proposed	Fate
Bulgaria	Republic or monarchy	May 1991	Social Democratic party in Parliament	Opposed by opposition Union of Democratic forces and withdrawn by initiators
Czechoslovakia	Czech-Slovak unity	March 1991	President Havel and others	Parliament cannot agree on question
Hungary	Recalling Parliament	December 1992	Initiative gets 100,000 signatures	Constitutional Court ruled against referendum on recall
Poland	Abortion	November 1992	Petition drive of 1.3 million	Parliament rejected referendum
Romania	Communist party and death penalty	January 1990	President Iliescu	"Second thoughts"—National Salvation Front saw no reason for one
Yugoslavia	Federal or confederal government	September 1990	President Jovic	Inability of Yugoslavia's six presidents to agree on a question.

SOURCE: Authors. Same as for table 6–3.

dum gathered enough support to be sent to the people. In a nationwide poll held in the same month, 74 percent of those polled (66 percent in Slovakia) supported holding a referendum. In late November, Havel proposed to Parliament a revision of the referendum law that would make a referendum mandatory if demanded by 500,000 Czech and 250,000 Slovak voters. Within a month, over 2 million signatures had been collected in a call for a referendum on the country's future organization.

In an interview of 24 January 1992, Havel described how his proposal was meant to overcome the Catch-22 of the current situation:

> [Under the original law] the question must be formulated by the parliament, and if the parliament is compelled to seek the view of the citizens . . . this means that it is not capable of reaching an agreement, and if it is not capable of agreeing on the merit of the matter, then it follows that it is even less capable of agreeing on the question which it will put forward to the public. The purpose of that amendment was to remove this illogical obstacle.[34]

Stalemate continued, however, and Havel failed to get approval for his change.

Throughout the rest of the year, public opinion supported a referendum and the preservation of the CSFR, but the two parties that won the June 1992 elections, the Movement for Democratic Slovakia and the Civic Democratic party in the Czech Republic, went about negotiating a split. On 25 November 1992, the Federal Assembly adopted a constitutional amendment permitting the dissolution of the federation without a referendum, thus paving the way for separation over the next few months. To the end, public opinion supported a referendum.

This is one of the rare cases where a referendum might have made it possible for a country to stay together. The ability of elites to avoid the referendum and to thwart mass opinion suggests one of the imperfections in the referendum device—it is powerless unless activated by an established authority.

The Former Soviet Union. A stalemate between reformers and powerful conservative remnants of the Soviet regime has paralyzed many of the former Soviet republics (especially in Russia, Belarus, Ukraine, and Moldova). The large number of proposed but aborted referendums designed to find ways to break the logjam (see table 6–9), along with the

---

34. Foreign Broadcast Information Service, Eastern European Unit, Czechoslovakia, 27 January 1992, "Havel on Parliament Draft Bill, Referendum Issue," p. 12.

TABLE 6–9
Some Proposed Referendums in the Former Soviet Union, 1990–1993

Country	Topic	Date Proposed	Who Proposed	Fate
USSR	Economic plan	May 1990	Gorbachev and aides	No parliamentary approval for plan; Gorbachev changed course
USSR	Land reform	September 1990	Gorbachev	Change of course by Gorbachev
USSR[a]	Union Treaty	September 1990	Gorbachev	Boycotted by six republics; held in nine others
Belarus	Dissolution of Supreme Soviet	January 1992	Petition by democratic parties	Parliamentary maneuvers
Belarus	CIS Security Pact	April 1992	Parliamentary opposition	Parliamentary maneuvers
Lithuania	Citizenship	December 1991	Nationalist public group	Parliamentary opposition
Moldova	Moldovan independence	December 1992	President Snegur; parliamentary majority	No need—parliamentary opposition dissolves
Moldova	New constitution	March 1993	President Snegur; parliamentary majority	Stalemate as of end of 1993

(Table continues)

213

TABLE 6-9 (continued)

Country	Topic	Date Proposed	Who Proposed	Fate
Russia	Preserve Russia	February 1991	Yeltsin	Fears about how autonomous republics would react
Russia[a]	Elect president	February 1991	Yeltsin	Boycotted by pro-Communist and nationalist areas such as Bashkiria, North Ossetia, Oryoly, Smolensk, Tatarstan, and Tuva; held elsewhere
Russia	Private land	June 1992	Democratic Russia—million signatures	Victim of stalemate between Yeltsin and Parliament
Russia	President vs. Congress	January 1993	Yeltsin	Endless bickering between Yeltsin and legislature leading to modified questions
Ukraine	Dissolve Parliament	September 1992	Opposition Rukh	Failed to get 3 million signatures
Ukraine	Confidence in president and Parliament	June 1993	Response to striking miners	Elections called without referendum; also opposition of president

SOURCE: Authors. Same as for table 6-3.

low success rate of governmental reform referendums that do come to fruition (for example, Russia in April 1993 or Lithuania in May 1992), suggests that referendums do little to solve these kinds of problems in these kinds of polities. Elites already in conflict can find too many ways to derail or defuse referendums and can ignore inconvenient results.

Conclusion

Although referendums appear to be the ultimate method for checking the pulse of democracy, they are inherently limited by the machinations of elites who can decide if and when to hold them, what will be asked, what will be said through the media, how success will be defined, and whether to abide by the results. With all these defects, referendums might be thought useless; yet they spoke eloquently and powerfully against communism in Poland and Hungary in the late 1980s and in the USSR in 1991. Referendums played an important part in getting Communists out of power in these pivotal countries.

Referendums also bestowed legitimacy on independence movements by allowing them to counter claims that their desire for independence was extremist or a minority opinion. In the best of circumstances, elites took them more seriously and tried to find a peaceful path to independence. In the worst of circumstances, elites countered with force. In the USSR, for example, the referendums in the Baltic states in February and March 1991 probably caused Gorbachev to rethink his strategy for the Union Treaty, but they also contributed to the reactionary coup attempt of August 1991. The failure of this coup then made it possible for the Baltic and other republics to leave the Soviet Union. In Yugoslavia, where referendums were met by force, they served as the shouting accompanying the deadly shoving match among the Yugoslavian nationalities. In at least one instance, a referendum was used to hold two republics together (Montenegro's decision to remain with Serbia). But in Czechoslovakia, where a referendum might have brought groups together, elites wanting separate republics maneuvered to prevent a referendum. All in all, referendums in this part of the world have been much better at ripping apart than tying together, and in doing so, they often foster emotions that can lead to violence.

Referendums are not very useful for breaking governmental deadlocks because elites who are at odds have many ways to sabotage them. Yet, in a few instances referendums have helped to reconstitute authority. The most conspicuous example is Yeltsin's presidency referendum of 17 March 1991. His success in this referendum was fundamental to his ability to thwart the coup attempt of August 1991 and his continuing ability to lay claim to power in the Soviet Union. The 25 April 1993 Russian referendum had no immediate meliorative effect on the legitimacy crisis, but Yeltsin's success in this referendum undoubtedly played a part in his garnering support from the military and abroad during his confrontation with the Russian Parliament in October 1993. Nevertheless, these are probably the exceptions rather than the rule. In most cases, it is very easy for bickering elites to eviscerate referendums or to ensure their defeat.

Referendums can allow public opinion to flower, and during times of transition, these blooms can ease the way to democracy if decision makers decide not to trample them underfoot with force and violence. There are dangers, however. In the giddiness of transitions, referendums can proliferate, creating chaotic gardens as each group jostles for its own space. Elites can prune and shape public opinion in ways that make a mockery of it. And the flower, some might say weed, of nationalism grows more robustly in the referendum garden than the flower of governmental reform. Nevertheless, referendums have been and will continue to be important devices for democratic transitions.

Bibliography

American Association for the Advancement of Slavic Studies. *Current Digest of the Post-Soviet Press*, various issues, 1992–1993. Columbus, Ohio: AAASS.

——. *Current Digest of the Soviet Press, 1990–1992.* Columbus, Ohio: AAASS.

Bozoki Andras, "Political Transition and Constitutional Change in Hungary." In *Post-Communist Transition: Emerging Pluralism in Hungary,* edited by Andras Bozoki, Andras Korosenyi, and George Schopflin. New York: St. Martin's Press, 1993.

Commission on Security and Cooperation in Europe. *Presidential Elections and Independence Referendums in the Baltic States, the Soviet Union, and Successor States.* Washington, D.C.: CSCE, 1992.

Estoniia. Tallinn, Estonia, 1991–1993.

Foreign Broadcast Information Service. *Daily Report, East Europe,* various issues, 1986–1993.

——. *Daily Report, USSR,* 1986–1993.

Jasiewicz, Krzysztof, and Tomasz Zukowski. "The Elections of 1984–89 as a Factor in the Transformation of the Social Order in Poland." *Democratization in Poland, 1988–90: Polish Voices,* edited by George Sanford. New York: St Martin's Press, 1992.

Molodezh' Estonii. Tallinn, Estonia, various issues, 1991–1993.

New York Times, various issues, 1986–1993.

Potichnyj, Peter. "The Referendum and Presidential Elections in Ukraine." *Canadian Slavonic Papers* 33, no. 2 (June 1991): 123–38.

Pravda (Moscow), various issues, 1991–1993.

Radio Free Europe/Radio Liberty, *Daily Reports,* various issues, 1991–1993.

Slider, Darrell. "The First 'National' Referendum and Referenda in the Republics: Voting on Union, Sovereignty, and Independence." *Journal of Soviet Nationalities,* forthcoming.

Wambaugh, Sarah. *Plebiscites since the World War.* Washington, D.C.: Carnegie Endowment for International Peace, 1933.

Washington Post, various issues, 1987–1993.

7
Direct Legislation in the American States

David B. Magleby

Although the United States is one of five democracies that have never held a nationwide referendum, direct legislation—the processes of popular referendum and initiative—is permitted in varying forms in just over half its states. During the past two decades, direct legislation has become an important feature in over fifteen states and now influences the political agenda of the entire nation.

The agenda of initiative activists has helped move direct legislation to center stage in American politics. Votes on gun control, abortion, automobile insurance, homosexual rights, and taxes are often taken as national bellwethers. Not surprisingly, many groups affected by a measure in a particular state invest heavily in supporting or opposing the measure, thus reinforcing the sense that a vote in a single state has consequences well beyond that state. The powerful agenda-setting possibilities of direct legislation have in turn encouraged greater use of the process by more issue activists and politicians. In recent elections, the number of statewide ballot questions has risen to the point that some question the ability of voters to handle the length of the ballots.

While use of direct legislation has increased, only one state has adopted the process since 1978, and only five states have adopted some form of direct legislation since 1918. Since the late 1970s, Hawaii, New Jersey, Minnesota, and Rhode Island have seriously considered adopt-

I acknowledge the assistance of election officials in the twenty-seven direct legislation states for their willingness to provide data. Eugene C. Lee and Don Norton provided helpful comments. Research assistance was provided by Scott Baxter, Camie Christiansen, Rob Karlinsey, Quin Monson, Paul M. Peterson, and Kevin Wilkinson.

ing the process, but only Mississippi has actually done so.[1]

Direct legislation in the United States is largely a product of the Progressive Era (c. 1890–1920); more than 80 percent of the states that permit some form of initiative and popular referendum adopted the process during the first two decades of the twentieth century.[2] While direct legislation has generated more interest in the past fifteen years, the renewed interest has not led other states to adopt the process.

This chapter examines the dynamics of direct legislation in the United States. Topics discussed include the widely varying rules and procedures for use of the process and their implications, the appeal of the process and an explanation for its increased use, the subject matter of initiatives, the extent and nature of citizen participation in the process, the implications of the initiative for other institutions of government, and a general assessment of direct legislation as it operates today.

Defining Direct Legislation in the United States

Figure 7–1 presents the states that use the various forms of direct legislation. The *initiative* process permits citizens to draft laws *(statutory initiative)* and in some states constitutional amendments *(constitutional initiative)*, which are later decided by the voters in an election. If the proposed law goes directly to the ballot, the process is called the *direct initiative*. If the state permits the legislature to consider and possibly adopt the proposed law or constitutional amendment, the process is called the *indirect initiative*. As a general rule, in states that provide both the statutory and the constitutional initiative, initiative sponsors will seek to define their measure as a constitutional initiative because of its higher legal standing.[3] Constitutional initiatives can be changed only by a subsequent vote of the people; statutory initiatives can often be changed by votes of the legislature. Only five states do not allow the legislature to amend or repeal statutory initiatives.[4] Moreover, the

---

1. Mississippi actually readopted the initiative. The state first adopted the initiative in 1916, but the state supreme court declared the initiative law unconstitutional in 1922. Unsuccessful efforts to challenge that ruling in the 1980s led to passage of a new law reestablishing the initiative.

2. David B. Magleby, "Taking the Initiative: Direct Legislation and Direct Democracy in the 1980s," *PS: Political Science and Politics,* vol. 21 (1988), pp. 601–2.

3. David B. Magleby, *Direct Legislation: Voting on Ballot Propositions in the United States* (Baltimore: Johns Hopkins University Press, 1984), pp. 35–36.

4. Philip L. Dubois and Floyd F. Feeney, *Improving the California Initiative Process: Options for Change* (Berkeley: California Policy Seminar, University of California, 1992), p. 70.

FIGURE 7-1

PROVISIONS FOR INITIATIVE AND POPULAR REFERENDUM IN THE UNITED STATES

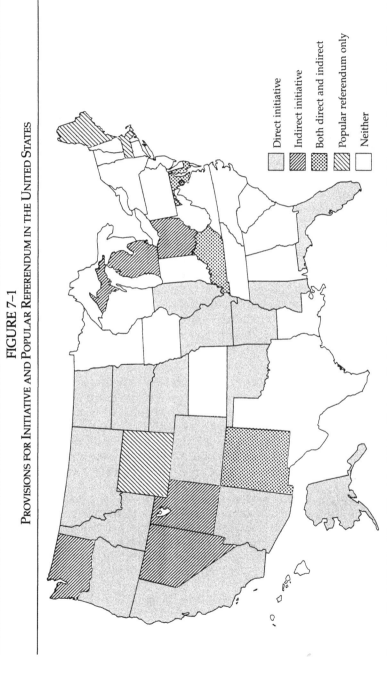

Direct initiative

Indirect initiative

Both direct and indirect

Popular referendum only

Neither

SOURCE: David B. Magleby, *Direct Legislation: Voting on Ballot Propositions in the United States* (Baltimore: Johns Hopkins University Press, 1984), pp. 38–39. Mississippi Constitution, Section 273, and Mississippi Code Annotated, Section 23-1-71.

tendency to use the constitutional initiative in states like California has increased since 1978.[5] In states that provide both the direct and the indirect initiative process, the direct initiative is used most because it eliminates the need to compromise and provides more unmediated access to voters.[6]

In its broadest definition, a referendum is any vote of the people on a proposed law, policy, or public expenditure. From the very beginning of the American republic, a view has prevailed that voters ought to decide on major constitutional questions at the state level, through *constitutional referendums.* Rhode Island, for instance, submitted the U.S. Constitution directly to the voters for approval.[7] Today, voters in all states but Delaware must formally approve changes in the state constitution,[8] and voters in some states sometimes cast ballots on proposed amendments to the U.S. Constitution, for example, the Equal Rights Amendment in the 1980s.[9] State legislatures often place *legislative referendums* on the ballot; these measures are essentially statutory changes for which they desire a ratifying vote of the people; in some states, they include bond measures to raise revenue, often for designated purposes.[10]

The type of referendum most akin to the initiative is the *popular*

---

5. Eugene C. Lee, "Representative Government and the Initiative Process," in John Kirlin and Donald Winkler, eds., *California Policy Choices*, vol. 6 (Los Angeles: University of Southern California, School of Public Administration, 1990), p. 228.

6. See Magleby, *Direct Legislation;* Dubois and Feeney, *Improving the California Initiative Process;* and Lee, "Representative Government and the Initiative Process."

7. Of the original thirteen colonies, only Massachusetts and New Hampshire submitted their state constitutions directly to the voters for ratification. Likewise, only Massachusetts required the direct vote of the people to change its constitution. Madison argued strongly for this provision to be included in the Virginia Constitution, but originally it was not. By the Civil War, however, all new states and most original states required voter approval for constitutional changes. See Thomas E. Cronin, *Direct Democracy: The Politics of Initiative, Referendum, and Recall* (Cambridge: Harvard University Press, 1989), pp. 41–43.

8. Magleby, *Direct Legislation*, p. 36.

9. Patrick B. McGuigan, "When in Doubt, Vote No" (Paper presented at the annual meeting of the American Political Science Association, Washington D.C., August 1986).

10. Legislative referendums in the American states are equivalent to the facultative referendums in Western European nations described by Vernon Bogdanor in chapter 3. The measures are placed on the ballots by actions of the legislature and governor, not, as in the case of popular referendums, by petitions signed by voters.

referendum, which permits citizens to place an action of the legislature or local government on the ballot for a ratifying vote of the people. Here, as with the initiative, the trigger mechanism is the petition process, in which voters sign their names to petitions to force a vote on a government action. Most states that provide the initiative in some form also provide the popular referendum, because proponents of direct legislation often see the initiative as the means to correct legislative "sins of omission" while the popular referendum permits citizens to correct legislative "sins of commission."[11] Three states provide only the popular referendum, and two states provide the initiative without the popular referendum.

With only one exception, the states that adopted some form of direct legislation before 1914 adopted both the initiative and the popular referendum. In contrast, only half the eight states that adopted the process after 1915 chose to provide both the initiative and the popular referendum. States have become increasingly less likely to see the initiative and popular referendum as part of a package. States have also become more enamored with the indirect initiative since 1915. Of states that adopted some form of initiative after 1915, half provide the indirect initiative only. In contrast, just one of eighteen states that adopted the initiative before 1915 grants only the indirect initiative. In short, in the early going states were much more likely to embrace all aspects of direct legislation and provide the most direct forms of the process. In later years, those states that have adopted the process have been more inclined to adopt only parts of it and have been more interested in indirect forms of the initiative. Two states, however, that have given recent serious attention to adopting the initiative, Minnesota and New Jersey, have focused on the direct initiative and popular referendum. While many states permit both the initiative and the popular referendum, it is the initiative that is much more frequently used. Since 1980, there have been roughly five initiatives for every popular referendum.

Petitioners can and sometimes do use the direct initiative as a popular referendum because the process is less constraining, especially in the time limitation for petitions. The best-known example of this is the 1964 vote on open housing in California.[12] This initiative essentially vetoed the action of the legislature, which had passed a measure pro-

---

11. Gilbert Hahn and Stephen C. Morton, "Initiative and Referendum: Do They Encourage or Impair Better State Government?" *Florida State University Law Review,* vol. 5 (1977), pp. 926–27.

12. Raymond E. Wolfinger and Fred I. Greenstein, "The Repeal of Fair Housing in California: An Analysis of Referendum Voting," *American Political Science Review,* vol. 63 (1969), p. 755; Reitman v. Mulkey, 387 U.S. 369 (1967).

hibiting racial discrimination in the sale of residential housing. By a large majority, Californians voted for this constitutional initiative and thereby against the antidiscrimination law, an action later overturned by the courts.

As figure 7–1 illustrates, direct legislation is much more common in the western states.[13] This geographic concentration is in part a historical artifact. The western states were in the early stages of their political development during the Progressive Era, and hence were more open to these new processes. The West was also a stronghold of the Progressive movement. Progressive reformers, whose agenda included such reforms as the direct election of U.S. senators, the direct primary, and nonpartisan local elections, were also champions of the initiative, referendum, and recall.[14] Because of the Progressives' "passion for the more democratic, anti-institutional political reforms," it is not surprising that this region remains the most committed to direct legislation.[15] In contrast, only six states in the Northeast and South have adopted any form of direct legislation, and then such adoption is only partial, like Maryland's use of the popular referendum but with no provisions for the initiative; Florida's and Mississippi's use of the initiative only; and Georgia's and Louisiana's provision of the recall only.[16]

The politics surrounding Mississippi's adoption of the initiative manifest the lingering concerns of many elected officials about direct legislation. Mississippi adopted the direct initiative, both statutory and constitutional, and referendum in 1916. But both the initiative and the referendum were declared unconstitutional only six years later by the state supreme court because they had been enacted as a single general measure rather than as several specific constitutional changes.[17] In 1990, two state legislators decided to test the decades-old ruling by circulating initiative petitions for a state lottery. When the secretary of state refused to put the measure on the ballot, the legislators and the

13. Charles M. Price, "The Initiative: A Comparative State Analysis and Reassessment of a Western Phenomenon," *Western Political Quarterly*, vol. 28 (1975), p. 246.

14. William B. Munro, ed., *The Initiative, Referendum and Recall* (New York: D. Appleton and Co., 1912), p. 1.

15. Arthur Stanley Link and Richard L. McCormick, *Progressivism* (Arlington, Ill.: Harlin Davidson Inc., 1983), p. 34.

16. David B. Magleby, "Opinion Formation and Opinion Change in Ballot Proposition Campaigns," in Michael Margolis and Gary Mauser, eds., *Manipulating Public Opinion* (Pacific Grove, Cal.: Brooks/Cole Publishing Company, 1989), p. 601; Cathy Hayden, "Initiative Shown, Amendment Passes," *Clarion Ledger* (4 November 1992).

17. Power v. Robertson, 93 So. 769, 130 Miss. 188 (1922).

attorney general challenged the action in the state courts. The state supreme court voted 6–0 to uphold the 1922 ruling.[18] Supporters of direct legislation then enacted a new law that permitted the process. Opponents of direct legislation in Mississippi included rural conservative members of the legislature and the black caucus. Black legislators feared that racially discriminatory measures would be put on the ballot by initiative, and rural House members feared that urban voters would raise their property taxes or reduce funding for rural road maintenance.[19]

Proponents of the initiative secured early passage of their proposal in the state Senate but failed on the first three votes in the House of Representatives. With each defeat, they watered down the provisions—abandoning statutory initiatives and popular referendums, while raising the signature threshold. To assuage the concerns of blacks, they added the requirement that one-fifth of the signatures must come from each of the five congressional districts (one of Mississippi's congressional districts has a majority black population).[20] To provide a greater role for themselves, the legislators permitted the legislature to place an alternative to each initiative on the ballot, allowing the voters to decide between the initiated proposal and the legislative alternative. In addition, they added a "supermajority" requirement that the majority voting in favor of a particular initiative must equal at least 40 percent of the total of all voters participating in that election. In 1993, the U.S. Department of Justice granted its approval of the new law, making it possible for Mississippi again to vote on initiatives.[21]

Legal Provisions for Direct Legislation in the American States

In the United States, the states are primarily responsible for their own election laws, and the initiative is no exception. States vary in their laws

---

18. Moore v. Molpus, 578 So.2d 624 (1991).

19. Sarah C. Campbell, "House Kills Voter Voice Amendment," *Clarion Ledger* (21 March 1992).

20. Some black legislators claimed, however, that the geographic distribution requirement would make it more difficult for black voters to get the necessary signatures in congressional districts where the majority of the population was white. See Hayden, "Initiative Shown, Amendment Passes."

21. Because Mississippi falls under the provisions of the national Voting Rights Act and its subsequent amendments, changes in state voting laws must be reviewed for possible discriminatory effects. See Jay Eubank and Sarah C. Campbell, "Lawmakers Vote for Initiative and Referendum Measure," *Clarion Ledger*, 9 May 1992.

governing direct legislation.[22] Some of the most important differences concern whether initiative proponents may amend the state constitution or are limited to statutory changes. Another important difference is whether the proponents of an initiative may take their proposition directly to the voters or whether they are required to give elected officials a chance to respond to the provisions of their measure first (direct versus indirect initiative).

One of the most important legal requirements in all direct legislation processes is the signature threshold and related requirements. All forms of the initiative and popular referendum require that petitioners gather sufficient signatures from registered voters to meet a signature threshold, typically set as a proportion of the vote for governor in the previous gubernatorial election. Signature requirements range from a low of 2 percent in North Dakota for statutory initiatives to a high of 15 percent in Wyoming for statutory initiatives and popular referendums. Table 7–1 presents the signature thresholds for the direct legislation states and the number of initiatives and popular referendums that have appeared on the ballot since 1950.

The stringency of a state's signature threshold is inversely related to the frequency of measures qualifying for the ballot.[23] Thirteen states have a geographic distribution requirement for signatures on direct legislation petitions. The intent of this requirement is to force petitioners to demonstrate support for their measure outside a few heavily populated counties. The presence of a geographic distribution requirement appears to hamper proponents in getting their measures on the ballot. A simple comparison of the number of propositions that make

---

22. Magleby, *Direct Legislation*, p. 35.

23. To test for the relationship between signature requirements and whether the number of direct legislation options open to citizens (constitutional, statutory, or both) are related to the frequency of initiative use the following regression was run:

$$y = a + b_1x_1 + b_2x_2$$

Where y = number of measures on the ballot
        x_1 = number of direct legislation options
        x_2 = average signature threshold

The results of the model being tested are

$$y = 18.55 + 21.34 \text{ (options)} - 4.22 \text{ (threshold)}$$

The R^2 for the model is a statistically significant .479. Significant at a P value of .01. A model that included the independent variable geographic distribution was also computed, but the coefficient was not significant; however, the negative sign of the coefficient indicates that the presence of geographic distribution requirements and the number of measures making it to the ballot are inversely related.

TABLE 7–1
SIGNATURE REQUIREMENTS AND NUMBER OF INITIATIVES AND REFERENDUMS
QUALIFYING FOR BALLOT IN SELECTED STATES, 1950–1992
(percent of vote in a preceding candidate election)

	Statutory Initiative	Consti-tutional Initiative	Popular Referendum	Average Signature Threshold	Number of Initiatives and Referendums
North Dakota	2	4	2	2.7	95
Maryland[a]	—	—	3	3.0	14
Massachusetts[a]	5	5	2	4.0	32
Colorado	5	5	5	5.0	63
Kentucky	—	—	5	5.0	0
California	5	8	5	6.0	127
Oregon	6	8	4	6.0	97
Missouri[a]	5	8	5	6.0	24
Washington	8	—	4	6.0	69
Montana[a]	5	10	5	6.7	49
South Dakota	5	10	5	6.7	31
Ohio[a]	6	10	6	7.3	28
Nebraska[a]	7	10	5	7.3	24
Michigan	8	10	5	7.7	48
Arkansas[a]	8	10	6	8.0	40
Florida[a]	—	8	—	8.0	8
Illinois	—	8	10[b]	9.0	10
Oklahoma	8	15	5	9.3	38
Alaska[a]	10	—	10	10.0	22
Arizona	10	15	5	10.0	54
Idaho	10	—	10	10.0	13
Maine	10	—	10	10.0	22
New Mexico	—	—	10	10.0	2
Nevada[a]	10	10	10	10.0	24
Utah[a]	10	—	10	10.0	14
Mississippi[a]	—	12	—	12.0	0
Wyoming[a]	15	—	15	15.0	3
Median	8	10	5	7.5	

NOTE: An empty cell indicates that the state does not permit use of the device.
a. Geographic requirement.
b. Nonbinding, advisory.
SOURCE: The numbers of initiatives and popular referendums on the ballot since 1950 were obtained from Graham, *A Compilation of Statewide Initiative Proposals on Ballots through 1976*; Magleby, *Direct Legislation: Voting on Ballot Propositions in the United States*, p. 43, as well as from interviews with election officials in all twenty-seven initiative and popular referendum states.

it to the ballot in the fourteen states without a geographic distribution requirement with the thirteen states that have one also demonstrates the large hurdle that geographic distribution requirements place in the way of initiative proponents. Since 1950, the states without a distribution requirement have averaged forty-eight propositions per state (initiatives and popular referendums), while the states with the requirement have averaged twenty-two per state.

Other important procedural rules include the time period a measure can remain in circulation, the process whereby the measure is given its official title and summary, limitations on the subject matter that may be part of the measure, and whether the vote necessary for success is a simple majority of those voting on the measure, a majority of those voting in the election, or a supermajority of 60 percent or more of those voting in the election. Initiative petitions typically may circulate for up to 120 days, but the time limitation can be as short as 50 days or as long as 360 days. Popular referendum petitions typically have a shorter time period for circulation, averaging about 90 to 120 days.

Because initiatives are proposed laws or constitutional amendments, they can be very lengthy and technical in their wording. All states provide a short summary of the proposal, and most states give a short title as well. In some states, the proponents are permitted to title and summarize their own measures, but in most states this task is left to election officials. The process of summarizing and titling initiatives is often challenged in court. Yet with regard to "procedural defects such as . . . title and summary requirements, most states either prohibit post-election review under the 'election cures all' doctrine or place a higher burden of proof on the challengers."[24]

States also quite commonly limit the subject matter of initiatives and popular referendums either by excluding some subjects from the process or by requiring that each measure be limited to a single subject. As direct legislation evolves, other procedural rules arise to address abuses or concerns. Individuals cannot be named to office in California via the initiative, for example, and at least four states "require that a measure may not encompass more than a single subject."[25] This provision in California was the result of a 1948 initiative that attempted to build a winning coalition by including several different subjects, for

---

24. James D. Gordon and David B. Magleby, "Pre-election Judicial Review of Initiatives and Referendums," *Notre Dame Law Review*, vol. 64 (1989), pp. 313–34.

25. Ibid., p. 303.

example, gambling, reapportionment of the state legislature, surface mining, and retirement pensions.[26]

The vote needed for enactment of direct legislation also varies among the states. Some states require a majority of those voting on the measure, others a majority of those voting in the election, and still others an extraordinary majority of those voting in the election. At least one state requires a majority vote in two consecutive elections for a constitutional initiative to take effect. In 1988 and 1990, for instance, Nevada voters approved a constitutional initiative banning income taxes. When Minnesota voted on whether to adopt the initiative process in 1980, 53.2 percent of those voting on the question voted for the proposal, but a quarter of a million persons who voted in the election failed to vote on the question. Hence the affirmative vote was only 46.7 percent of all voters in the election. Since Minnesota law requires that a majority of those voting in the election vote affirmatively for changes in the state constitution, the proposal for a statewide initiative failed.[27]

A few states used to have limitations on paid signature solicitation, but in 1988 the U.S. Supreme Court declared them unconstitutional.[28] In those states (for example, Colorado), which once allowed only volunteer signature collectors, paid signature solicitors now operate legally. Changes in interpretation of California law now permit signature solicitation by mail. Some political consulting firms that specialize in direct mail fund-raising are now paid to circulate petitions to place an initiative on the ballot along with a request, in the same mailing, for campaign contributions to fund the solicitation and subsequent campaign. One recent study of the process found that direct mail signature solicitation has spread to most states that do not require petition circulators to notarize their petitions.[29] Another common practice is for paid petition circulators to circulate several petitions simultaneously. The strategy involves asking citizens if they are interested, for example, in voting on school vouchers, gay rights, the auto insurance industry, or a tax on tobacco. Citizens may choose to sign as many of the petitions as they wish.[30]

---

26. Perry v. Jordan, 34 Cal.2d 330 (1949).

27. Charles Backstrom, "Popular Vote on Populist Amendments" (Paper presented at the annual meeting of the American Political Science Association, Denver, Colorado, September 1983), p. 3.

28. Meyer v. Grant, 486 U.S. 414 (1988).

29. California Commission on Campaign Financing, *Democracy by Initiative: Shaping California's Fourth Branch of Government* (Los Angeles: Center for Responsive Government, 1992), p. 153.

30. For a discussion of recent developments in signature solicitation, see Charles M. Price, "Signing for Fun and Profit: The Business of Gathering Petition Signatures," *California Journal* (November 1992), pp. 545–48.

Only registered voters may sign petitions, except in North Dakota, which does not have voter registration. There is a wide variation in how states verify petition signatures, ranging from verifying each signature to verifying random samples of signatures. States routinely check for duplicate signatures and evidence of petition fraud.

Expanded Use of Direct Legislation

Table 7–2 summarizes initiative activity by state. Holding aside Mississippi, which only recently readopted the process, four more states permit the statutory initiative than permit the constitutional initiative. For the period since 1898, the average total number of statutory initiatives for each state is forty-five, and the average total number of constitutional initiatives for each state that permits this form of initiative is forty-one—a rough parity in the frequency of statutory and constitutional initiatives. In the aggregate, there is also little difference in the passage rates for statutory and constitutional initiatives: statutory initiatives have been enacted about 40 percent of the time, and constitutional initiatives about 36 percent of the time.

There are some differences among the states in rates of passing initiatives. All three initiatives that have appeared on the Wyoming ballot have passed, while only two of Utah's sixteen initiatives (13 percent) have been approved by the voters. States with higher initiative pass rates include Wyoming, Florida, Idaho, Illinois, Massachusetts, and Montana. Most of these states have either recently adopted or activated the process (Wyoming, Florida, and Illinois) or have had few initiatives on the ballot (Idaho).

There has been a resurgence of the use of the initiative since the mid-1970s. Figure 7–2 plots the use of the initiative in the United States by decade, with a projection for the 1990s based on number of measures decided between 1990 and 1992.

The use of direct legislation grew dramatically in the first few years of its existence. Between 1910 and 1919, a record-setting 269 measures went to a vote, and 98 were approved. Use of direct legislation declined in the 1920s, rose again in the 1930s, fell precipitously in the 1940s and 1950s, and bottomed out in the 1960s. In the 1950s and 1960s, an average of fewer than eight initiatives passed per election cycle, down from an average of nearly twenty per election cycle in the 1920s. But these patterns reversed themselves in the 1970s, when the number of measures on the ballot grew faster than the number of propositions passed by the voters. Based on projections from the 1990 and 1992 elections, the 1990s will set new records for direct legislation activity.

The growth in initiative activity has been widespread. States like

TABLE 7-2
INITIATIVE PROPOSITIONS SUBMITTED TO THE VOTERS IN THE UNITED STATES, 1898–1992

State	Statutory Initiatives			Constitutional Initiatives			Totals		
	No. proposed	No. approved	Percent approved	No. proposed	No. approved	Percent approved	No. proposed	No. approved	Percent approved
Alaska	20	9	45.0	0	0	—	20	9	45.0
Arizona	78	28	35.9	55	24	43.6	133	52	39.1
Arkansas	26	13	50.0	58	28	48.3	84	41	48.8
California	121	42	34.7	115	36	31.3	236	78	33.1
Colorado	48	21	43.8	99	32	32.3	147	53	36.1
Florida	0	0	0	8	5	62.5	8	5	62.5
Idaho	17	11	64.7	0	0	—	17	11	64.7
Illinois	1	1	100.0	10	6	60.0	11	7	63.6
Maine	30	10	33.3	0	0	—	30	10	33.3
Massachusetts	40	19	47.5	2	2	100.0	42	21	50.0
Michigan	11	8	92.9	54	17	61.5	65	25	38.5

Missouri	20	6	30.0	38	11	28.9	58	17	29.3
Montana	50	31	62.0	8	3	37.5	58	34	50.0
Nebraska	22	4	18.2	16	8	50.0	38	12	31.6
Nevada	16	7	43.8	18	9	50.0	34	16	47.1
North Dakota	151	60	39.7	34	19	55.9	185	79	42.7
Ohio	10	3	30.0	48	12	25.0	58	15	25.9
Oklahoma	31	8	25.8	47	14	29.8	78	22	28.2
Oregon	158	55	34.8	116	34	29.3	274	89	32.5
South Dakota	35	9	25.7	6	3	50.0	41	12	29.3
Utah	16	2	12.5	0	0	—	16	2	12.5
Washington	96	46	47.9	0	0	—	96	46	47.9
Wyoming	3	3	100.0	0	0	—	3	3	100.0
Total	1,000	396	39.6	732	223	36.0	1732	659	38.1

— indicates state does not permit use of the device.

SOURCE: For 1900–1976, Virginia Graham, "A Compilation of Statewide Initiative Proposals Appearing on Ballots through 1976" (Washington, D.C.: Congressional Research Service); for 1977–1991, interviews with election officials in each state; for 1992, Free Congress Foundation.

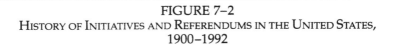

FIGURE 7–2
HISTORY OF INITIATIVES AND REFERENDUMS IN THE UNITED STATES,
1900–1992

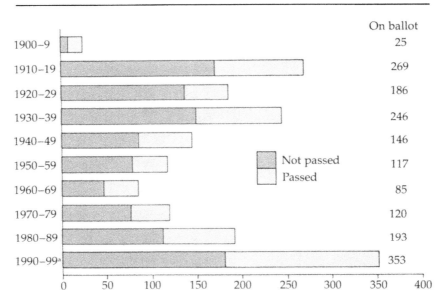

a. Projected.
SOURCE: For 1990–1976, Virginia Graham, "A Compilation of Statewide Initiative Proposals Appearing on Ballots through 1976" (Washington, D.C.: Congressional Research Service); for 1977–1984, Sue Thomas, "A Comparison of Initiated Activity by State," *Initiative Quarterly*, vol. 3 (1984), pp. 8–10; for 1985–1992, state election officials.

South Dakota and Utah, which have rarely used initiatives in the past, have recently voted on measures more frequently. More initiative-prone states like California, Oregon, and Washington have seen even heavier use of the process. The growth in numbers of initiatives going before the voters is only part of the explanation for increased use of the initiative. An even more dramatic expansion of activity has occurred at the petition circulation phase. Figure 7–3 presents the number of initiatives titled, qualified, and adopted for California between 1912 and 1992.

California's drop in the use of the initiative closely mirrors that in other states during the 1940–1969 period. For instance, the state passed only two initiatives during the 1950s. California, like the nation, saw more measures qualified and adopted in the 1970s and even more dur-

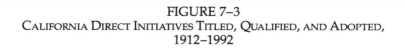

FIGURE 7–3
CALIFORNIA DIRECT INITIATIVES TITLED, QUALIFIED, AND ADOPTED,
1912–1992

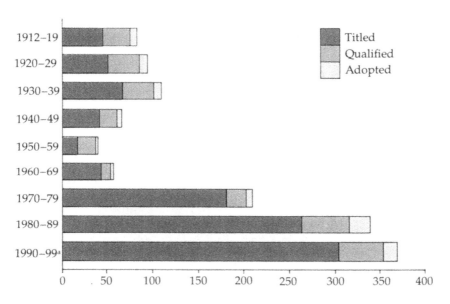

a. Projected.
SOURCE: March Fong Eu, "A History of the California Initiative Process," Office of the Secretary of State, November 1992.

ing the 1980s. But the greatest growth in initiative activity has been at the beginning stages of the process—the titling and petition-circulation phases. More measures were titled in the 1970s than in the previous four decades combined, and even though only seven measures made it to the ballot and won voter approval during the 1970s, the number of initiatives started has continued to increase during the 1980s and early 1990s.

There are several explanations for the recent increase. One is that the process was rediscovered in the 1970s by issue activists as a tool for achieving their policy goals. Conservatives used the initiative to make tax cutting a national movement, and liberals did the same with the nuclear freeze movement. Other groups discovered the same benefits, and if they were not able to push their issues in several states, then they used a single state as a means to generate media attention and interest in it. Advocates of both conservative and liberal policies have used initiatives. In 1992, for instance, voters took more conservative positions by curbing taxes and government spending and broadening the rights of crime victims, while taking liberal positions on abortion issues.

Politicians have also championed specific initiatives or adoption of the process for their own purposes. States without the process have seen such gubernatorial candidates as Bill Clements of Texas and Al Quie of Minnesota advocate it to establish their populist credentials. In states that already have the initiative, prominent politicians have used it to further their political careers. In California's 1990 gubernatorial campaign, candidates Diane Feinstein, John Van de Kamp, and Pete Wilson all sponsored initiatives; Van de Kamp, indeed, supported three separate measures. In 1992, the governors of Colorado and Michigan also actively supported ballot initiatives. Gubernatorial candidates' use of the initiative to broaden their electoral base goes back at least to 1974, when candidate Jerry Brown helped sponsor a campaign reform initiative in California. State legislators, especially in the minority party, also sponsor initiatives. For a politician, the initiative process is a way to heighten visibility, appeal to issue constituencies that might otherwise not vote in an election, and raise money from issue activists.

The growth in initiative activity is also partly explained by the expansion and professionalization of the initiative industry. For decades, initiative campaigns have employed professional managers, petition circulators, media consultants, pollsters, and the like. Since the 1970s, the number of such professionals has proliferated, and the industry has expanded to include litigation, direct mail fund-raising and petition signature collection. Given the large amounts of money spent on initiative campaigns, it is not surprising that such an industry has developed.

One new tactic in the initiative industry is to sponsor counter-initiatives that appear to cover the same issue as a competing initiative but actually are intended to defeat the original initiative by getting more votes. The strategic purposes of counter-initiatives include confusing the voters so they will vote No on both measures, and making the ballot so long that voters out of frustration and fatigue vote No on all measures.[31] If opinion strongly supports an initiative, then a counter-initiative seeks to gain more Yes votes, typically by going only part way toward the objective of the original initiative. Use of the counter-initiative dates back at least to 1968, but the strategy grew even more popular in 1988 and 1990.

---

31. Susan A. Banducci, "Voter Confusion and Voter Rationality: The Use of Counter Proposals in the Direct Democracy Process" (Paper presented at the annual meeting of the American Political Science Association, Chicago, Illinois, September 1992), p. 7.

The growth in the initiative industry raises questions about whether the process is any longer a grass-roots process. Whether we have reached the point at which many initiatives come from the initiative industry's efforts to increase business by proposing its own measures is unclear, but the use of counter-initiatives suggests that this may be happening.[32]

The initiative industry is involved not only in getting measures on the ballot but also in running campaigns and in defending or challenging the measures in the courts should they be approved by the voters. Not surprisingly, one large component of the industry is lawyers, who assist at all stages. The only check on the initiative in most states is the court system, which has become the enforcer and adjudicator of the process. Lawyers participate in disputes over the titling and official description, in the signature gathering process, and eventually in litigation over the legality or constitutionality of the measures.[33]

Courts have assumed the role of overseer. The Mississippi courts were not alone in questioning the constitutionality of the initiative process. In an early case that went all the way to the U.S. Supreme Court, the Oregon law was challenged as violating the U.S. Constitution's guarantee that states provide a "republican form of government."[34] However, unlike the Mississippi State Supreme Court in 1922, which held that the enactment of the initiative had violated the state constitution, the U.S. Supreme Court in 1912 declared that direct legislation does not violate the federal Constitution.[35] One former Oregon Supreme Court justice has recently argued that courts should revisit the matter of whether the initiative, because it is prone to "unbridled interest and passion," confirms the founders' fears of direct democracy and their preference for republican government.[36]

While courts have been generally liberal in permitting states to adopt direct legislation, they have not hesitated to declare unconstitutional some measures approved by the voters. Between 1960 and 1980, only three initiatives approved by the voters of California were not

---

32. Bill Ainsworth, "Initiative Wars: If You Can't Beat 'Em, Swap 'Em," *California Journal* (March 1990), pp. 147–49.

33. Gordon and Magleby, "Pre-election Judicial Review of Initiatives and Referendums," p. 302.

34. U.S. Constitution, Art. IV, sec 4.

35. Pacific States Telephone and Telegraph Company v. Oregon, 233 U.S. 118 (1912).

36. Hans A. Linde, "When Initiative Lawmaking Is Not 'Republican Government': The Campaign against Homosexuality," *Oregon Law Review*, vol. 72 (1993), p. 32.

declared partly or entirely invalid by state or federal courts.[37] The high level of judicial review of initiatives in California became an issue itself during gubernatorial elections and played a role in the defeat of three California Supreme Court judges in the election of 1986.[38] California is not alone in the frequent judicial review of measures adopted by direct legislation, and substantive questions of constitutionality are only about one-quarter of the cases that go before the courts. The remainder of the cases deal with procedural issues like violations of rules on petition circulation, disputes over the official title or description, or whether the content violates limitations on the subject matter of initiatives.[39]

Another reason for the initiative's popularity is that it is a favorite of the news media. Initiatives and initiative activists can make great copy. The proponents, often outside the political mainstream, tend to behave differently from politicians. Their opponents frequently include powerful individuals and institutions. Ballot issues are usually controversial—issues the state legislature does not wish to deal with. Human interest stories, including those about initiative sponsors, are particularly popular in the age of "infotainment." Moreover, the outcome of an initiative has real consequences, or at least more predictable consequences than candidate elections.

While public opinion is mixed on some aspects of the process, most people jealously guard their right to vote on initiatives and referendums. Public support for the initiative process has declined somewhat in California, down from 83 percent who felt proposition elections were a good thing in 1979 to 66 percent in 1990. The 1990 poll of Californians found support for some reforms of the process, but a majority opposed substituting the indirect initiative for the direct initiative.[40] Even supporters of the process in general have concerns about whether "many people will not be able to cast an informed ballot" and fear "that special interests will gain power by spending money to promote only their side of an issue."[41] After facing a series of very

---

37. Data through 1980 are reported in David B. Magleby, *Direct Legislation*, p. 203. See also Gordon and Magleby, "Pre-election Judicial Review of Initiatives and Referendums," p. 301.

38. Julian N. Eule, "Judicial Review of Direct Democracy," *Yale Law Journal*, vol. 99 (1990), p. 1582.

39. Gordon and Magleby, "Pre-election Judicial Review of Initiatives and Referendums," p. 302.

40. Mervin Field and Mark DiCamillo, "Declining Majority Supportive of the Initiative System," *California Poll* (Press release), 12 September 1990, p. 1.

41. Large majorities held these positions in polls conducted in New Jersey

lengthy ballots, it is not surprising that "only one in five Californians (21 percent) thinks the typical voter understands most or all of the propositions that are put before them in statewide elections."[42] In Los Angeles County, the number of state and county ballot propositions between 1980 and 1992 averaged twenty-eight, and in general elections alone the average was thirty-two measures.

Agenda Setting by Initiative

The agenda for direct legislation issues is primarily concerned with matters of state and local government but sometimes extends to national and even international issues, such as the use of nuclear weapons or advisory votes on foreign policy decisions.[43]

No particular ideology has captured the initiative agenda in the American states. Issues pushed by conservatives include tax reduction, opposition to expanding the rights of homosexuals, and school choice. Liberals have sponsored measures to protect the environment, to preserve abortion rights, and to limit the death penalty. Table 7–3 divides statewide initiatives since 1978 into subject matter areas.

Since the late 1970s, when the surge in initiative activity accelerated, the most common subject matter for initiatives has been taxes and government spending; and three-fifths of all initiatives have concerned government spending, public morality, or political reform. Initiatives that seek to regulate business or labor or that deal with the environment often generate the most campaign spending but constitute only about one-quarter of all initiatives. Initiatives on civil rights or civil

---

in 1979 and California in 1982. Equally large majorities supported the view that the "public should decide, when representatives are afraid of offending certain interest groups" and that "if people could vote on issues, they would become interested in politics and participate in government." Data are from the *New Jersey Poll #38* (Rutgers, N.J.: Eagleton Institute of Politics, Rutgers University, October 1979); and the *California Poll #8206* (San Francisco: Field Institute, October 1982).

42. Mark DiCamillo and Mervin Field, "Voters Think Most Statewide Ballot Propositions Are Not Understandable to the Average Person. Most Expect to Spend Relatively Little Time Reading the Long November Election Ballot Pamphlet," the *California Poll* (Press release), 24 October 1990, p. 1.

43. One student of direct legislation has speculated that if the United States were to adopt a national initiative process, the agenda would likely include such issues as a balanced budget amendment, affirmative action, the death penalty, gun control, congressional pay raises and term limits, clean air, school prayer, and public financing of elections (Cronin, *Direct Democracy*, pp. 179–80).

TABLE 7–3
COMPARISON OF SUBJECT MATTER OF QUALIFIED INITIATIVES IN THE
UNITED STATES, 1978–1992

Subject	Total	Percentage
Government or political reform	77[a]	19
Public morality	58	15
Revenue or tax or bond	105	26
Regulation of business and labor	65	16
Civil liberties or rights	20	5
Health, welfare, housing	19	5
Environment or land use	35	9
Education	9	2
National policy	11[b]	1
Total	399	99

a. Seventeen of the forty-four were term-limit measures on the ballot in 1990 and 1992.
b. Eight of the eleven appeared on the 1982 ballot.
SOURCE: For 1978–1984, Sue Thomas, *Initiative Quarterly*, vol. 3 (1988), p. 8. For 1985–1986, Sue Thomas, *Monthly Initiative Bulletin*, vol. 3 (August 1988), p. 11. For 1987–1988, Sue Thomas, *Monthly Initiative Bulletin*, vol. 3 (August 1988), p. 11. For 1989–1992, Free Congress Foundation.

liberties, health, welfare, or education are relatively rare. Despite an occasional well-known national policy issue (for example, the nuclear freeze), national policy initiatives have constituted only 1 percent of all initiatives since 1978. Of the eleven national policy initiatives that have appeared on the ballot since 1978, eight were nuclear freeze votes on 1982 ballots.

What have been the most frequent subjects for initiatives in the 1990s? The 1990 and 1992 elections saw a jump in the number of initiatives on governmental and political reform; nearly 30 percent dealt with this topic. An impressive seventeen initiatives limiting the terms of elected officials appeared on ballots in 1990 and 1992. Term limitations alone constituted 11 percent of all initiatives decided in this period. In the early 1990s, several initiatives also dealt with public morality, especially gambling and abortion. In sum, the issue agenda of the early 1990s shows an even greater concentration of initiative activity in governmental and political reform, public morality, and taxing and spending policy, and comparatively few initiatives in other areas. Only three initiatives in the 1990s dealt with civil rights or civil liberties—although at least one, Colorado's gay rights initiative, received a great deal of national attention.

Issue activists who succeed in getting a measure on the ballot in one state can encourage similar groups in other states to do the same. The June 1978 vote on property taxes in California (Proposition 13) generated such intense national and international interest that tax cutters in more than a dozen states placed similar measures on the 1978 and 1979 ballots. Proposition 13 also spurred a variety of proposals for constitutional amendments to set general spending limits, require a balanced federal budget, or index tax brackets. The focus on lowering taxes was not limited to ballot initiatives but spread to state legislatures as well. During the 1978 and 1979 legislative sessions, thirty-seven states reduced property taxes, twenty-eight states cut income taxes, and thirteen states restricted sales tax collections; income and sales tax cuts together surpassed $4 billion.[44] Political commentators frequently argued that the passage of Proposition 13 signified a new move toward conservatism, a resurgent middle class, a tax-cutting tendency, and a message that the public desired less government.[45] A more recent example of this phenomenon is the series of term-limitation initiatives voted on in various states since 1990. Voters in Oklahoma were the first to impose term limits. By 1992, voters in sixteen other states had followed suit. These initiatives typically place a twelve-year limit on the

---

44. David O. Sears and Jack Citrin, *Tax Revolt: Something for Nothing in California* (Cambridge: Mass: Harvard University Press, 1985), pp. 261–63.

45. Proposition 13 made news not only in the United States but abroad as well. Reporting on the California campaign, the *Economist* (London) titled its editorial on Proposition 13 "Taxes Overboard" and concluded that "California's vote, like most things Californian, was just bolder, better, more innovative—in short a harbinger of things to come" (17 June 1978), p. 11. This same theme was echoed in cover stories for both *Time* and *Newsweek*. The *Newsweek* article, titled "The Big Tax Revolt," characterized the California tax revolt as "the new gut issue in American politics" (5 June 1978), p. 24. Even though political commentators did not agree on the causes and consequences of Proposition 13's passage, all agreed that it was a major political event. *Time's* review article on the 1978 general election began as follows: "Taxes, taxes, taxes! Ever since the resounding triumph of California's Proposition 13 last June, the nation has been shuddering with a kind of tax cutting fever" (20 November 1978), p. 16. See also "Is There a Parade?" *Nation*, vol. 227 (14 October 1978), pp. 363–64; "Conservatism," *U.S. News and World Report*, vol. 84 (23 January 1978), pp. 24–25. Not all commentators agreed that the country was turning conservative or that Proposition 13 was evidence of fundamental shifts in voter attitudes. For examples of contrary views, see Everett C. Ladd, "What the Voters Really Want," *Fortune*, 18 December 1978, pp. 40–44, 46, 48; Curtis B. Gans, "Conservatism by Default," *Nation*, vol. 227 (14 October 1978), pp. 372–74; and Tom Bethell, "The Changing Fashions of Liberalism," *Public Opinion*, vol. 2 (January/February 1979), pp. 41–46.

number of consecutive terms a legislator can serve in the state legislature, the U.S. Congress, or both.

In many respects, California is seen as a leader both in the issue agenda of initiatives and in the development of the process. Part of the reason is the interest the media have taken in California initiatives. But while many of the trends discussed in this chapter are most evident in California, they are visible in several other states as well.

Not surprisingly, targets of initiatives, such as tobacco companies, automobile insurance companies, and trial lawyers, see the vote in a single state on a measure hostile to their interests as a potential problem in several states, especially if the initiative passes. That is why early votes on initiatives targeted at specific groups or industries often generate high campaign expenditures. The opponents of such a measure seek to defeat the idea before it becomes a national movement. In cases where the industry or affected groups think their chances of defeating the measure are slight, they will follow the old adage "If you can't beat them, join them" and sponsor counter-initiatives that go part way in limiting toxins, reducing automobile insurance costs, strengthening environmental requirements, or whatever the issue is.

In most states, if the ballot presents two competing measures on the same topic and if both measures get majorities, the measure with the most votes takes effect. For instance, in California during 1988, voters passed two campaign finance reform initiatives; one was more comprehensive, including provisions on some topics omitted by the other measure. Proponents of the more comprehensive measure, which came in second to the counter-initiative, asserted that their measure should take effect in areas where the other initiative was silent, but the courts disagreed.

As noted, the initiative has seen increased use in the American states. But polls show that rarely do the initiatives on the ballot reflect the problems that voters view as most important. In 1992, for example, voters indicated that the economy, unemployment, and the deficit were the most important problems facing the nation.[46] In California, the state's economy and unemployment were listed as the most important problems facing the state. Yet the initiative is poorly suited to getting the economy working or reducing unemployment. Sometimes, initiatives deal with topics that interest only a few. Whether a state may allow the use of bear traps (Colorado) or permit nondentists to fit people with dentures (Oregon and Idaho) are examples of initiatives that went before the voters but probably concerned very few.

---

46. American National Election Study, Center for Political Research, University of Michigan (1992).

In the United States, an area of longstanding concern has been initiatives targeted at racial or other minorities. James Madison warned that the passions of the majority could become dangerous in a direct democracy.[47] The best-known example of such an initiative is California's vote on open housing in 1964, in which a majority voted to strike from state law recently enacted antidiscrimination regulations governing the sale of residential housing.[48] Some states have voted on initiatives to limit school busing to achieve school desegregation, and at least three states have banned public funding of abortions, a policy that has a disproportionate effect on racial minorities.[49]

Racial minorities are not the only minority groups that have been the target of initiatives. Linguistic minorities have been the subject of "English as the official language" initiatives in at least five states. Homosexuals have sponsored initiatives to establish antidiscrimination ordinances and have also been the subject of initiatives seeking to limit those rights. An example of the latter is the unsuccessful 1978 California initiative that provided for dismissal of gay or lesbian public school teachers. The 1992 vote in Colorado, which overturned local ordinances that protected gays from discrimination, is another example of the clash between minority groups and majoritarian direct democracy. Generally, however, the more extreme the measure, the less the chance of passage. For example, Oregon's 1992 initiative that required state and local governments to discourage homosexuality and the 1986 California initiative that would quarantine all AIDS victims lost by large margins.

Is direct legislation a danger to the rights of minorities? The answer seems to be yes, unless the courts are able and willing to protect these groups from attacks by direct legislation. In new democracies where traditions of antimajoritarian judicial protection of religious, ethnic, racial, and other groups may not exist, the potential for danger to minorities is greater.

Women are also often the subject of initiatives. Many western states led the way in adopting women's suffrage, and four states—

---

47. James Madison, *Federalist*, No. 10, in Clinton Rossiter, ed., *The Federalist Papers* (New York: New American Library edition, 1961), pp. 77–84.

48. See discussion of this proposition in the section "Defining Direct Legislation in the United States."

49. Magleby, *Direct Legislation*, p. 185; Derrick A. Bell, Jr., "The Referendum: Democracy's Barrier to Racial Equality," *Washington Law Review*, vol. 54 (1978); and Michele Arington, "English-Only Laws and Direct Legislation: The battle in the States over Language Minority Rights," *Journal of Law and Politics*, vol. 7 (1991).

Colorado, Oregon, Wyoming, and Arizona—did so by initiative.[50] More recently, women's rights advocates have taken an interest in the initiative process because it has become a battleground for reproductive freedom. Since 1990, voters in four states have decided statewide measures on abortion. Half the measures sought to limit abortion, while the other half tried to codify or broaden abortion rights. In all four cases, the voters decided to uphold a woman's right to an abortion, a major disappointment for conservative groups.

Because initiative issues are so hotly contested, often with very large sums of money spent on them, it is not surprising that an initiative can dominate the agenda of a particular election. Media preoccupation with some initiatives also reinforces the public's focus on initiatives and reduces focus on candidates. Examples of the high stakes of initiatives include the five insurance initiatives, on which more than $101 million was spent in California in 1988. In contrast, $29 million was spent on the California governor's race in 1990. Spending by insurance companies was extraordinary, but in 1988, the National Rifle Association (NRA) spent $8 million in Maryland on a handgun registration vote, and cigarette companies spent $21 million in California on a tobacco tax increase. Both the NRA and the tobacco companies lost.

Citizen Participation in Direct Legislation

Direct legislation involves citizens in a range of activities, including circulating and signing petitions, campaigning for and against measures, and voting on them. Even in the states with the most demanding signature thresholds, the required signatures do not exceed a small fraction of the vote cast for governor in the preceding election. Yet this does not mean that it is easy to gather enough signatures to qualify a measure for the ballot. Few individuals are so committed to an issue that they will invest the time and energy and risk the rebuffs sometimes experienced by petition circulators. This may be one reason why many issue activists in several states now employ paid signature solicitors.

People who sign petitions do so for a variety of reasons, ranging from genuine support of the measure to wanting to appease the solicitor. Surprisingly little research has been done on the signature solicitation process, especially in recent years. Earlier studies found that as many as half of those who signed petitions later voted against the mea-

---

50. Cronin, *Direct Democracy,* p. 97.

sure.[51] More recent reports from legislative hearings or court proceedings suggest that most people who sign petitions do not read what they sign but depend on the representation of the solicitor on what they are signing.[52]

While some initiatives continue to be pressed mainly by unpaid issue activists, it is now common for sponsors in California and other initiative states to retain professional petition circulators to help them acquire the necessary signatures. Paying for petition circulators and other parts of the initiative effort takes money, and contributions to initiative campaigns are another way individuals can participate in direct legislation. The findings of a recent study of sources of campaign contributions for the California initiative process are presented in figure 7-4.

Two-thirds of all money spent on California initiatives in 1990 came from business interests, while only 12 percent came from individuals. The remaining money came from political groups, office holders, and broad-based issue groups. Labor unions played a minimal role in 1990 initiatives, contributing only 1 percent to the campaigns. If the eighteen most expensive initiatives in California are examined, an even larger share of the money came from business groups—83 percent—and on these highly contested initiatives, individual contributors gave only 8 percent of the money.[53] Moreover, these supporters make large contributions. In the 1992 election, 67 percent of all money donated came in amounts of $100,000 or more, and 37 percent of this money came in chunks of $1 million or more. Likewise, though small contributions of $1,000 or less account for 78 percent of the number of contributions received, they account for only 6 percent of the money contributed to initiative campaigns.

In the case of the eighteen most expensive initiatives in California history, large contributions are even more predominant.[54] In 1990 alone, one donor, the brewer Annheuser-Busch, spent $8.3 million on two California alcohol tax initiatives.[55] Most money spent by business

51. Herbert M. Baus and William B. Ross, *Politics Battle Plan* (New York: Macmillan Co., 1968); Joseph F. La Polambara, *The Initiative and Referendum in Oregon: 1938–1948* (Corvallis, Oregon: Oregon State University Press, 1950); Allen R. Wilcox and Leonard B. Weinberg, "Petition-signing in the 1968 Election," *Western Political Quarterly*, vol. 24 (1971), pp. 731–40.

52. Magleby, *Direct Legislation*, p. 54; and Cronin, *Direct Democracy*, pp. 62–64.

53. California Commission, *Democracy by Initiative*, p. 271.

54. Ibid., pp. 279–80.

55. "State's Initiative Process Being Taken Over by Wealthy," *Bay Area Reporter*, 30 April 1992.

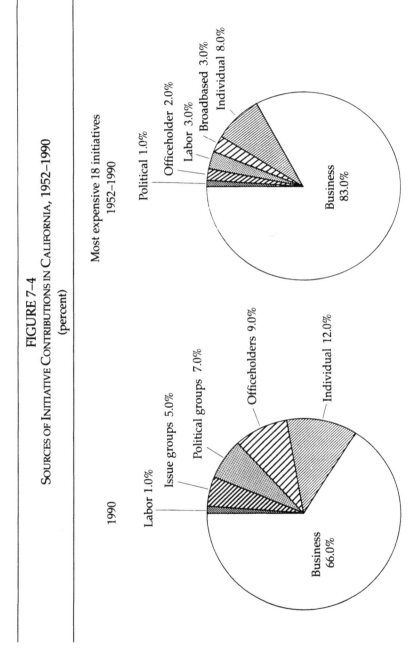

FIGURE 7–4
SOURCES OF INITIATIVE CONTRIBUTIONS IN CALIFORNIA, 1952–1990
(percent)

Most expensive 18 initiatives
1952–1990

Political 1.0%
Officeholder 2.0%
Labor 3.0%
Broadbased 3.0%
Individual 8.0%

Business
83.0%

1990

Labor 1.0%
Issue groups 5.0%
Political groups 7.0%
Officeholders 9.0%
Individual 12.0%

Business
66.0%

SOURCE: California Commission on Campaign Financing Data Analysis Project.

interests in initiative campaigns is spent to defeat measures with the exception of some recent efforts to sponsor counter-initiatives as a means of defeating an initiative by winning more votes for the watered-down version sponsored by business.[56]

As a result, citizen participation in direct legislation in most states is confined largely to voting on the measures put on the ballot with the assistance of the initiative industry and to responding to the campaigns financed by a few individuals or groups willing to make large contributions.

One frequent argument made in support of adopting the initiative is that the process will lead to greater voter turnout. Some contend that people will be more likely to vote if they get to decide policy issues or when controversial and highly visible issues are placed on the ballot.[57] Yet the evidence is that initiatives do not systematically increase turnout.[58] Maine provides a good example because it permits initiatives to occur in elections with candidates (even-numbered years) and in statewide elections when no elective offices are contested. A recent study found that "turnout in Maine is much lower in odd-numbered years (that is, years with no candidate elections), even when there are highly controversial issues on the ballot."[59] This is not to deny that in some states in some instances, a highly controversial measure may increase turnout, but such instances are rare.

The differences in turnout between presidential and midterm elections and between primary and general elections are well known. Initiative activists try to time the appearance of their ballot question to maximize its chances of success. Conservative tax cutter Howard Jarvis placed his Proposition 13 on a June 1978 primary ballot in an election with no statewide Democratic contests, because he believed it would maximize the chances of passage. California is the only state to vote on initiatives and popular referendums in primary elections, a practice dating to 1970, which some have urged be abandoned.[60] One problem with voting on initiatives in general elections only is that the already

---

56. Tom E. Thomas, "Has Business 'Captured' the California Initiative Agenda?" *California Management Review*, vol. 33 (1990), pp. 131–47.

57. Cronin, *Direct Democracy*, pp. 67–68.

58. Magleby, *Direct Legislation;* and David H. Everson, "Initiatives and Voter Turnout" (Paper presented at the annual meeting of the American Political Science Association, New York, New York September 1981). See also table 2–6.

59. Dave Kehler, Amy L. Yonowitz, and Christy Almanzor, "Initiatives and Voter Turnout," *Initiative and Referendum Analysis* (Princeton, New Jersey: Public Affairs Research Institute of New Jersey, Inc., 1992), p. 3.

60. Lee, "Representative Government and the Initiative Process," pp. 239–40.

long ballots would become even longer.

Several states have recently liberalized their absentee voting laws, making it easier to request and use an absentee ballot. If more and more voters were to vote by absentee ballot, it could alter the dynamics of opinion changes, which occur frequently in initiative campaigns. Voters who go to the trouble of requesting an absentee ballot are likely to be better informed about the measures, or, as one observer described it, "pre-informed."[61] Some local governments have even gone so far as to permit an entire election on an initiative or referendum to be conducted through the mail, but no state has yet done so.[62]

Some states permit special elections to decide direct legislation measures. California governor Ronald Reagan did this with a tax-cutting measure in 1973, and Governor Jerry Brown did the same with a spending limitation measure in 1979. In 1993, Governor Pete Wilson placed a conservative school voucher measure on a special election ballot. Generally, special elections in California are held in November of odd-numbered years, when many local governments are electing officials or deciding local measures. One exception was Governor George Deukmejian's proposal to hold a special election on reapportionment in December of 1983. The California Supreme Court canceled it because it would interfere with the "orderly conduct" of the June 1984 primary election. Moreover, reapportionment occurs in the year following each national census (held every tenth even-numbered year) rather than periodically throughout the decade following the census, and this limitation on state legislatures on when they may redistrict is equally binding on the statutory initiative.[63]

California's experience suggests that only about one in four persons of voting age will vote in special elections and that those who do vote will not be very representative of voters in general elections. Voters in special elections are likely to be better informed and politically more knowledgeable than voters in regular elections.[64]

In regular elections, some voters skip a particular candidate election or some ballot questions. I have called the percentage of voters who do this "drop-off." The range of drop-off in candidate elections and on ballot propositions is detailed in table 7–4.

Drop-off in candidate contests ranges between 2 and 12 percent.

61. Ibid., p. 240.
62. David B. Magleby, "Participation in Mail Ballot Elections," *Western Political Quarterly*, vol. 40 (March 1987), pp. 79–91.
63. Legislature of the State of California v. Deukmejian, 194 Cal. Rptr. 781, (1983).
64. Magleby, *Direct Legislation*, p. 88.

TABLE 7–4
AVERAGE GENERAL ELECTION DROP-OFF IN CALIFORNIA, MASSACHUSETTS,
AND WASHINGTON BY TYPE OF CONTEST, 1970–1992
(percent)

	California	Massachusetts	Washington
President	3	2	2
Senator	4	4	4
Representative	7	11	7
Governor	2	5	3
Lt. governor	5	5	9
Attorney general	6	6	9
Secretary of state	6	9	9
Treasurer	8	12	11
Auditor (controller)	7	16	12
Average Drop-off by Category of Proposition			
Initiatives	8	8	10
Referendums	a	10	13
Legislative propositions	14	12	17
All propositions	13	14	14

a. California did not vote on any popular referendum in the period 1970–1992.
SOURCE: State of California, *Statement of the Vote, 1970–92* (Sacramento: Office of the Secretary of State, 1970–92); Commonwealth of Massachusetts, *Election Statistics, 1970–92* (Boston: Office of the Secretary of the Commonwealth, 1970–92); State of Washington, *Abstract of Votes, 1970–92* (Seattle: Office of the Secretary of State, 1970–92).

Voters participate in nearly identical proportions for races for president and U.S. senator, and their rate of drop-off increases as they move down the ballot to less visible offices. As many as 16 percent of Massachusetts voters on average drop off when voting for auditor. For ballot questions, drop-off falls between 8 and 17 percent. Initiatives aside, drop-off is related to ballot order—earlier ballot questions have lower drop-off than later ones. The rate of drop-off for all propositions is remarkably similar, at 13–14 percent on average; and the lower rate of drop-off for initiatives is also consistently 8–10 percent.

While drop-off is not large on most initiatives, direct legislation is one of the reasons state ballots are so long. The initiative process often requires a subsequent vote of the people to repeal or modify an earlier successful initiative. A successful 1922 initiative permitting chiropractors to practice in California is an example of an initiative that has necessitated subsequent votes. Because of technical changes in the area regulated by the initiative, the legislature has asked voters to consider seven changes in the past seventy years.[65] Moreover, one indirect result of direct legislation is that it encourages legislatures to push to the ballot matters they could resolve themselves.[66] Examples of such issues are the initiatives that allowed nondentists to fit people with dentures in Idaho, permitted self-serve gas stations in Oregon, and the recriminalization of marijuana in Alaska.

Ballot length can also add to voter confusion. In San Francisco during the 1988 general election, for example, voters were asked to decide fifty-two separate ballot questions (twenty-nine statewide propositions, twenty-three local questions). While only nineteen of these measures were initiatives, the length of the ballot added to voter fatigue and confusion. Given the number of decisions to be made, it is not surprising that the 1988 ballot pamphlet was 159 pages long, a record broken in 1990 when the California pamphlet was printed in two volumes with a combined length of 221 pages.[67] California voters are not alone in dealing with long pamphlets: the 1990 Arizona pamphlet was 224 pages in length. Few would argue that even well-informed voters will take the time to sort through so many separate issues, and the political science literature suggests that most voters lack the interest or inclination.[68] Voting fatigue may also foster negative voting. Two scholars who have recently studied the initiative process in California recommend "no more than six statewide initiatives on any single ballot," as a way of addressing the problem of lengthy ballots.[69]

Voting on ballot questions is different from voting in candidate elections because the effects of partisanship and candidate appeal are largely absent. These voting cues simplify the voting choice in candidate elections; and while voters may consider candidates' positions on issues in their candidate voting, these stands are often of less importance than party labels and personal qualities. Parties occasionally take strong positions on ballot questions, but their normal tendency is to avoid alienating voters by taking no position. Prominent entertainers and politicians, including some major elected officials, often make en-

---

65. California Commission, *Democracy by Initiative*, p. 95.

66. Lee, "Representative Government and the Initiative," pp. 231–32.

67. Charles Price and Robert Waste, "Initiatives: Too Much of a Good Thing?" *California Journal* (March 1991), p. 117.

68. Cronin, *Direct Democracy*; and Arthur Lupia, "Political Information, Political Behavior, and Policy Outcomes in Direct Legislation" (Paper presented at the annual meeting of the American Political Science Association, Washington, D.C., August 1991).

69. Philip L. Dubois and Floyd Feeney, "Improving the California Initiative Process: Options for Change," *CPS Brief*, vol. 3 (November 1991), p. 3.

dorsements in initiative campaigns. These endorsements can be important but can also backfire, as in the case of an advertisement by the actress Angela Lansbury opposing the 1990 California term-limit initiatives. Her advocacy became controversial because she is not a Californian nor is she a U.S. citizen. When the advertisement became an issue, she withdrew her opposition to the initiatives.[70]

Credibility of the communicator as well as the believability of the message is important to initiative campaigns. Those who have the resources to influence these campaigns sometimes have an incentive to mislead or confuse voters.[71] Two scholars who have studied these problems extensively have called for true identification of initiative sponsors, disclosure of the use of paid signature gatherers, limits on the length of the ballot, and placing counter- and conflicting initiatives together on the ballot. They also recommend that the secretary of state be authorized to point out that these initiatives deal with similar subject matter and make clear that if more than one measure passes, the one with the most votes takes effect. Finally, they suggest that voter information materials be written at the reading level of a high-school graduate.[72]

Because voters have fewer cues in referendums than in candidate elections, it is not surprising that voting intentions are more likely to shift during initiative campaigns, and voters are more susceptible to short-term forces. Voters are also more likely to decide how they will vote later in initiative campaigns than in candidate contests. Voters rely heavily on political advertising to make up their minds on initiatives, but for politically interested and well-educated citizens the voter pamphlet is a popular source of information.[73] One reason the pamphlet is not more widely used is that much of it is written in highly technical language, ranging up to the eighteenth-grade level.[74]

Looking at polls over time for candidate and proposition elections, I found that, on average, about 70 percent of voters change their opinions on ballot measures during campaigns, compared with 26 percent who shift in candidate elections.[75] The most common pattern of opin-

---

70. Interview with Robert M. Stern, Matthew Stodder, and C. B. Holman, Newport, California, 21 July 1993.

71. Arthur Lupia, "Busy Voters, Agenda Control and the Power of Information," *American Political Science Review*, vol. 86 (1992), pp. 390–403.

72. Dubois and Feeney, *Improving the California Initiative Process*, p. 170.

73. Philip Dubois, Floyd Feeney, and Edmond Constantini, "A Voter Survey about the California Ballot Pamphlet," *CPS Brief*, vol. 5 (August 1993), p. 5.

74. Magleby, *Direct Legislation*, pp. 118–19.

75. Magleby, "Opinion Formation and Opinion Change," p. 110.

ion change is from "soft" early support for an initiative to a large majority in opposition to the measure on election day. On only a small percentage of initiatives are voters likely to hold strong opinions that make them much less susceptible to the campaign. Voters are more likely to be undecided late during campaigns on initiatives in comparison with candidate races. On the eve of a highly contested 1982 Michigan election, only 10 percent of the voters were undecided how they would vote for the U.S. Senate, but more than 50 percent were undecided how they would vote on two hotly contested initiatives.[76] Part of the reason for late decisions is the complexity of many initiatives. In a study of the 1976 California nuclear power initiatives, two scholars estimate that less than one-third of the voters were well enough informed to make an educated judgment in the voting booth.[77]

Given the volatility of opinion on initiatives, it is not surprising that campaign spending is important.[78] Yet on fewer than one in five measures do both sides spend the same.[79] Greater spending on the No side is most effective, but heavy Yes spending also makes a difference. If opponents spend more, or if spending is roughly even, the measure is defeated more than 80 percent of the time. If the proponents spend a disproportionate amount of money, their chance of success climbs from roughly one in three to one in two.[80]

The single best predictor of initiative voting is liberal or conservative ideology. Not surprisingly, voters try to integrate the measure into their general political outlooks. If the measure is understood across a liberal-conservative spectrum, then ideology becomes an important part of the voting calculus. Voters, however, often respond more to factors like the cost of the proposal, its perceived necessity, their feelings about the supporters or opponents, and confusion about the measure's costs and consequences.

Voters appear to be generally skeptical of initiatives, rejecting about two-thirds of the measures that make it to the ballot. Table 7–5 contrasts the passage rates for legislative referendums and popular initiatives in a dozen states since 1898.

---

76. Ibid., p. 104.

77. Deborah R. Hensler and Carl P. Hensler, *Evaluating Nuclear Power* (Santa Monica, Calif.: RAND Corporation, 1979), p. 70.

78. Daniel H. Lowenstein, "Campaign Spending and Ballot Propositions: Recent Experience, Public Choice Theory and the First Amendment," *UCLA Law Review*, vol. 86 (1982), pp. 505–641.

79. Magleby, *Direct Legislation*, p. 148.

80. Ibid.; David B. Magleby, "Campaign Spending in Ballot Proposition Election" (Paper presented at the annual meeting of the American Political Science Association, Washington, D.C., August 1986).

TABLE 7–5
VOTER APPROVAL RATES FOR INITIATIVES AND LEGISLATIVE PROPOSITIONS FOR TWELVE STATES, 1898–1992

State	From the Legislature			By Petition		
	Number proposed	Number approved	Percent approved	Number proposed	Number approved	Percent approved
Alaska	21	12	57.1	20	9	45.5
Arizona	164	91	55.5	135	51	37.8
Idaho	22	20	90.9	17	11	64.7
Maine	147	107	72.8	33	13	39.4
Arkansas	94	48	51.1	84	41	48.8
Oregon	322	186	57.8	274	89	32.5
Michigan	107	65	60.7	65	26	40.0
Montana	62	37	60.0	58	34	58.6
California	541	342	63.2	236	79	33.5
Oklahoma	224	117	52.2	78	22	28.2
Ohio	142	84	59.2	53	14	26.4
Nebraska	257	173	67.3	38	12	31.5
Total	2,103	1,282	61.0	1,091	401	36.8

SOURCES: For 1898–1978, Austin Ranney, "The United States of America," in David Butler and Austin Ranney, eds., *Referendums: A Comparative Study of Practice and Theory* (Washington, D.C.: American Enterprise Institute, 1978), p. 77. Much of Ranney's data are drawn, in turn, from Graham, *A Compilation of Statewide Initiative Proposals Appearing on Ballots through 1976, 1979–1992*, Offices of the Secretaries of State, from each state.

About three of every five measures put on the ballot by state legislatures were approved by the voters, and there is remarkably little variation among the twelve states in the proportion passed. In contrast, only one-third of measures placed on the ballot by popular petitions in these same states was approved by voters.[81] There is much more deviation among states in this regard. Only 26 percent of Ohio's initiatives have been approved, while 65 percent of Idaho's initiatives have passed. Voters in only two states, Idaho and Montana, are more likely to approve than reject an initiative. The tendency of voters to reject far more initiatives than legislative proposals indicates voter skepticism about direct legislation. This may be one reason why campaign spending on the negative side is more effective. An alternative explanation is that voters are status quo oriented and therefore oppose the changes often proposed in initiatives. While many measures proposed by legislatures call for change as well, their changes are often more moderate in scope, and there is typically less opposition to them.

Political and Institutional Consequences of Direct Legislation

The reformers who established direct legislation in the American states attempted to place these processes outside the reach of checks and balances except for judicial review. There is no gubernatorial veto of an initiative, the legislature plays no formal role in deciding a direct initiative, and the people can abandon prior institutional arrangements through the constitutional initiative. Some have called the initiative the fourth branch of government, but this label seems mistaken, because the initiative is largely a separate governmental process with profound consequences for the other institutions and processes of government.[82]

From the very beginning of direct legislation in the United States, however, the courts have ruled on the legitimacy of the process and adjudicated disputes about its implementation. Courts today resolve disputes about petition circulation, official titles and summaries, whether the proponents have complied with particular legal provisions (for example, whether the measure concerns a single subject), whether its content includes areas not permitted in initiatives, and similar issues. Courts are also called on to decide whether initiatives vio-

---

81. Voters at the local level, at least in California, are much more likely to pass initiatives than at the statewide level. Over 60 percent of local initiatives in California between 1983 and 1988 passed; see David Hadwiger, "When the Initiative Comes to Town: California Cities and Citizen-sponsored Ballot Measures," *Western City*, vol. 65 (May 1989), pp. 60–65.

82. California Commission, *Democracy by Initiative*, p. 2.

late state constitutions or the U.S. Constitution.

As important as courts are to the implementation of initiatives, they are even more important in deciding on the constitutionality of the measures approved by the voters. American courts have not been timid in declaring successful initiatives unconstitutional, either in whole or in part. Judicial review sometimes places courts in the politically difficult position of overturning a vote of the people. Because many state supreme courts are popularly elected, this can be an act of personal political importance to the justices.[83]

The initiative also has consequences for legislatures. As an institution, the initiative process is much more popular than the state legislature.[84] As a result of recent initiatives, many states now have term limitations that were enacted after campaigns emphasizing the negative views many voters have of legislatures. Other initiatives encouraged by similar sentiments include measures for campaign reforms and new reapportionment processes.

Another effect of the initiative process on state legislatures is that it elevates some issues to the legislature's agenda either before they are voted on by the people (when the legislature is seeking to deflect support for the proposal by adopting some version of it) or after a measure is passed and must be implemented. Some sponsors of initiatives are themselves legislators who are frustrated by the procedures of the legislature or who desire wider visibility.

Finally, governors are also affected by direct legislation. They must alter their political agendas as initiative activists put issues on the state ballot, and they must live within the constraints of successful initiatives. Governors unable to get their way with the legislature also use the process to circumvent legislative obstacles.[85] Beginning in 1970, 15 percent of proposed initiatives were put forward by state officeholders.[86] The state taxing and spending constraints experienced in California are very much the result of Proposition 13 and related measures in the late 1970s and early 1980s. In 1992, Colorado voters enacted an initiative that requires a vote of the people before taxes can be raised at the state or at the local level. An even more extensive constraint on state government, especially state legislatures, is the recent spate of term-limit initiatives.

83. See Eule, "Judicial Review of Direct Democracy," p. 1582.
84. David B. Magleby, "Legislatures and the Initiative: The Politics of Direct Democracy," *State Government*, vol. 59 (1986), p. 32.
85. Lee, "Representative Government and the Initiative Process," p. 226.
86. Charles Bell and Charles Price, "Are Ballot Measures the Magic Ride to Success?" *California Journal*, vol. 13 (1988), p. 382.

Conclusion

There is much to learn from the experience of the American states with direct legislation: the frequency of its use in several states provides a rich body of experience, and the variations in the rules facilitate true comparative analysis useful for both established and new democracies. While American experience with direct legislation in states and localities is extensive, the United States has yet to have a national referendum; and the debate over establishing such a process reveals that many Americans have not yet fully embraced this form of democracy. Indeed, the continuing debates over whether to establish a national initiative, like the debates in states that have recently considered adopting the initiative, reveal the reservations many elites hold about direct legislation.

The idea of a national initiative or popular referendum has been around for many years but has never come close to realization. Congressional hearings were held on the idea in 1977, and Jack Kemp advocated it in his 1980 presidential campaign and in his book *An American Renaissance*.[87] Many liberals, however, have feared the dangers the process poses for minorities and the disadvantaged; and many conservatives also have philosophical reservations about it on the national level, especially as it might affect foreign policy. Many in both camps prefer to work through existing representative institutions. This does not mean that some leader wishing to reinforce his populist credentials will not press the idea in the future. Moreover, the public favors a national initiative: Gallup polls in 1977 and 1981 found 57 and 52 percent of national samples favoring it.[88] More recent polls have found pluralities favoring a national advisory referendum and over 60 percent favoring a binding referendum.[89]

Interest in referendums has grown over the past two decades in the United States and around the world, and in many places the use of

---

87. Jack Kemp, *An American Renaissance: A Strategy for the 1980s* (New York: Berkeley Publishing Company, 1981).

88. Cronin, *Direct Democracy*, pp. 174–76.

89. The wording of the later question was, Should the nation "conduct national referendums or votes on major issues and require the government to treat a referendum approved by a majority of all registered voters in the same manner as legislation passed by Congress?" *Americans Talk Issues, #22: Improving Democracy in America* (Washington, D.C.: Americans Talk Issues Foundation, 1993). Survey conducted by Market Strategies and Greenberg-Lake/The Analysis Group, 10–15 March 1993.

the referendum device has increased as well.[90] With greater use, however, the implications of a long ballot for informed and rational decision making by voters has caused concern. Increased use also has implications for legislatures, executives, and courts. In the American states, the courts more than legislatures or governors deal with direct legislation by regulating the implementation of the rules and procedures and by deciding on the constitutionality of the measures adopted. Indeed, aside from the voters, the only real check on direct legislation is the courts, and they have played that role aggressively. But courts are also constrained by direct legislation in that elected judges find it increasingly hard to limit the wishes of voters.

As with other forms of electioneering, the initiative industry in the United States has applied campaign technology to direct legislation. What was once a state-by-state process has become multistate in focus and even international in scope. Campaign consulting firms now openly advertise for business in several initiative states and have even set up shop in places as distant as Russia. While there are important political variations across state and national boundaries, some professional consultants for direct legislation campaigns have convinced clients around the world that these differences are less important than the skill that comes from experience with the use of computers, polls, mailing lists, petition circulation, electronic advertising, and the like. As direct legislation spreads, the campaigns in other polities will be increasingly influenced by the approach to campaigns in the American states.

Direct legislation is a powerful agenda-setting device. Those who can successfully jump the hurdles of the signature-gathering process and who have sufficient funds to mount a campaign can have a major voice in making public policy. The proponents of initiatives can win in terms of public exposure, fund-raising, and a possible legislative response, even though they most often lose at the ballot box. This powerful agenda-setting function has pushed many individuals and groups to use the initiative as their preferred political tactic. The initiative relates to the political agenda in another way as well. It is potentially a useful way to resolve fundamental political or constitutional questions. All but one of the fifty states put constitutional changes before the voters; and when hotly contested matters of fundamental law or public policy arise, direct legislation can serve the useful purpose of resolving conflict.

---

90. Austin Ranney, "Referendums: New Practice and Old Theory" (Working paper) (Berkeley: Institute of Governmental Studies, University of California, 1991). See also chapters 1 and 2 of this book.

Yet, the direct legislation measures voted on in the American states have not been broadly representative of the issue concerns of most voters, and the voting process is prone to the kinds of limitations discussed earlier in this chapter. As Eugene Lee recently wrote,

> To be critical of the initiative is not to excuse the failings of the legislature, the weaknesses of the executive branch, or the excesses of the electoral process. It is to suggest, rather, that instead of being a positive response to these shortcomings, the initiative itself contributes to them. . . . The initiative is part of the problem. Turned on its head, "direct democracy" is no longer democratic.[91]

These reservations aside, direct legislation has become an enduring part of the political culture and will continue to play an important part in the politics of these states and communities.

Much of the battle of direct legislation is definition: which side can more effectively define the issue for voters in ways they will understand and remember. This often means that the campaign on an initiative focuses on only one part of the actual proposal. It is therefore problematic to conclude that the vote on a particular initiative or referendum reflects an understanding of the issue more broadly defined. The American system, reflecting the antirepresentative views of the Progressives, allows voters to vote on the text of laws rather than on general policy questions. As a result, voters may prefer a policy but reject an initiative that embodies that policy.

Political reforms often have unintended consequences that may be more important than other results. In the case of direct legislation, the process in several American states is now a high-stakes battleground for well-funded interests. Some measures reflect a grass-roots citizen activism, but they are often defeated at the ballot box by the targeted interests who can spend large amounts of money on campaigns against them. While direct legislation can be a safety valve against the failures of representative democracy, comparatively few initiatives fall into the safety-valve category. For voters, direct legislation affords an opportunity to respond to issues placed on the ballot in increasing numbers, sometimes with multiple initiatives on the same subject. These issues, however, reflect a narrow range of interests and are often complex and confusing. Voters are typically inclined to vote against initiatives but still want to keep the process. While the initiative has had some beneficial consequences for the institutions of the states that use it, it has

---

91. Lee, "Representative Government and the Initiative," p. 248.

fundamentally altered the relationships between the institutions and the people and among the institutions themselves. Direct legislation has been and will continue to be an important part of the way politics is done in many American states.

8
Conclusion
David Butler and Austin Ranney

The preceding chapters show the diversity in the practice and theory of referendums in the polities that have used the device most. For the student of comparative government, however, they nevertheless suggest some significant generalizations.

Generalizations

1. Five major democracies have never had a nationwide referendum: India, Israel, Japan, the Netherlands, and the United States.[1] No obvious common characteristic distinguishes these five from other nations, and that observation underlines a central fact about referendums. Universal judgments about their nature and impact must, for the most part, be avoided. As the preceding chapters have shown, in most countries referendums are unique, both in origin and in consequences. There are no universal rules; at the most, there are some widely observed tendencies.

2. Only a few political systems—notably, Switzerland and some states in the United States—have used referendums regularly and frequently as major devices for making authoritative political decisions. Politics in those systems is quite different from politics in places where referendums have been employed infrequently, often as a last resort—a category that includes most nations.

3. The impact of the referendum device on the policies and institutions of democratic polities depends in good part on the degree to which its use is controlled by elected officials. In nations such as the United Kingdom and the Scandinavian democracies, in which referen-

---

1. In 1977–1978, bills were introduced in Congress to provide for nationwide referendums demanded by a number of voters equal to at least 3 percent of the vote for president in the most recent election. The bills failed to get out of committee, but Gallup polls taken at the time showed a 57 percent majority favoring such referendums.

dums are held only when elected governments call them and governments word the propositions and define the voters' choices, referendums rarely shape the basic character of parties, legislatures, cabinets, and the other institutions of representative government. Referendum elections in these countries are substantially less frequent and less important than candidate elections. Conversely, in polities such as Switzerland, Italy, and some American states, in which ordinary voters can, by signing petitions in sufficient numbers, launch new measures, or require popular approval of measures enacted by governments, or both, public policies and representative institutions have been powerfully affected by referendums and the threat of referendums.

4. Politicians usually dislike referendums—although there are occasions, such as those described in chapters 3 and 5, when party leaders turn to them as last-ditch devices for resolving issues so contentious that, if left to the ordinary ways of party government, they might shatter the established parties altogether. Referendums take decisions out of established hands, and elected leaders can never control—or be responsible for—their outcomes. Thus, in Britain in 1972, Roy Jenkins resigned from the deputy leadership of the British Labour party when his colleagues decided to endorse a referendum on European Community membership; he protested that referendums were wrong because they could not be limited to one subject; because they divided parties and produced inconsistent government; and because they were likely to be invoked as a weapon against progressive legislation (see chapter 3).

Recent experience, however, does not justify such fears. The vast majority of Western-style democracies rarely use the device. Apart from Switzerland and Italy, none has held frequent nationwide referendums. No country, except perhaps Norway, has had its party or governmental system upset by referendums; no country, except perhaps Ireland, has had progressive legislation frustrated—or accelerated—by referendums.

5. Yet referendums are not unimportant. In South Africa and in Chile, they opened the door to a transformation of the regimes' basic characters. On a more modest scale, they brought about changes in the electoral system in Italy and New Zealand that the politicians did not want. In Canada, a referendum rejected a modification of the federal system that the politicians did want. And where the Soviet Union once held sway, referendums have been used repeatedly to express nationalist claims and establish the legitimacy of new nations and constitutions. In Russia especially, the 1993 referendum played a vital role in President Boris Yeltsin's battle with Parliament over economic reform.

The cohesion and development of the European Community have been at stake in critically close popular votes, twice in Denmark and once in France.

6. Frequent recourse to referendums can contribute to a special political culture in which politicians are inhibited, for good or ill, from acting as representatives. They can avoid making difficult and unpopular decisions by referring divisive issues to the people; they make other decisions, while they are secure in knowing that those decisions may be overruled by the people. As chapters 4 and 7 make clear, in Switzerland and the high-user American states, those ever-present possibilities shape politicians' strategies in ways that are largely unknown in low-user political systems.

In chapter 3, Vernon Bogdanor contrasts the use of the referendum in France and in Italy. In France, the president uniquely has authority to call a referendum unilaterally; there the device has added significantly to presidential power over policy making. In Italy, Switzerland, and some American states, the people have authority to call a referendum unilaterally; thus in those polities the device has become a major constraint on the power and actions of elected officials.

7. Even in the low-user systems, however, most politicians regard the referendum device, in James Callaghan's words, as "a rubber life raft into which we may all have to climb." When that happens, everyone has to turn to a new form of politics, in which party cues to the public are much less effective than usual and coalitions of interested groups on both the Yes and No sides have to learn how to work together, often across established lines of political cleavage, in formal or informal umbrella organizations.

8. Referendum campaigns are usually organized quite differently in Switzerland and the Western states of America from most other polities. Since referendums in the former polities are frequent, and often closely contested for high stakes, well-established firms of professional campaign consultants are employed by interest groups to collect signatures, raise money, buy newspaper space and television time, and plan and execute campaign strategies and tactics.

9. Successful referendums, like laws enacted by legislatures, do not always produce the consequences expected by either their advocates or their opponents. For example, after the Swedes voted eighty-five to fifteen in 1955 against driving on the right, the government waited twelve years and then made the change (without having another referendum). In Switzerland, as chapter 4 shows, the political class has been skillful in evading awkward referendum decisions. In America, the courts have disallowed some policies approved in referendums as well as some enacted by legislatures; thus the courts have

used the power of judicial review to override direct expressions of the popular will by referendum majorities as well as indirect expressions of that will by the actions of elected representatives.

10. The unpredictability of referendums should not be exaggerated. The vast majority of referendums have been sponsored by governments and have produced the voting outcomes desired by those governments. That is certainly true for some authoritarian regimes (the Chilean referendum of 1988 is a shining exception), but it is also largely true for democratic systems (although chapter 5 shows Australia as another exception, with thirty-six government defeats in forty-four referendums and with almost all referendums producing votes in the 60–40 percent range). Some leading examples of popular majorities rejecting government positions include the defeat of de Gaulle's referendum in 1969; the Danish vote on the Maastricht Treaty in 1992; and the defeat of the New Zealand establishment in 1992 and 1993. Nevertheless, referendum decisions unwanted by (and sometimes embarrassing for) the leaders of representative assemblies are far more common in Switzerland and in the high-user American states.

11. Some referendum decisions have had clearly adverse consequences—although all the obvious examples are confined to American states (for example, California's Proposition 13). But the same states also offer many examples of decisions by elected representatives that have had clearly adverse consequences. Neither direct democracy nor representative democracy (nor, for that matter, any nondemocratic form of government), it seems, can guarantee good decisions all the time.

12. Anxieties about referendums have perhaps been more extreme in Britain than in any other traditional democracy. Burkean myths about representative government have long come readily to British politicians' lips, but even the most institutionally conservative politicians have looked favorably on the referendum device when they calculated that it might further their policies, which otherwise would be blocked by the established processes. Thus, in the 1992–1993 controversy over Britain's approval of the Maastricht Treaty, Margaret Thatcher and other opponents demanded a referendum (despite their previous criticism of the device). The Conservative and Labour leadership, however, united against a referendum, quoting high constitutional principles to block a move that they feared would lead to the treaty's defeat.

13. Like many other users of referendums, Britain knows how volatile the public can be on referendum questions. In 1975, for example, polls showed the public moving from an 8 percent No margin in January to a 34 percent Yes majority in May. But when the active cam-

261

paign was launched in the four weeks before the June poll, despite a much more professional effort by the Yes forces, there was a slight falling off in the Yes majority to the final margin of 66 to 34. In 1979, a favorable Yes vote in the Scottish referendum on devolution seemed certain until the winter of discontent caused a plummeting in the Labour party's rating—and since the Labour leadership was the main advocate of devolution, the issue failed to win enough votes.

14. The major democratic polities, Italy and some American states excepted, have not significantly increased their use of referendums in recent years. Conversely, except for Ireland between 1928 and 1937, nowhere has the right to hold a referendum been withdrawn or narrowed. Politicians may privately be reluctant to transfer responsibility to the general public, but evidently they see no reason to take the risk of saying so publicly.

15. Referendums came into fashion in the United States at the turn of the twentieth century, as the Progressives sought ways to counter the corruption endemic in many state governments and to end boss control of big-city politics. The referendum, the initiative, the recall, and the direct primary (regarded by some as the most radical reform of the lot) were intended to give power over specific issues to the people over the politicians. As chapter 7 shows, the states' experience in this regard has been limited at best; nevertheless, the referendum has remained an occasional vehicle for protest. Much the same has been true in Italy, as shown in 1993, when, in defiance of the dominant parties, the voters passed a referendum calling for a major transformation of the electoral system.

16. Campaigns can make a difference in the outcome of referendum elections as in the outcome of elections for candidates and parties. Opinion polls in Canada, Denmark, and France in 1992, for example, showed a fall off in Yes support in the last few weeks, in the first two cases denying the government its expected victory.

17. These outcomes militate against the contention that opinion polls offer an economical substitute for referendums. Opinion polls do offer a continuous measure of public opinion on major issues. But many people vote differently when faced with a choice of government in a general election from the way they vote in a by-election, when only a single seat is at stake and the voters can send a message to elected leaders without going so far as to remove them from office. Similarly, voters may say one thing to a pollster when they know what they say will not have any real-life consequences, but they may well say another at the end of a serious referendum campaign, when they know that the outcome will control what government does or refrains from doing.

On Balance

We do not end this book as unalloyed advocates or unrelenting critics of referendums. We recognize that referendums are not panaceas, not universal remedies for all the ills of democracy. But referendums have been useful in ameliorating some crises and in resolving some questions that established representative institutions could not manage. If hopes are dupes, fears may be liars. The consequences of most referendums discussed in this book seem to have been beneficial.

Politicians as a class—indeed, the leaders and even the institutions of representative government—are again in low repute in most democratic nations. Further cries for matters to be referred directly to the people are bound to be heard in many countries in the years to come. We do not expect that all of the cries will—or should—be ignored.

Nationwide Referendums, 1793–1993

In the following list an attempt is made to record all nationwide referendums through 1993 in independent countries except for Australia and Switzerland, which have had more referendums than all other countries put together. (Swiss referendums are listed in chapter 4; referendums in Australia and New Zealand are listed in chapter 5). The data in many cases are of uncertain quality. Totalitarian and managed referendums are not segregated from scrupulously reported democratic referendums. Moreover, the data are often derived from newspaper reports or uncheckable works of reference. Quite apart from possible errors of transcription, it is often unclear whether the turnout and percentages voting Yes are based on all registered voters or only on valid votes. All countries that were members of the United Nations in 1993 are mentioned here, together with a few obvious additions. Appendix B lists referendums bearing on the sovereignty of subordinate or colonial territories.

APPENDIX A: NATIONWIDE REFERENDUMS, 1793–1993

Region and Nation	Date	Subject	Percent Yes Vote	Percent Turnout of Electorate
Europe[a]				
Andorra (2)	28 May 1982	New electoral system (PR 2.2, majority system 31.9, mixed system 23.4)	51.9	—
	14 Mar. 1993	New constitution	74.2	75.7
Austria (2)	10 Apr. 1938	Approve Anschluss	99.7	99.7
	5 Nov. 1978	Approve nuclear power	49.5	64.1
Belgium (1)	12 Mar. 1950	Return of Leopold III	57.6	92.4
Bulgaria (3)	19 Nov. 1922	Approve trials for "war crimes"	97.1	—
	8 Sept. 1946	End monarchy	95.1	89.2
	16 May 1971	Approve constitution	99.7	99.7
Denmark (16)	14 Dec. 1916	Cession of Virgin Islands	64.2	38.0
	6 Sept. 1920	Incorporation of North Schleswig	96.9	50.1
	23 May 1939	Voting age 23 not 25 and Landsthing abolished	91.9[b]	48.9
	28 May 1953	New constitution	78.4	58.3
	28 May 1953	Voting age 23 not 21	54.6	62.2
	30 May 1961	Voting age 21 not 23	55.0	37.2
	25 June 1961	Agricultural acquisition law	38.4	73.0
	25 June 1961	Smallholders law	38.6	73.0
	25 June 1963	Municipal preemption	39.6	73.0
	25 June 1963	Nature conservancy law	42.6	73.0

Country	Date	Measure	% Yes of votes cast	Turnout
	24 June 1969	Voting age 18 not 21	21.2	63.6
	2 Oct. 1972	Join European Community	63.3	90.1
	19 Sept. 1978	Voting age 18 not 20	53.9	63.4
	27 Feb. 1986	Approve Single European Community Act	56.2	74.8
	2 June 1992	Maastricht Treaty	49.0	68.7
	18 May 1993	Maastricht Treaty	56.8	86
Estonia (5)	17–19 Feb. 1923	Restore religious instruction	71.7	66.2
	19 Aug. 1932	Constitutional reform	49.2	90.5
	10 June 1933	Presidential government	32.6	66.5
	14 Oct. 1933	Presidentialism with ministerial responsibility	72.6	77.9
	8 Jan. 1936	Convene constituent assembly	76.1	80
Finland (1)	29 Dec. 1931	Abolish prohibition of alcoholic beverages	70.5	44.4
France[c] before 1900 (10)	4 Aug. 1793	Approve constitution	99.3	26.7
	6 Sept. 1795	Approve constitution	95.6	13.7
	30 Aug. 1799	Approve constitution	63.8	3.8
	7 Feb. 1800	Approve Napoleon as consul	99.9	43.1
	2 Aug. 1802	Approve Napoleon as consul for life	99.8	51.2
	18 May 1804	Approve Napoleon as emperor	99.7	43.3
	30 May 1815	Restore imperial constitution	99.7	18.8
	21 Dec. 1851	Ten-year presidency	92.1	79.7
	21 Nov. 1852	Restore empire	96.9	79.7
	8 May 1870	Parliamentary rule	83.1	83.5
France[c] after 1900 (12)	21 Oct. 1945	Assembly to draft constitution	96.3	79.9
	21 Oct. 1945	Interim power for assembly	66.8	79.9
	5 May 1946	Approve constitution	47.1	80.7

(Table continues)

267

APPENDIX A (continued)

Region and Nation	Date	Subject	Percent Yes Vote	Percent Turnout of Electorate
	13 Oct. 1946	Approve constitution	53.2	68.8
	29 Sept. 1958	Approve constitution	79.2	84.9
	8 Jan. 1961	Algerian self-determination	75.3	76.5
	9 Apr. 1962	Agreement with Algiers	90.7	75.6
	28 Oct. 1962	Direct election of president	61.7	77.2
	27 Apr. 1969	Senate power and regional devolution	46.8	80.6
	23 Apr. 1972	Expand European Economic Community	67.7	60.7[e]
	6 Nov. 1988	New Caledonia deal	80.0	37.0
	20 Sept. 1992	Maastricht Treaty	51.0	69.7
Germany (6)	20 June 1926	Confiscation of royal property	92.3[d]	39.3
	22 Dec. 1929	Repudiation of war guilt (reparations)	94.5[d]	14.9
	12 Nov. 1933	Approve Nazi government	93.4	92.2
	19 Aug. 1934	Approve Hitler as leader and chancellor	88.2	94.7
	29 Mar. 1936	Approve Reichstag list and Führer	98.1	98.9
	10 Apr. 1938	Approve Anschluss	99.0	99.7
German Democratic Republic (1)	16 Apr. 1968	Approve constitution	94.5	98.1
Greece (8)	19 Nov. 1862	Election of Prince Alfred as king	95.4	—
	5 Dec. 1920	Return of King	98.6	—
	14 Apr. 1924	Institute republic	70	—
	3 Nov. 1935	Restore monarchy	97.9	—
	1 Sept. 1946	Return of George II	69	90
	29 Sept. 1968	Approve constitution	91.9	77.7

Country	Date	Measure		
	29 July 1973	Institute republic	77.2	74.7
	8 Dec. 1974	End monarchy	69.2	75.6
Hungary (5)	26 Nov. 1989	Postpone presidential election	50.0	55
	26 Nov. 1989	Ban Communist organizations	95.1	55
	26 Nov. 1989	Disclose Communist assets	95.4	55
	26 Nov. 1989	Disband Communist militia	94.9	55
	29 July 1990	President elected	13.9	85.9
Iceland (4)	19 Oct. 1918	Union with Denmark	92.6	43.8
	21 Oct. 1933	End prohibition of alcoholic beverages	57.7	45.3
	29 May 1944	Separate from Denmark	98.5	98.4
	29 May 1944	Institute republic	98.5	98.4
Ireland (18)	1 July 1937	Approve constitution	56.5	68.3
	17 June 1959	Abolish proportional representation	48.2	58.4
	16 Oct. 1968	Increase variation in electorates	39.2	62.9
	16 Oct. 1968	Abolish proportional representation	39.2	63.0
	10 May 1972	Join European Community	83.1	70.9
	7 Dec. 1972	Lower voting age to 18	84.6	50.7
	7 Dec. 1972	Remove special position of church	84.4	50.7
	12 May 1974	Repeal divorce law	40.9	88.1
	5 July 1979	New adoption law	99.0	28.0
	5 July 1979	University representation in Senate	92.4	28.0
	7 Sept. 1983	Abortion ban	66.9	54.3
	14 June 1984	Enfranchise resident noncitizens	75.4	45.8
	26 June 1986	Permit divorce	36.5	62.7
	26 May 1987	Single European Community Act	69.9	—
	19 June 1992	Maastricht Treaty	57.3	68.7

(Table continues)

269

APPENDIX A (continued)

Region and Nation	Date	Subject	Percent Yes Vote	Percent Turnout of Electorate
	25 Nov. 1992	Abortion information	64	—
	25 Nov. 1992	Abortion travel	67	—
	25 Nov. 1992	Abortion when life of mother at stake	34	—
Italy (31)				
	24 May 1929	Approval of fascist regime	98.3	89.5
	26 Mar. 1934	Approval of fascist regime	99.9	99.5
	2 June 1946	End monarchy	54.3	89.1
	12–13 May 1974	Repeal divorce law[e]	59.1	88.1
	11 June 1978	Repeal state financing of parties[e]	43.7	81.3
	11 June 1978	Repeal antiterrorist legislation[e]	23.3	81.4
	17 May 1981	Repeal abortion law	32.1	79.8
	17 May 1981	Modified abortion law	11.5	79.8
	17 May 1981	Repeal antiterror law	14.8	79.8
	17 May 1981	Repeal arms licensing	14.0	79.8
	17 May 1981	Abolish life sentences	22.7	79.8
	9 June 1985	Amend wage-indexing	45.7	78.0
	8 Nov. 1987	Repeal nuclear law	80.6	65.2
	8 Nov. 1987	Repeal nuclear plant subsidy law	79.7	65.2
	8 Nov. 1987	Repeal foreign nuclear tie	71.8	65.2
	8 Nov. 1987	Magistrate's liability	85.0	65.2
	8 Nov. 1987	Trial of ministers	85.1	65.2
	18 June 1989	United European government	88.0	—
	3 June 1990	Reject one hunting law[e]	92.3	43.3
	3 June 1990	Reject pesticide law	92.5	43.3
	3 June 1990	Reject another hunting law	92.3	43.3

Country	Date	Description		
	9 June 1991	Abolish multiple preference voting	95.6	62.5
	9 June 1991	Electoral reform	95.6	62.5
	18 Apr. 1993	Environment rules	—	77.0
	18 Apr. 1993	Repeal proportional representation for Senate election	82.7	77.0
	18 Apr. 1993	End state finance of parties	90.3	77.0
	18 Apr. 1993	Depenalize drugs	55.3	77.0
	18 Apr. 1993	State bank changes	89.8	77.0
	18 Apr. 1993	End Tourist Ministry	82.2	77.0
	18 Apr. 1993	End Agriculture Ministry	70.1	77.0
	18 Apr. 1993	End Enterprise Ministry	90.1	77.0
Latvia (1)	Summer 1931	Religious rights	32.1	—
Liechtenstein since 1918		See chapter 4		
Luxembourg (3)	28 Sept. 1919	Confirm Grand Duchess	77.8	68.0
	28 Sept. 1919	Economic union with France not Belgium	73.0	65.3
	6 Jan. 1937	Restrictions on extremist parties	49.3	—
Norway (5)	13 Aug. 1905	Separation from Sweden	99.9	84.8
	12–13 Nov. 1905	Approve monarch	78.9	75.3
	6 Oct. 1919	Retain prohibition	61.6	66.5
	19 Oct. 1926	Repeal prohibition	55.8	64.8
	24–25 Sept. 1972	Join European Community	46.5	77.6
Poland (5)	30 June 1946	Abolish Senate	68.0	87.6
	30 June 1946	Make economic system permanent	77.1	87.6
	30 June 1946	Approve Baltic and eastern frontiers	91.4	87.6[d]
	29 Nov. 1987	Approve economic reforms	64.0	67.3
	29 Nov. 1987	Approve political reforms	69.0	67.3

(Table continues)

271

Region and Nation	Date	Subject	Percent Yes Vote	Percent Turnout of Electorate
Portugal (1)	19 Mar. 1933	Approve constitution	99.1	97.6
Romania (7)	10 May 1864	Constitutional change	99.8	51.2
	2 May 1866	Prince Charles Louis as reigning prince	99.9	—
	24 Feb. 1938	Approve constitution	99.9	92
	2 Mar. 1941	Approve Antonescu government	99.9	—
	9 Nov. 1941	Approve Antonescu government	99.9	
	3 Nov. 1986	Unilateral arms reduction	100	99.9
	8 Dec. 1991	New constitution	69.1	77.3
Russia (6)	17 Mar. 1991	Direct election of president	69.9	75.1
	25 Apr. 1993	Confidence in Yeltsin	57.4	65.0
	25 Apr. 1993	Approve economic policy	53.7	65.0
	25 Apr. 1993	Early presidential election	49.1	65.0
	25 Apr. 1993	Early Congress election	70.6	65.0
	12 Dec. 1993	Approve new constitution	54.8	58.4
Soviet Union (1)	17 Mar. 1991	Preserve Soviet Union	75.3	73.0
Spain (4)	6 July 1947	Approve succession law	95.1	94.0
	14 Dec. 1966	Approve constitution	95.9	98.2
	15 Dec. 1976	Approve political reform program	94.2	77.7
	12 Mar. 1986	Stay in NATO	52.6	59.4
Sweden (3)	6 Oct. 1922	Prohibition of alcoholic beverages	49.0	51.1
	16 Oct. 1955	Drive on right	15.2	53.2

Country	Subject	Date		
	Alternative pension plans (1)	13 Oct. 1957	47.7	—
	(2)		36.7	72.4
	(3)		15.6	—
Switzerland	See chapter 4			
Turkey (4)	Approve constitution	9 July 1961	61.2	78.5
	New Constitution	7 Nov. 1982	91.5	—
	Amnesty for politicians	6 Sept. 1987	50.2	92
	Advance local elections	25 Sept. 1989	35	—
United Kingdom (1)	Stay in European Community	5 June 1975	67.2	64.5
Africa[f] and Near East[f]				
Algeria (6)	Approve assembly's powers	20 Sept. 1962	99.6	81.5
	Approve constitution	8 Sept. 1963	99.6	82.7
	Approve national charter	27 June 1976	98.5	91.4
	Approve constitution	19 Nov. 1976	99.2	92.9[a]
	Amend national charter	16 Jan. 1986	98.3	95.9
	Constitutional change	23 Feb. 1989	74	70
Benin (2)	Approve constitution	5 Jan. 1964	99.8	92.1
	Approve constitution	31 Mar. 1968	93.2	81.2
Botswana (1)	Independent election supervisor	26 Sept. 1987	Yes	—
Burundi (3)	New constitution	18 Nov. 1981	97.4	—
	Endorse Unity Charter	5 Feb. 1991	89.2	96.2
	Approve constitution	9 Mar. 1992	90.0	97.1

(Table continues)

273

Region and Nation	Date	Subject	Percent Yes Vote	Percent Turnout of Electorate
Cameroon (2)	21 Feb. 1960	Approve constitution	58.8	76.6
	21 May 1972	Unite East and West Cameroon into one republic	99.9	98.5
Central African Republic (2)	1 Feb. 1981	New constitution	99.4	—
	21 Nov. 1986	One-party constitution	90	—
Chad (1)	19 Dec. 1989	Endorse president and constitution	99.4	92
Comoros (2)	28 Oct. 1977	Continue Ali Soilih as president	56.6	92.2
	1 Oct. 1978	Approve Federal Islamic Constitution	99.3	—
Congo (4)	8 Dec. 1963	Approve constitution	86.1	91.7
	24 June 1973	Approve constitution	94.6	77
	8 July 1979	New constitution	—	—
	15 Mar. 1992	Constitutional change	96	70+
Egypt (19)	23 June 1956	Approve constitution and Nasser	99.8	—
	20 Feb. 1958	Approve union with Syria	99.9	—
	15 Mar. 1965	Reelect Nasser and approve policies	99.9	98.2
	2 May 1968	Approve March 30 statement	99.9	99.8
	15 Oct. 1970	Approve President Sadat	90.4	84.8
	1 Sept. 1971	Approve Federation of Arab Republics	99.9	97.2
	11 Sept. 1971	Approve constitution	99.9	—
	15 May 1974	Approve "October paper"	99.9	—

	10 June 1976	Approve extension of presidential term	99.9	95.7
	16 Sept. 1976	Reelect Sadat and approve policies	99.9	95.8
	10 Feb. 1977	Approve decree against rioters	99.4	96.7
	21 May 1978	Approve measures against opposition	97.8	85.2
	19 Apr. 1979	Dissolve assembly	99.9	90
	19 Apr. 1979	Approve treaty with Israel	99.9	90
	22 May 1980	Constitutional change	99.9	87
	10 Sept. 1981	Security measures	99.5	91.6
	13 Oct. 1981	Approve President Mubarak	98.5	81
	11 Oct. 1990	Approve fresh elections	92.7	—
	4 Oct. 1993	Approve another term for President Mubarak	96.8	—
Equatorial Guinea (2)	29 July 1973	Approve constitution	99	—
	15 Aug. 1982	New constitution	95	—
Gambia (2)	Nov. 1965	Approve republican constitution	65.98	62.3
	20 Apr. 1970	Republican constitution	74.3	84.8
Ghana (4)	17 Apr. 1960	Approve republican constitution	88.4	54.3
	24 Jan. 1964	One-party state	99.9	96.5
	31 Mar. 1978	Approve no-party constitution	55.6	—
	28 Apr. 1982	Lift ban on parties	90	60
Ivory Coast (1)	Nov. 1986	New constitution	—	—
Iraq (1)	Aug. 1921	Approve Feisal as king (consultation through headmen)	96	—
Liberia (2)	7 Oct. 1975	Limit presidential term	—	98.6
	3 July 1984	Constitutional change	90+	80+
Libya (1)	1 Sept. 1971	Approve Federation of Arab Republics	98.6	94.6

(Table continues)

275

Region and Nation	Date	Subject	Percent Yes Vote	Percent Turnout of Electorate
Madagascar (2)	8 Oct. 1972	Approve constitution	95.6	84.3
	21 Dec. 1975	Approve constitution	94.6	91.7
Malawi (1)	14 June 1993	End one-party rule	63.2	67
Mali (1)	26 June 1974	Approve constitution	99.7	67
Mauritania (1)	12 July 1992	End one-party rule	95	86
Morocco (7)	7 Dec. 1962	Approve constitution	95.3	84.2
	24 July 1970	Approve constitution	89.7	93.1
	1 Mar. 1972	Approve constitution	98.7	92.9
	23 May 1980	Royal age of majority to 16	99.7	96.9
	30 May 1980	Constitutional change	96.7	91.2
	31 Aug. 1984	Federate with Libya	99.9	—
	1 Dec. 1989	Extend Parliament by two years	99.9	95.8
Niger (2)	14 June 1987	Approve national charter	99.6	—
	24 Sept. 1989	New constitution	99.3	95.0
Ruanda (1)	17 Dec. 1978	New constitution	89.9	—
São Tome (1)	22 Aug. 1990	New constitution	Yes	79.4
Senegal (2)	3 Mar. 1963	Approve constitution	99.5	—
	2 Feb. 1970	Reinstate post of prime minister	99.9	94.9
Seychelles (1)	9 June 1989	Third term for president	96.2	91.0

Sierra Leone (2)	5 June 1978	Approve one-party constitution	97.1	96.2
	Aug. 1991	Approve multiparty democracy	60	75
Somalia (2)	20 June 1961	Merger of two Somalias	90.6[a]	—
	25 Aug. 1979	New constitution	89.9	—
South Africa (4)	5 Oct. 1960	Change to republic	52.3	90.7
	2 Nov. 1983	Presidential constitution	66.3	75.6
	17 Mar. 1992	Constitutional reform	69.0	—
	17 Mar. 1992	Approve moves to end apartheid	66.8	—
Sudan (2)	15 Sept. 1971	Approve President Numeiry	98.6	92.9
	3 Apr. 1977	Reelect Numeiry and approve policies	99.1	—
Syria (7)	25 June 1949	Four questions on constitution reform	90+	60+
	10 July 1953	New powers for president	99.7	86.8
	20 Feb. 1958	Approve union with Egypt	99.9	—
	1 Sept. 1971	Approve Federation of Arab Republics	96.4	89.7
	12 Mar. 1973	Approve constitution	97.8	88.9
	8 Feb. 1978	Reelect President Assad and approve policies	99.9	97
	11 Feb. 1985	Endorse President Assad	99.9	—
Togo (4)	9 Apr. 1961	Approve constitution	—	95
	5 May 1963	Approve constitution	98.3	90.6
	9 Jan. 1972	Reelect President Eyadema	99.9	98.6
	30 Dec. 1979	New constitution	99.9	—
Tunisia (1)	Nov. 1974	Life presidency for Bourguiba	99.9	96.8
Upper Volta (3)	27 Nov. 1960	Approve constitution	99.5	90.2

(Table continues)

APPENDIX A (continued)

Region and Nation	Date	Subject	Percent Yes Vote	Percent Turnout of Electorate
	14 June 1970	Approve constitution	98.4	75.9
	27 Nov. 1977	Approve constitution	98.7	78.6
Zaire (3)	27 June 1964	Approve constitution	92	—
	4 June 1967	Approve constitution	97.8	—
	28 July 1984	Endorse President Mobutu	99.9	—
Zambia (1)	17 June 1969	Constitutional change entrenched clauses	53	91
Asia[h]				
Bangladesh (2)	30 May 1977	Approve constitution and President Zia	98.9	85
	21 Mar. 1985	Continue president's term	94.5	71.5
Burma (1)	15–31 Dec. 1973	Approve constitution	94.4	91.1
Cambodia (4)	7 Feb. 1955	Approve Sihanouk and independence	99.8	—
	1958	Reduce numbers of representatives	99	—
	5 June 1960	Approve Shihanouk and his policies	99.9	91.8
	30 Apr. 1972	Approve republican constitution	97.5	75
Iran (4)	10 Aug. 1953	Dissolve Majlis	99.9	—
	26 Jan. 1963	Shah's reform program	99.9	92
	30 Mar. 1979	Islamic republic	99.3	—
	1979	New constitution	99.5	65

Country	Date	Subject		
Maldives (2)	Mar. 1968	Republic, not sultanate	90	—
	23 Sept. 1988	Reelect President Mamoun	96.4	—
Nepal (1)	2 May 1980	Retain advisory council	54.8	67
Pakistan (1)	19 Dec. 1984	Presidential rule and Islamic constitution	98	62
Philippines (11)	11 Mar. 1947	Approve American business rights	88.4	40
	27 July 1973	Approve Marcos and martial law	90.7	—
	27 Feb. 1975	Approve restructuring of local government	69.0	90.7
	27 Feb. 1975	Approve Marcos's handling of martial law	87.6	90.7
	27 Feb. 1975	Approve continuance of martial law	86.7	90.7
	16 Oct. 1976	Approve continuance of martial law	97.9	97.2
	16 Oct. 1976	Approve constitutional amendment	90.6	97.2
	18 Dec. 1977	Approve Marcos as president and prime minister	89.5	98
	7 Apr. 1981	Expand president's term and power	79.5	66
	27 Jan. 1984	4 constitutional amendments	80–85	—
	2 Feb. 1987	Approve draft constitution	76.4	87
South Korea (6)	17 Dec. 1962	Approve constitution	78.6	85
	18 Oct. 1969	Third term for president	65.1	75.9
	21 Nov. 1972	Approve constitution	92.2	90.0
	12 Feb. 1975	Support constitution and president	74.4	79.8
	22 Oct. 1980	New constitution	91.6	95.5
	9 Oct. 1987	Constitutional change	95.0	—
South Vietnam (1)	23 Oct. 1955	Depose Emperor Bao Dai	98.9	—
Sri Lanka (1)	22 Dec. 1982	New constitution	54.6	70.9

(Table continues)

Region and Nation	Date	Subject	Percent Yes Vote	Percent Turnout of Electorate
North and South America[i]				
Argentina (1)	25 Nov. 1984	Treaty with Chile	81	73
Bolivia (1)	11 Jan. 1931	Approve constitution	—	—
Brazil (4)	6 Jan. 1963	Full power for president	84.2	66.2
	25 Apr. 1972	Republic, not monarchy	87	—
	21 Apr. 1993	Approve presidential system	68.9	—
	29 Sept. 1898	Prohibition of alcoholic beverages	51.3	44.0
Canada (2)	27 Apr. 1942	Military conscription	63.7[j]	71.3
	26 Oct. 1992	Approve constitutional accord	45.6	—
Chile (5)	30 Aug. 1925	Approve constitution	94.7	86.3
	4 Jan. 1978	Approve Pinochet's defense of Chile's stand	78.4	91.4
	11 Sept. 1980	Approve regime	69.0	92.9
	5 Oct. 1988	Extend president's term	43.0	—
	30 July 1989	Approve constitutional changes	85.7	—
Colombia (2)	1 Dec. 1957	Approve constitution	94.6	72.3
	25 May 1990	Set up constitutional assembly	90	—
Cuba (1)	15 Feb. 1976	Approve constitution	99.0	98.7
Ecuador (2)	15 Jan. 1978	New constitution (24.9% spoiled ballots)	58.1	90
	1 July 1986	All independents to stand	30.4	—

Country	Date	Measure	% Yes	% Turnout
Guatemala (1)	22–24 June 1935	Extend president's term	99.9	—
Guyana (1)	10 July 1978	Abolish referendums for constitutional change	97.4	70.7
Haiti (6)	12 June 1918	New constitution	Yes	—
	10 Jan. 1928	Constitutional change	Yes	—
	14 June 1964	Life presidency for Duvalier	100.0	—
	31 June 1971	Confirm Duvalier's power to choose successor	100.0	—
	27 Mar. 1987	New constitution	—	99.0
	9 Mar. 1988	Approve constitution	99	—
Mexico (2)	4 Dec. 1863	Approve Emperor Maximillan	99	—
	Dec. 1867	Amend constitution (votes never counted)	—	—
Newfoundland (1)	Nov. 1915	Approve prohibition	82.4	71.3
Panama (3)	15 Dec. 1940	Approve constitution	—	—
	23 Oct. 1977	Approve canal treaty with United States	67.4	94
	24 Apr. 1983	Constitutional amendments	87.8	—
Paraguay (1)	4 Aug. 1940	Approve constitution	92.4	—
Peru (2)	18 June 1939	Amend constitution	87.4	—
	31 Oct. 1993	Approve constitution	55.0	—
Suriname (1)	10 Sept. 1987	New constitution	93	70
Uruguay (13)	1916	9-man council not presidency	No	—
	25 Nov. 1917	Approve constitution	95.2	—
	19 Apr. 1934	Approve constitution	95.6	54.9

(Table continues)

Appendix A (continued)

Region and Nation	Date	Subject	Percent Yes Vote	Percent Turnout of Electorate
	27 Mar. 1938	Approve constitutional amendments	93.8	55
	29 Nov. 1942	Approve constitution	77.2	66.9
	24 Nov. 1946	Approve constitutional amendments	42.6[k]	79.9
	1958	Restore presidency	No	—
	25 Nov. 1962	Restore presidency	No	73
	16 Dec. 1966	Return to presidential government	64.9	70
	28 Nov. 1971	Two constitutional amendments	30	92
	10 Sept. 1987	Amnesty for politicians	57	77
	16 Apr. 1989	Index pensions	Yes	—
	13 Dec. 1992	Approve privatization	30	—
Venezuela (1)	15 Dec. 1957	Approve President Perez's rule	86.6	—
Australia and New Zealand[l]				
Australia (39)	See chapter 5			
New Zealand[m,o] (13)	17 Nov. 1908	Prohibition continuation	32.9	—
	17 Nov. 1908	Prohibition reduction	38.7[m]	79.8
	7 Dec. 1911	Prohibition	55.8[n]	83.5
	10 Dec. 1914	Prohibition	49.0	84.6
	30 Apr. 1919	Prohibition	48.6	—
	9 Mar. 1949	Off-track betting	68.0	56.3
	9 Mar. 1949	Maintain 6 pm drink curfew	75.5	56.5

3 Aug. 1949	Maintain conscription	77.8	61.5
23 Sept. 1967	Three-, not four-year parliaments	68.1	71.2
23 Sept. 1967	Longer drinking hours	64.5	71.2
19 Sept. 1992	Retain electoral system	84.7	55.2
19 Sept. 1992	4 alternative systems	70.5	55.2
6 Nov. 1993	Approve MMP election law	53.8	82.6

— = no data available.

a. European countries that have not had nationwide referendums are Albania, Cyprus (on June 8, 1975, a referendum in the Turkish part of Cyprus approved permanent partition, with 99.4 percent voting Yes and with a 70 percent turnout), Czechoslovakia, Malta (which had a referendum before independence), Netherlands, Soviet Union, West Germany (the constitution provides for referendums at the *Land* level, and two have been held under *Land* constitutions; see chap. 1, n. 5).

b. This referendum was lost because it secured the support of only 44.5 percent of the total electorate, not the 45 percent then required by the Danish Constitution. In 1953, the requirement was reduced to 40 percent.

c. The figures are for metropolitan France only.

d. These were popular initiatives. The 1926 affirmative vote represented only 36.4 percent of the electorate, and the 1929 vote represented only 14.1 percent of the electorate. The approval of 50 percent of the electorate was required.

e. Popular initiative. Despite receiving more than 90 percent in Yes votes, the three Italian referendums in 1990 failed because the turnout was less than 50 percent.

f. African and Near Eastern countries that have not had nationwide referendums are Angola, Bahrain, Botswana, Cape Verde*, Djibouti,* Ethiopia, Gabon,* Guinea,* Guinea-Bissau, Israel, Ivory Coast,* Jordan, Kenya, Kuwait, Lebanon, Lesotho, Malawi, Mauritius, Mozambique, Nigeria, Oman, Qatar, Rwanda,* Saudi Arabia, South Yemen, Swaziland, Tanzania, Uganda, United Arab Emirates, and Yemen. Those followed by an asterisk (*) held a referendum before independence.

g. A two-thirds majority was required; hence the 1965 proposal was defeated.

h. Asian countries that have not had nationwide referendums are Afghanistan, Bhutan, China, Formosa, India, Indonesia, Japan, Laos, Malaysia, Mongolia,* Nepal, North Korea, Singapore,* Thailand, and Vietnam. Those followed by an asterisk (*) held a referendum before independence.

i. North and South American countries that have not had nationwide referendums are Argentina, Bahamas, Barbados, Bermuda, Costa Rica, Dominican Republic, El Salvador, Grenada, Honduras, Jamaica (which had a referendum before independence), Mexico, Nicaragua, Trinidad, and the United States (see chapter 4).

j. Only 29 percent voted Yes in Quebec.

(Table continues)

k. One alternative received 42.6 percent, another 37.2 percent, and 25.1 percent voted for neither. The preferred proposal secured the support of only 29.1 percent of the registered voters and thus failed because it did not receive the 35 percent required by the constitution.

l. Australasian and oceanic countries that have not had nationwide referendums are Fiji, Gilbert Islands, Nauru, Solomon Islands, Tuvalu, Papua New-Guinea, Tonga, and Western Samoa (which had a referendum before independence).

m. From the days before independence in 1907, New Zealand general elections were accompanied by votes on liquor licensing. In the seventeen general elections since 1919, New Zealanders have been asked to choose between (a) the status quo in liquor licensing (b) state purchase of liquor, and (c) prohibition. In 1919, the votes were (a) 44.4 percent, (b) 5.8 percent, and (c) 49.7 percent. Support for prohibition steadily declined, and by 1975, the votes were (a) 69.2 percent, (b) 14.9 percent, and (c) 15.9 percent.

n. A 60 percent vote of Yes was required to give effect to the 1908–1914 referendums.

o. 70.5 percent vote for a mixed member proportional system

Referendums in Subordinate Territories, 1552–1993

In the following list, an attempt is made to list those referendums in colonial or dependent territories that affected the boundaries or allegiance of the territory, or its independence, or its preindependence constitutions. (In some of the nineteenth-century referendums in France and Italy listed here, the territories were technically nations.) There have been many referendums on other questions in component states of federations and a few in colonies. For the United States, see chapter 7; for Australia, see chapter 5.

The reservations made in appendix A about the accuracy of the figures also apply here. A dash indicates that data are not available.

APPENDIX B: REFERENDUMS IN SUBORDINATE TERRITORIES, 1552–1993

Nation and Territory	Date	Subject	Percent Yes Vote	Percent Turnout of Electorate
Australia				
Cocos Islands	6 Apr. 1984	Integrate with mainland	88.5	—
New South Wales (New England only)	29 Apr. 1967	Make New England a separate state	45.8	92.5
Western Australia	8 Apr. 1933	Secede from Australia Constitutional convention	66.2	92
Austria				
Salzburg	29 May 1921	Join with Germany	98.7	—
Tyrol	24 Apr. 1921	Join with Germany[a]	98.7	—
Vorarlberg	11 May 1919	Join with Switzerland	87.5	—
Belgium				
Rwanda	Sept. 1961	Approve institution of Mwami[b]	20.2	—
	Sept. 1961	Approve present Mwami[b]	20.2	—
Canada				
Northwest Territory	12 Apr. 1982	Divide territory	55.9	—
	4 May 1982	Divide into two		
Quebec	20 May 1980	Approve independence	40.4	84.1
China				
Mongolia	20 Oct. 1945	Independence from China	97.8	98.4

Cyprus				
Turkish part	5 May 1985	Separatist constitution	70.2	78.3
Denmark				
Faroes	14 Sept. 1946	Separate from Denmark[a]	50.1	66.4
Greenland	17 Jan. 1979	Approve home rule	73.1	63.2
	23 Feb. 1982	Withdraw from European Community	53.0	75
St. Thomas and St. John	9 Jan. 1868	Cession to United States[c]	98.2	—
Ethiopia				
Eritrea	25 Apr. 1993	Approve independence	99.8	98.2
Finland				
Aaland Isles	June 1919	Union with Sweden (unofficial)	45.5	96.4
France (before 1900)				
Avignon	7–24 July 1791	Join with France	66[d]	—
Geneva	15 Apr. 1798	Join with France	—	—
Metz, Toul, and Verdun	1552	Stay with France	—	—
Mulhouse	Jan. 1798	Join with France	97.5	—
Nice	Dec. 1792	Join with France	100[d]	—
Nice	15 Apr. 1860	Join with France	99.3	85
Paris	3 Nov. 1870	Approve defense government	89.9	—
Savoie	8–20 Oct. 1792	Join with France	99.8	—
Savoie	22 Apr. 1860	Join with France	99.8	96.6
Switzerland	May 1802	Establish Helvetic Republic	43.9	49.7

(Table continues)

APPENDIX B (continued)

Nation and Territory	Date	Subject	Percent Yes Vote	Percent Turnout of Electorate
France (after 1900)				
Afars and Issas (French Somaliland)	28 Sept. 1958	Stay in French community	75.2	72.3
	19 Mar. 1967	Continue union with France	60.5	95.4
	8 May 1977	Independence from France	98.8	77.2
Algeria	28 Sept. 1958	Stay in French community	96.5	79.0
	6–8 Jan. 1961	Self-determination	65.9	58.8
	8 Apr. 1962	Approve Evian agreement	—	—
	1 July 1962	Independence on Evian terms	99.7	91.8
Chad	28 Sept. 1958	Stay in French community	99.2	65.8
Chandernagore	19 June 1949	Unite with India	98.0	60.8
Comoros	28 Dec. 1974	Approve independence	95.6	92.9
Congo	28 Sept. 1958	Stay in French community	99.4	78.8
Dahomey	28 Sept. 1958	Stay in French community	97.8	55.3
French Sudan	28 Sept. 1958	Stay in French community	97.6	45.3
Gabon	28 Sept. 1958	Stay in French community	92.1	77.5
Guinea	28 Sept. 1958	Approve independence	97.2	84.7
Ivory Coast	28 Sept. 1958	Stay in French community	99.9	97.5
Madagascar	28 Sept. 1958	Stay in French community	77.6	81.5
Mauritania	28 Sept. 1958	Stay in French community	94.2	83.9
Mayotte	8 Feb. 1976	Remain part of French Republic	99.4	83.3
	11 Apr. 1976	Remain French overseas territory (80 percent blank votes)	2.5	80.5

	Date		Yes %	Turnout %
New Caledonia	28 Sept. 1958	Stay in French community	98.1	75.6
Niger	13 Sept. 1987	Remain part of France	94.6	—
	28 Sept. 1958	Stay in French community	78.5	36
St. Pierre and Miquelon	24 Dec. 1941	Support Free French[g]	98.2	—
	28 Sept. 1958	Stay in French community	98.1	84.6
	7 Mar. 1976	Become French *departement*	91.5	43
Senegal	28 Sept. 1958	Stay in French community	97.8	81.1
Tahiti	Sept. 1940	Support Free French, not Vichy	99.7	—
Togo	28 Oct. 1956	Autonomy	93.4	76.7
Ubangi-Shari	28 Sept. 1958	Stay in French community	99.0	78.8
Western Samoa	11 May 1961	Approve constitution[b]	86.3	77.6
	11 May 1961	Approve independence under constitution[b]	85.4	77.6
Netherlands				
Curaçao	19 Nov. 1993	Future status:	—	58.0
		Preserve Netherlands Antilles Federation	73.6	—
		Independence	0.5	—
		Province of Netherlands	8.0	—
		Autonomy under Dutch crown	17.9	—
Nigeria				
Midwest region	13 July 1963	Creation of midwest region	98.2	90.2
Philippines				
13 provinces	17 Apr. 1977	Reject autonomy for region	97.9	—
13 provinces	16 Nov. 1989	Increased autonomy	No	<50
5 provinces	29 June 1990	Increased autonomy	—	—

(Table continues)

289

APPENDIX B (continued)

Nation and Territory	Date	Subject	Percent Yes Vote	Percent Turnout of Electorate
South Africa				
Ciskei			—	—
K. Williamstown			—	—
Mafeking			—	—
Natal	10 June 1909	Merge with new South Africa	58.2	75.1
Southwest Africa	17 May 1977	Approve independence scheme	94.9	64.9
Thaba 'nchu			—	—
Soviet Union		See chapter 6		
Spain				
Andalusia	28 Feb. 1980	Increased autonomy	93.3[b]	60.4
Basque region	5 Oct. 1979	Increased autonomy	94.7	58.9
Catalonia	25 Oct. 1979	Increased autonomy	88.1	59.7
Equatorial Guinea	15 Dec. 1961	Autonomous government under Spain	57.3	91.6
Galicia	21 Dec. 1980	Increased autonomy	77.3	26.2
Sweden				
St. Bartholomew	Oct. 1877	Cession to France	99.7	67.9
Turkey				
Kars, Batum, and Ardahan	July 1918	Unite with Turkey	97.8	—

Uganda				
Buyoaga and Bugangadzi	4 Nov. 1964	Unite with Bunyoro (stay with Uganda, 20.5 percent; be a separate district, 0.7 percent)	78.8	—
United Kingdom				
Cameroons				
North	7 Nov. 1959	Decide later, not merge with Nigeria[b]	62.3	—
North	11–12 Feb. 1961	Merge immediately with Nigeria	59.8	83.6
South	11–12 Feb. 1961	Merge with Cameroon[b]	70.4	94.1
Gibraltar	10 Sept. 1967	Keep link with Britain	99.6	95.8
Imperial Australia				
Four colonies				
New South Wales	3 June 1898	Approve confederation	51.9	43.5
South Australia	4 June 1898	Approve confederation	67.4	30.9
Tasmania	3 June 1898	Approve confederation	81.3	25
Victoria	3 June 1898	Approve confederation	82.0	50.3
Total			67	—
Six colonies				
New South Wales	28 June 1899	Approve revised constitution	56.1	63.4
Queensland	2 Sept. 1899	Approve revised constitution	55.4	64.8
South Australia	29 Apr. 1899	Approve revised constitution	79.4	54.4
Tasmania	27 July 1899	Approve revised constitution	94.4	41.8
Victoria	27 July 1899	Approve revised constitution	94.0	56.3
Western Australia	31 July 1900	Approve revised constitution	69.4	67.1
Total			72.4	—
India				
Junagadh	24 Feb. 1948	Join India, not Pakistan	99.9	94.7

Nation and Territory	Date	Subject	Percent Yes Vote	Percent Turnout of Electorate
Northwest Frontier	6 July 1947	Join Pakistan, not India	99.9	51.0
Sylbet	6 July 1947	Join Pakistan, not India	56.5	—
Ionian Isles	23 Sept. 1863	Unite with Greece	99	—
Jamaica	19 Sept. 1961	Approve West Indies federation	46.2	60.4
Malta	1870	Political rights for ecclesiastics	96	59.8
	11–12 Feb. 1956	Approve integration with Britain	77.0	59.1
	2–4 May 1964	Approve independence constitution	50.7	79.7
Newfoundland	3 June 1948	(1) Responsible government	45.1 ⎫	
		(2) Join Canada	40.5 ⎬	88.4
		(3) Stay under commission	14.4 ⎭	
	22 July 1948	Join Canada, not responsible self-government	52.3	84.9
Northern Ireland	8 Mar. 1973	Stay in United Kingdom	98.9	58.7
Scotland	1 Mar. 1979	Approve devolution	51.6[c]	63.6
Shetland	17 Mar. 1976	Freedom to opt out of Scottish devolution[1]	89.9	71.5
Singapore	1 Sept. 1962	Three types of merger with Malaysia (25.8 percent blank votes)	(1) 70.8 ⎫ (2) 1.6 ⎬ (3) 1.8 ⎭	89.4
Southern Rhodesia	27 Oct. 1922	Self-government, not join South Africa	59.3	78.5
	9 Apr. 1953	Approve Central African Federation	63.5	82.1
	26 July 1961	Approve constitution	65.8	76.5

292

	5 Nov. 1964	Approve constitution	89.3	61.9
	20 June 1969	Become republic	81.0	92.4
	20 June 1969	Approve constitution	72.5	92.4
Togo	9 May 1956	Join with Ghana[b]	58.1	83.6
Tuvalu (Ellice Islands)	Aug.–Sept. 1974	Separate from Gilbert Islands	92.8	94
Wales	1 Mar. 1979	Approve devolution	20.9	58.8
United States				
American Samoa	7 Aug. 1972	Elect own governor	17.3	28.2
	4 Aug. 1973	Elect own governor	34.3	23.6
	18 June 1974	Elect own governor	48.2	17.2
	31 Aug. 1976	Elect own governor	69	24
Federated States of Micronesia	12 July 1978	All-Micronesia constitution	61.6	78.8
	21 June 1983	Compact of Free Association with United States	79.0	63.2
Guam	30 Jan. 1982	Six choices of status (48.5 percent prefer commonwealth)	48.5	38
Marshall Islands	7 Sept. 1983	Compact of Free Association with United States	58.5	83.5
Northern Marianas	17 Jan. 1975	Approve commonwealth status	78.5	86.5
Palau	10 Feb. 1983	Compact of Free Association with United States	55.6[1]	88.2
	4 Sept. 1984	Compact of Free Association with United States	66.9[1]	—
	30 July 1987	Compact of Free Association with United States	67.9[1]	—

(Table continues)

APPENDIX B (continued)

Nation and Territory	Date	Subject	Percent Yes Vote	Percent Turnout of Electorate
	4 Oct. 1987	Compact of Free Association with United States	73.3[1]	—
	6 Feb. 1990	Compact of Free Association with United States	60.8[1]	—
Philippines	14 May 1935	Approve independence constitution	96.7	—
Puerto Rico	4 June 1951	Prepare commonwealth constitution	76.5	65
	3 Mar. 1952	Approve constitution	81.9	58.2
	23 July 1967	Commonwealth, not statehood (38.9 percent) or independence (0.6)	60.5	65.8
	14 Nov. 1993	Future status:		
		Commonwealth	48.4	—
		Statehood	46.2	—
		Independence	4.4	—
Virgin Islands	6 Mar. 1979	Increased self-government	44.0	38
	Nov. 1981	New constitution	No	50
Yugoslavia		See chapter 6		
League of Nations Territorial Plebiscites				
Allenstein	11 July 1920	Join Germany, not Poland	97.8	87
Klagenfurt	10 Oct. 1920	Join Austria, not Yugoslavia	59.0	95.8
Marienwerder	11 July 1920	Join Germany, not Poland	92.1	87

Saar	13 Jan. 1935	Join Germany, not France	90.3	97.9
Schleswig, North	10 Feb. 1920	Join Denmark, not Germany	75.4	91.5
Schleswig, South	14 Mar. 1920	Join Germany, not Denmark	80.2	90.6
Sopron (Oedenburg)	17 Dec. 1921	Join Hungary, not Austria	65.1	89.5
Upper Silesia	20 Mar. 1921	Join Germany, not Poland	59.7	97.5

International Control Commission

Saar	23 Oct. 1955	Approve Europeanization statute	32.2	93.3

a. Unofficial referendum; no action followed.
b. Under United Nations supervision.
c. The cession did not take place until a new agreement in 1916, which was endorsed by 99.9 percent of the voters in an unofficial referendum in St. Croix.
d. Votes by whole communes.
e. Since those voting No (56.1 percent) were only 28.2 percent of the whole electorate, this vote was taken as a Yes.
f. Guinea was the only French territory to vote against President de Gaulle's first referendum and thus to opt for immediate independence. But all French territories took part in that referendum.
g. The vote was 783 to 14, but since 215 ballots were spoiled, only 77.3 percent of all ballots were in favor.
h. There were also votes in Reggio, Modena, and Guastalla. Full figures are not available.
i. Unofficial (postal) referendum.
j. Failed because some provinces voted No.
k. Only 32.9 percent of the Scottish electorate voted Yes, so the referendum failed.
l. A 75 percent majority was needed to ratify the compact, so the referendum was defeated.

Index

Abortion, 3, 66, 80, 82–85, 90, 172, 238, 241, 242
Abrogative referendum (Italy), 18, 32, 62–65, 89, 95
Aitkin, Don, 160, 164
Alaska, 248
Albania, 176n, 177, 206, 207, 208, 209
Alcohol advertising and sales, 3, 74, 171–72, 243
Algeria, 52, 57, 58, 89
Andalusia, 28
Andreotti, Giulio, 62, 89
Antonescu, Ion, 176n, 177, 181
Appenzell-Inner Rhodes, 99
Appenzell-Outer Rhodes, 99
Arington, Michele, 241n
Arizona, 242, 248
Arkansas, 20
Armenia, 176n, 187, 188, 189, 190, 193, 195, 201
Arterton, F. Christopher, 12, 21
Ascherson, Neal, 182n
Atlee, Clement, 36
Auriol, Vincent, 48
Austen, John, 17, 22
Australia
    campaign costs, 161
    constitutional amendment referendums, 159–60
    decreasing use of referendums, 20
    dispute over monarchy vs. republic, 161–62
    double-majority requirement, 160
    electoral system, referendums on, 170
    entrenchment, 166
    influence of U.S. Progressive movement, 158
    interest groups in referendums, 158
    narrow vote margins, 4, 162
    nationwide referendums, 1906–1988, 155–56
    state and territorial referendums, 1903–1992, 167–68
    voters' information, 163
    world's second-greatest user of referendums, 98
Australian Capital Territory, 170
Austria, 4, 24, 25, 26, 28, 31, 32–33, 87, 89, 90, 91, 176n
Azerbaijan, 176n, 180n, 188, 190, 192–93, 195, 203

Backstrom, Charles, 228n
Banducci, Susan A., 234n
Barber, Benjamin, 12, 15, 22
Basque country, 28
Belau (Palau), 2
Belgium, 24, 25, 26, 87
Bell, Derrick A., Jr., 241n
Belarus, 188, 196, 202, 212
Belorussia. See Belarus
Berglund, Sten, 76
Biel, Walter, 107
Bjørklund, Tor, 70, 71
Board, Joseph, 76
Bogdanor, Vernon, 44, 47, 89, 92, 221n, 260
Borre, Ole, 72
Bosnia-Herzegovina, 206, 207, 209
Boundary disputes, 2
Bozoki, Andras, 185n, 186, 216
Brazil, referendum of 21 April 1993, 8
Brown, J. F., 182n
Bryce, James, 34, 46, 92
Bulgaria, 176n, 182, 183
Butler, David, 17, 21, 22, 39, 40, 87

A NOTE ON THE BOOK

This book was edited by Dana Lane, Ann Petty, and Cheryl Weissman
of the AEI Press. The figures were drawn by Hördur Karlsson.
The text was set in Palatino, a typeface designed by the twentieth-century
Swiss designer Hermann Zapf. Coghill Composition Company,
of Richmond, Virginia, set the type, and Edwards Brothers, Incorporated,
of Ann Arbor, Michigan, printed and bound the book,
using permanent acid-free paper.

The AEI Press is the publisher for the American Enterprise Institute for Public Policy Research, 1150 17th Street, N.W., Washington, D.C. 20036; *Christopher C. DeMuth*, publisher; *Dana Lane*, director; *Ann Petty*, editor; *Cheryl Weissman*, editor; *Lisa Roman*, editorial assistant (rights and permissions).

www.ingramcontent.com/pod-product-compliance
Lightning Source LLC
Jackson TN
JSHW011932131224
75386JS00041B/1340